The Pepin Press
P.O. Box 10349
1001 EH Amsterdam
The Netherlands
T +31 20 420 20 21
F +31 20 420 11 52
mail@pepinpress.com
www.pepinpress.com

Project coordinator: Femke van Eijk
Photography: Randal Scobie, René de Haan (cover, p. 1, 352)
Lithography: Van Osch studio & litho BV, Sang Choy pte. ltd.
Collection and text: Tassenmuseum Hendrikje
Copy editing: Dorine van den Beukel, Dik van de Heuvel
Translations: LocTeam, The Big Word
Design: Kitty Molenaar
Cover design: Pepin van Roojen

ISBN
english edition   90 5496 109 0
french edition   90 5496 115 5
dutch edition   90 5496 112 0
spanish edition   90 5496 117 1
italian edition   90 5496 113 9
german edition   90 5496 114 7
japanese edition   90 5496 116 3

10 9 8 7 6 5 4 3 2 1
2009 08 07 06 05 04

Manufactured in Singapore

Bags
Sacs
Tassen
Bolsos
Borse
Taschen
バッグ

THE PEPIN PRESS

Contents 4

Sommaire 5

Inhoud 5

Contenido 6

Indice 6

Inhaltsverzeichnis 7

目次 7

English

français   nederlands

Español   Italiano

deutsch　　　　　　　　　　　　　　　　日本語

Preface

Préface

Voorwoord

Prefacio

Prefazione

Vorwort

序文

Probably only a few people stop to consider that an apparently everyday object such as the handbag has an extraordinarily rich history and has undergone remarkable development in its many centuries of existence. This book charts the evolution of the bag used for carrying personal items from the late Middle Ages to modern times, with special focus on the fashion and social trends that have influenced the development of the bag.

The bags are divided into chapters according to their function, material or shape. Their broad range of styles and uses make the bag a fascinating accessory. There are chapters devoted to special kinds of leather and plastics, and there are examples of bags decorated with fine embroidery or set with precious stones. Space has also been devoted to the influence of styles from the applied arts, and this book shows modern classics and handbags from leading designers as well.

All the bags in this book are from the Hendrikje Bag Museum in The Netherlands. Like many museums, this one originated from a zeal for collecting. What began as a personal fascination grew to an extensive collection showcasing the bag as an exciting accessory in constant development.

The museum has a collection of more than 2,500 bags, which makes it the largest bag museum in Europe. The bags are displayed there in both permanent and changing exhibitions. The museum also encourages young designers by regularly holding exhibits of their work and selling their bags.

Hendrikje Ivo
Hendrikje Bag Museum
Amstelveen, The Netherlands

www.museumofbagsandpurses.com

English

Seuls bien peu sans doute prennent la peine de penser qu'un objet d'apparence aussi ordinaire que le sac à main possède une histoire extrêmement riche et a considérablement évolué au cours de ses nombreux siècles d'existence. Cet ouvrage retrace, de la fin du Moyen Âge à l'époque moderne, le chemin parcouru par le sac d'effets personnels et s'intéresse tout particulièrement aux modes et tendances de société qui ont influencé son développement.

Les sacs sont classés en chapitres selon leur fonction, leur matériau ou leur forme. Le vaste éventail de styles et d'usages du sac en fait un accessoire des plus fascinants. Certains chapitres sont entièrement consacrés à des cuirs ou plastiques spéciaux, d'autres présentent des sacs ornés de broderies fines ou sertis de pierres précieuses. L'influence des styles d'arts appliqués trouve également sa place, à travers des classiques modernes et les sacs à main de grands créateurs.

Tous les sacs présentés ici viennent du Musée des sacs Hendrikje aux Pays-Bas. Comme bien d'autres musées, il est né de la passion d'un collectionneur, dont la fascination toute personnelle a donné lieu à une immense galerie où le sac est un accessoire passionnant en constante évolution.

Avec sa collection de plus de 2 500 sacs, le Musée des sacs est le plus grand du genre en Europe. Les articles y sont présentés au public dans des expositions permanentes et temporaires ; le musée encourage également les jeunes créateurs à présenter régulièrement leur travail et à vendre leurs modèles.

Hendrikje Ivo
Musée des sacs Hendrikje
Amstelveen, Pays-Bas

www.museedessacs.com

Maar weinigen zullen erbij stilstaan dat een op het oog zo alledaagse voorwerp als de tas een buitengewoon rijke geschiedenis heeft, en in de vele eeuwen van zijn bestaan een opmerkelijke ontwikkeling heeft doorgemaakt. In dit boek is de wordingsgeschiedenis van de tas in kaart gebracht – van de late Middeleeuwen tot de dag van vandaag – met aandacht voor de mode en sociaal-maatschappelijke ontwikkelingen die op de ontwikkeling van de tas van invloed zijn geweest.

De tassen zijn per hoofdstuk ingedeeld naar functie, materiaal of vorm. De grote variatie hierin maakt de tas een boeiend accessoire. Zo zijn er hoofdstukken gewijd aan bijzondere leersoorten en kunststoffen, en zijn er voorbeelden van tassen die zijn versierd met fijn borduurwerk of bezet met edelstenen. Ook is er ruime aandacht voor de invloed van stijlen in de toegepaste kunst en toont het boek de moderne klassiekers en tassen van vooraanstaande ontwerpers.

Alle tassen in dit boek zijn afkomstig van Tassenmuseum Hendrikje. Zoals veel musea is ook dit tassenmuseum ontstaan uit verzamelwoede. Wat begon als een persoonlijke fascinatie, is uitgegroeid tot een uitgebreide collectie die laat zien dat de tas een spannend gebruiksvoorwerp is met een immer voortdurende ontwikkeling. Het museum heeft een collectie van meer dan 2500 tassen, en is daarmee het grootste tassenmuseum van Europa. De tassen worden er in vaste en wisselende tentoonstellingen getoond. Het museum stimuleert jonge ontwerpers door regelmatig tentoonstellingen van hun werk te organiseren en hun tassen te verkopen.

Hendrikje Ivo
Tassenmuseum Hendrikje
Amstelveen, The Netherlands

www.tassenmuseum.nl

français

nederlands

Probablemente sólo unos pocos se paran a pensar que detrás de un objeto aparentemente tan cotidiano como un bolso de mano se esconde una historia extraordinariamente rica y que a lo largo de sus varios siglos de existencia ha experimentado un desarrollo importante. Este libro muestra la evolución de la bolsa empleada para transportar efectos personales desde la Edad Media hasta la época moderna, y hace especial hincapié en las tendencias de la sociedad y la moda que han influido en el desarrollo del bolso.

Los bolsos se dividen en capítulos según su función, material o forma. La amplia variedad de estilos existente convierten al bolso en un accesorio apasionante. Algunos capítulos tratan sobre los distintos tipos de cuero y de plástico, y se presentan ejemplos de bolsos decorados con delicados bordados o con piedras preciosas. También se dedica un capítulo a la influencia de estilos procedentes de las artes aplicadas, y el libro presenta bolsos clásicos modernos, así como bolsos de diseñadores destacados.

Todos los bolsos que aparecen en el libro provienen del Hendrikje Bag Museum (Países Bajos). Al igual que sucedió con otros museos, éste tiene su origen en el celo coleccionista, pues lo que comenzó como una fascinación personal pasó a convertirse en una generosa colección que mostraba que el bolso es un accesorio estimulante en continuo desarrollo.

El museo dispone de una colección de más de 2.500 ejemplares que lo convierte en el mayor museo de bolsos de Europa. En él, estos accesorios se muestran en exposiciones permanentes y en exposiciones temporales. Asimismo, el museo anima a los jóvenes diseñadores mediante la organización de exposiciones de sus trabajos y la venta de los bolsos que diseñan.

Hendrikje Ivo
Hendrikje Bag Museum
Amstelveen, Países Bajos

www.museumofbagsandpurses.com

Español

Probabilmente, pochi si soffermano a pensare che un oggetto di uso quotidiano apparentemente banale come la borsetta ha una storia straordinariamente ricca e ha vissuto un notevole sviluppo nei molti secoli della sua esistenza. Questo volume traccia l'evoluzione della borsa come contenitore di piccoli effetti personali dalla fine del Medioevo all'epoca contemporanea, con particolare attenzione alla moda e agli avvenimenti sociali che ne hanno influenzato lo sviluppo. Le borse sono suddivise in capitoli a seconda della loro funzione, del materiale di cui sono fatte e della loro forma.

L'immensa varietà di stili e di utilizzi di questi accessori racchiude il segreto del loro fascino. Vi sono capitoli dedicati a pellami e plastiche speciali, e vi si trovano esempi di borsette decorate con fini ricami o con pietre preziose. Si è dedicato anche uno spazio all'influenza degli stili artistici in voga nelle diverse epoche, e il volume comprende anche i classici moderni e borsette ideate da famosi stilisti.

Tutte le borsette riprodotte in questo libro sono conservate al Museo della Borsetta Hendrikje, nei Paesi Bassi. Come molti altri musei, anche questo è nato dalla passione di un collezionista. In seguito, quella che era iniziata come una fascinazione personale si è sviluppata fino a diventare una vasta collezione che illustra lo sviluppo, ancora in corso, di questo affascinante accessorio.

Con una collezione di oltre 2.500 borse e borsette, il museo Hendrikje è il più grande museo della borsetta d'Europa. A fianco della collezione permanente, vi si tengono anche mostre temporanee. Inoltre, il museo promuove e sostiene i giovani stilisti organizzando regolarmente esposizioni del loro lavoro e mettendo in vendita le loro creazioni.

Hendrikje Ivo
Museo della Borsetta Hendrikje
Amstelveen, Paesi Bassi

www.museumofbagsandpurses.com

Italiano

Nur wenige von uns haben sich wahrscheinlich jemals über einen so alltäglichen Gebrauchsgegenstand wie die Handtasche Gedanken gemacht. Dabei umfasst die Geschichte der Handtasche viele Jahrhunderte und bemerkenswerte Entwicklungen. Dieses Buch stellt die Entwicklung der Tasche als Utensil zur Beförderung persönlicher Gegenstände vom späten Mittelalter bis in die heutige Zeit dar und stellt dabei besonders die Mode- und Gesellschaftstrends in den Vordergrund, die in der Geschichte der Tasche von Bedeutung waren. Die Taschen werden nach Kapiteln getrennt entsprechend ihrem Verwendungszweck, den verwendeten Materialien und ihrer Form vorgestellt. Ihre breite Palette an Stilen und Funktionen machen die Handtasche zu einem faszinierenden Accessoire. Es gibt Kapitel über Taschen aus Leder und Kunststoffen und andere zu Taschen aus feiner Stickerei oder Edelsteinen. Andere Kapitel widmen sich den Einflüssen der jeweils aktuellen Stile der angewandten Kunst. Schließlich werden auch einige moderne Taschen-Klassiker sowie Modelle führender Designer gezeigt.

Alle hier in diesem Buch aufgeführten Taschen stammen aus dem Hendrikje-Taschenmuseum in den Niederlanden. Wie es bei vielen Museen der Fall ist, entstand dieses Museum aus einer großen Sammelleidenschaft heraus. Was als persönliches Hobby begann, wurde über die Jahre zu einer umfangreichen Sammlung, die zeigt, dass die Tasche ein ausgesprochen interessantes Accessoire ist, das sich kontinuierlich verändert und entwickelt. Die Kollektion des Museums umfasst mehr als 2500 Stücke und macht das Museum damit zum größten Taschen-Museum in Europa. Die Stücke werden in Dauer- und Wechselausstellungen gezeigt. Außerdem unterstützt das Museum aufstrebende Designer durch regelmäßige Ausstellungen ihrer Modelle und deren Verkauf.

Hendrikje Ivo
Hendrikje Taschenmuseum
Amstelveen, Niederlande

www.taschenmuseum.com

おそらく皆さんの中でバッグのような日用品が並外れた豊かな歴史を持ち、何世紀にもわたってすばらしい発展を遂げてきたということを深くお考えになる方はそう多くはなでしょう。本書は中世後期から現代まで、個人の身の回り品を持ち運ぶために使用されてきたバッグ類の歩みを、その発展に影響を与えた流行や社会傾向に焦点を当てて紹介します。

バッグに関する記述は、その機能、素材、形などによって分類し各セクションにまとめました。幅広い様式と利用目的を持つバッグ類はとても興味深いアクセサリーといえます。本書は特殊なレザーやプラスチックに特記したセクションや見事な刺繍、宝石による装飾を施したバッグに関するセクションも設けています。また、応用美術面でバッグの様式が受けた影響についてのセクションもあり、近代クラシック、トップデザイナーが手がけたハンドバッグも余すところなく収めています。

本書に収録のバッグは全てオランダにあるヘンドリキア バッグ・パース博物館のコレクションです。多くの博物館同様、この博物館も収集に対する熱い情熱が発端でした。個人的なバッグに対する興味から始まったものが、今では膨大なコレクションとなり、バッグ類は今もなお常に進化し続ける興味深いアクセサリーとして展示されています。

この博物館は 2,500 点以上のバッグを有するヨーロッパ最大のバッグ博物館です。バッグ類は常時展示されているものとテーマに沿ってその都度展示されるものに分かれています。さらに、この博物館では新米デザイナーの作品展示や販売を定期的に行って若手デザイナー育成促進に努めています。

Hendrikje Ivo
Hendrikje Bag Museum
Amstelveen, The Netherlands

deutsch

日本語

500 years of bags

1500 - 1800, hanging bags and purses

Since earliest times, bags have been useful implements for both women and men. Because clothing as yet had no inside pockets, bags and purses were used for carrying money and other personal items. We can see how bags looked in past epochs from bags in museums and illustrations in paintings and prints and on carpets. Depending on their function, there were many different kinds of bags and purses: bags with frames, leather purses and pouch-like purses on long carrying cords. Apart from a few exceptions that hung from the shoulder, bags were carried on the belt or waistband. For men, the bag gradually fell into disuse with the arrival of pockets in men's clothing at the end of the sixteenth century and in the seventeenth century. With the exception of game bags and briefcases, bags became the exclusive domain of women in succeeding centuries.

From the sixteenth century on, women carried their purses also on a chatelaine, a hook with chains on which accessories could be hung, such as keys, a knife sheath and sewing materials. Because of the costly materials used, the chatelaine was a status-defining ornament as well as a practical accessory. In the course of the centuries, the form of chatelaines and the accessories that hung from them were constantly changing, but only at the beginning of the twentieth century was the chatelaine finally replaced by the handbag.

During the seventeenth, eighteenth and a large part of the nineteenth century, women's clothing was so voluminous that one or two loose pockets could be carried invisibly concealed under the skirt with no difficulty. Mostly these pockets were carried as a pair, one dangling from each hip. These tie pockets also remained popular until well into the nineteenth century.

1800 - 1900, new times, new bags

In the course of the 18th century, partly because of the discovery of Pompeii, everything related to the ancient Greeks and Romans had become popular. Under their

English

influence, the nature of fashion changed at the end of the century. Dresses became plain and the waist was raised. There was no longer space for tie pockets under this flimsy apparel, and their contents were moved to the reticule. The novelty was that the reticule was carried in the hand on a cord or chain; for the first few decades of the nineteenth century, it remained fashionable to carry bags in the hand. Reticules were made from all kinds of textiles, often by the women themselves.

Upon the arrival of new production methods with the advent of the Industrial Revolution, new materials such as papier-mâché, iron and cut steel were used to manufacture bags. The combination of these materials along with new technologies led to new kinds of bags. With the increase in travel came new bags for the modern traveller. Hand luggage for trains became the precursor of the handbag, which was not just taken on journeys but also used for making social calls and shopping.

1900 - today, the handbag

In the twentieth century, the bag changed further under the influence of a rapid succession of art trends and materials, but the emancipation of women was quite possibly an even greater influence. Because of women's increasing participation in the working world and, partly as a result, their growing mobility, the number of practical demands on the bag grew. Leather briefcases appeared for work, handy strolling and visiting bags in leather or plastic for daytime, elegantly shimmering evening bags and minaudières for evenings, and opera bags for the theatre.

Brand names began to play a major role in the twentieth century. Brands that have become world famous for their exclusive handbags and leather goods include Hermès, Louis Vuitton, Gucci and Prada. But the hand-bag is also now an important fashion accessory for designers and houses such as Chanel, Dior, Yves Saint Laurent, Versace, Donna Karan and Dolce & Gabbana. In contrast to previous centuries in which models could remain the same for decades, the bag has now become a fad that changes every season.

English

English

5 siècles de sacs

1500 - 1800, sacs et bourses suspendus

Depuis les temps les plus anciens, les sacs sont un accessoire des plus utiles pour les femmes autant que les hommes. Comme les vêtements n'étaient alors pas encore dotés de poches intérieures, les sacs et les bourses servaient à transporter son argent et tout autre objet personnel. On peut voir l'apparence qu'avaient ces sacs autrefois dans les musées et les illustrations des peintures, gravures ou tapisseries. Selon leurs fonctions, il existait de multiples sortes de sacs et de bourses : sacs à fermoirs, bourses en cuir ou en forme de bourse suspendue à de longs cordons. Sauf rares exceptions de modèles à l'épaule, les sacs se portaient à la ceinture. Pour les hommes, le sac est peu à peu tombé en désuétude avec l'introduction de poches dans les habits à la fin du seizième siècle et au dix-septième siècle. À l'exception des gibecières et des porte-documents, les sacs sont devenus l'apanage exclusif des femmes au cours des siècles suivants.

À partir du seizième siècle, les femmes portent leur bourse attachée à une châtelaine aussi, une agrafe dotée de chaînes auxquelles divers accessoires peuvent être accrochés, tels que des clés, un couteau dans sa gaine ou des ustensiles de couture. Réalisée dans des métaux précieux, la châtelaine est alors autant un bijou et un signe extérieur de richesse qu'un accessoire pratique. Si la forme des châtelaines et les objets qui y pendent n'ont cessé de changer au cours des siècles, ce n'est qu'au début du vingtième siècle que le sac a main s'impose définitivement.

Au dix-septième, dix-huitième et pendant une grande partie du dix-neuvième siècle, les vêtements féminins sont si volumineux qu'une ou deux poches peuvent aisément pendre, dissimulées sous les jupes. Ces poches vont en général par paires, une sur chaque hanche, et sont restées populaires jusque tard au dix-neuvième siècle.

1800 - 1900, à temps nouveaux, sacs nouveaux

Au dix-huitième siècle, notamment depuis la

français

découverte de Pompéi, tout ce qui rappelle les anciens Grecs et Romains est apprécié. Sous cette influence, la nature de la mode change à la fin du siècle. Les robes se simplifient et leur taille monte pour en faire des vêtements légers, ne laissant plus d'espace aux poches nouées en dessous dont le contenu est transféré aux réticules. Toute la nouveauté tient alors à la manière de porter ce dernier, à savoir à la main au bout d'un cordon ou d'une chaîne. Cette mode qui va durer toutes les premières décennies du dix-neuvième siècle. Les réticules sont coupés dans toutes sortes de tissus, souvent par les femmes elles-mêmes.

Avec l'introduction de nouvelles méthodes de production et l'avènement de la Révolution industrielle, de nouveaux matériaux comme le papier mâché, le fer et le fil d'acier coupé sont employés pour la fabrication des sacs. L'association de ces matières aux nouvelles technologies permet la création de sacs d'un genre nouveau.

Avec la multiplication des voyages, voient le jour de nouveaux sacs pour les voyageurs modernes. Les bagages à main pour le train sont les précurseurs du sac à main et servent en dehors des voyages pour les visites en société et le lèche-vitrines.

1900 – aujourd'hui, le sac à main

Au vingtième siècle, le sac poursuit sa transformation sous l'influence d'une succession rapide de tendances artistiques et de matériaux, mais aussi celle, sans doute encore plus importante, de l'émancipation féminine. Avec la présence accrue des femmes dans le monde du travail et la mobilité qui en découle, les exigences pratiques envers le sac se multiplient. C'est ainsi qu'apparaissent les porte-documents en cuir pour le travail, les sacs en cuir ou en plastique de promenade ou de visite pour la journée, les sacs du soir et minaudières scintillants et élégants pour les soirées et les sacs d'opéra pour le théâtre.

Les marques commencent à jouer un rôle majeur au vingtième siècle. Certaines sont devenues célèbres dans le monde entier pour leurs sacs à main et leurs articles de maroquinerie exclusifs comme Hermès, Louis Vuitton, Gucci et Prada. Mais le sac à main est désormais aussi un accessoire de mode important pour des créateurs et des maisons comme Chanel, Dior, Yves Saint Laurent, Versace, Donna Karan et Dolce & Gabbana. Contrairement aux siècles précédents où un modèle pouvait rester inchangé pendant des dizaines d'années, le sac est aujourd'hui éphémère et change à chaque saison.

500 jaar tassen

1500 - 1800, hangende tassen en beurzen

Vanaf de vroegste tijden waren tassen nuttige gebruiksvoorwerpen, zowel voor vrouwen als voor mannen.
Omdat kleding nog geen binnenzakken kende, gebruikte
men tassen en beurzen voor het meedragen van geld
en andere persoonlijke benodigdheden. Hoe tassen er
in afgelopen eeuwen uitgezien hebben, is af te leiden
van tassen in musea en van afbeeldingen op schilderijen,
prenten en tapijten.

Afhankelijk van hun functie waren tassen en beurzen er
in allerlei uitvoeringen: beugeltassen, leren beurzen en
buidelvormige beurzen aan lange trekkoorden. Behalve
enkele uitzonderingen die om de schouder werden gehangen, werden tassen aan de riem of gordel gedragen.
De tas raakte bij de man langzaam in onbruik met de
komst van binnenzakken in mannenkleding aan het
einde van de zestiende eeuw en in de zeventiende
eeuw. Met uitzondering van de jacht- en documenten-
tas werd de tas in volgende eeuwen het exclusieve
domein van de vrouw.

Vanaf de zestiende eeuw droegen vrouwen hun beurzen
ook aan een chatelaine: een haak met kettingen waaraan
accessoires gehangen konden worden, zoals sleutels,
een messenkoker en naaigerei. Door de kostbare
materialen was de chatelaine behalve een praktische
toevoeging ook een statusgevend sieraad. In de loop
van de eeuwen veranderen steeds de vorm van de
chatelaines en de accessoires die eraan werden
gehangen, maar pas aan het begin van de twintigste
eeuw werd de chatelaine definitief door de handtas
verdrongen.

Gedurende de zeventiende, achttiende en een groot
deel van de negentiende eeuw was de dameskleding
zo wijd, dat men zonder bezwaar onder de rok onzicht-
baar verborgen een of twee losse zakken kon dragen.
Meestal werden deze zakken gedragen als paar: één
op elke heup hangend. Vandaar dat ze dijzakken werden
genoemd. Ook de dijzak bleef tot ver in de negentiende eeuw populair.

nederlands

1800 - 1900, nieuwe tijden, nieuwe tassen

In de loop van de achttiende eeuw werd mede door de ontdekking van Pompeii alles wat met de Griekse en Romeinse Oudheid te maken had populair. Onder invloed daarvan veranderde aan het eind van de eeuw het modebeeld. Japonnen werden sluik en de taille ging omhoog. Voor de dijzak was onder deze fijne kleding geen plaats meer, en de inhoud ervan verhuisde naar de reticule. Nieuw was dat de reticule aan een koord of ketting in de hand gedragen werd; de eerste decennia van de negentiende eeuw bleef het modieus om tassen in de hand te dragen. Reticules werden uit allerlei soorten textiel veelal door vrouwen zelf gemaakt. Met de komst van nieuwe productiemethoden ten tijde van de Industriële Revolutie werden nieuwe materialen als papier-maché, ijzer en geslepen staal toegepast voor de productie van tassen. De combinatie hiervan met nieuwe technieken leverde nieuwe tasvormen op. Met de toename van het reizen kwamen er nieuwe tassen voor de moderne reiziger. De handbagage uit de trein werd de voorloper van de handtas die men niet alleen op reis meenam, maar ook gebruikte bij het afleggen van visites en bij het winkelen.

1900 - heden, de handtas

In de twintigste eeuw veranderde de tas verder onder invloed van elkaar snel opvolgende kunststromingen en materialen, maar van zo mogelijk nog grotere invloed was de emancipatie van de vrouw. Door haar toenemende deelname aan het arbeidsproces en de mede daardoor groeiende mobiliteit groeide het aantal praktische eisen aan de tas. Er kwamen leren documententassen voor naar het werk, handzame wandel- en visitetassen van leer of kunststof voor overdag, elegante glinsterende avondtassen en minaudières voor 's avonds, en operatasjes voor in het theater.

Merknamen zijn in de twintigste eeuw een grote rol gaan spelen. Merken die wereldberoemd zijn geworden vanwege hun exclusieve handtassen en lederwaren zijn Hermès, Louis Vuitton, Gucci en Prada. Maar ook voor modeontwerpers en modehuizen als Chanel, Dior,

Yves Saint Laurent, Versace, Donna Karan en Dolce & Gabbana is de tas tegenwoordig een belangrijk mode-accessoire. In tegenstelling tot vorige eeuwen, waarin sommige tasmodellen decennialang hetzelfde bleven, is de tas nu geworden tot een modeverschijnsel dat elk seizoen verandert.

500 años de bolsos

1500–1800: monederos y bolsos colgantes

Desde sus inicios, el bolso ha resultado un complemento útil tanto para mujeres como para hombres. Puesto que las prendas de vestir no disponían de bolsillos interiores como ocurre hoy en día, para transportar dinero y otros enseres personales se empleaban bolsos y monederos. El aspecto que tenían los bolsos en épocas anteriores se aprecia en los ejemplares conservados en museos, además de en las ilustraciones de cuadros y láminas, y en alfombras.

Según su función, encontramos diversos tipos de bolsos y monederos: bolsos de boquilla, monederos de piel y monederos tipo morral, que pendían de largos cordones. A excepción de algunos casos que colgaban del hombro, los bolsos se llevaban en el cinturón o en la pretina. Para el hombre, el bolso cayó paulatinamente en desuso con la aparición de bolsillos en la vestimenta masculina a finales del siglo XVI y durante el siglo XVII. Exceptuando las bolsas de caza y las maletas, en los siglos posteriores el bolso se convirtió en dominio exclusivo de la mujer.

A partir del siglo XVI, las mujeres llevaban el monedero colgado de una *chatelaine*, un gancho con cadenas del cual podían colgarse objetos tales como las llaves, una funda de navaja y el material de costura. Dado que éstos se realizaban con materiales costosos, además de resultar un accesorio práctico, la *chatelaine* era un ornamento que definía la condición social de su propietaria. En el transcurso de los siglos, la forma de las *chatelaines* y los accesorios que pendían de ellas cambiaban constantemente y no fueron sustituidos definitivamente por el bolso de mano hasta principios del siglo XX.

Durante los siglos XVII y XVIII, y gran parte del XIX, la indumentaria femenina era tan voluminosa que bajo la falda podía llevarse fácilmente uno o dos bolsillos de material no rígido sin que se vieran. Generalmente se empleaban dos bolsillos, uno sobre cada cadera. Estos bolsillos exteriores siguieron siendo muy populares hasta bien entrado el siglo XIX.

Español

1800–1900: nuevos tiempos, nuevos bolsos

En el transcurso del siglo XVIII, en parte debido al descubrimiento de las ruinas de Pompeya, todo lo relacionado con la antigua Grecia y la antigua Roma se puso de moda. Este hecho hizo cambiar la naturaleza de la moda a finales de siglo. Los vestidos se volvieron lisos y se elevó la cintura. Este ligero equipaje no dejaba espacio para los bolsillos exteriores, cuyo contenido pasó a transportarse en retículas. La novedad residía en que la retícula se llevaba en la mano o colgada de una cuerda o cadena. Durante las primeras décadas del siglo XIX, llevar los bolsos en la mano estaba de moda. Las retículas se elaboraban con los más diversos materiales y, a menudo, las confeccionaban las mismas mujeres.

Con la aparición de los nuevos medios de producción que trajo consigo la Revolución Industrial, en la producción de bolsos comenzaron a emplearse materiales no utilizados nunca anteriormente tales como el cartón piedra, el hierro y el acero cortado. De la combinación de estos materiales con las nuevas tecnologías surgieron tipos de bolsos novedosos.

Viajar se convirtió en una actividad frecuente y fue preciso diseñar nuevos tipos de bolsas para el viajero moderno. El equipaje de mano para los viajes en ferrocarril fue el precursor del bolso de mano, que no sólo se utilizaba en los trayectos largos, sino también cuando se iba de visita o se salía de compras.

1900: hoy, el bolso de mano

Si bien en el siglo XX el bolso siguió su evolución influido por la rápida sucesión de corrientes artísticas y por los nuevos materiales, hubo un factor posiblemente más decisivo: la emancipación de la mujer. Puesto que cada vez participaba de forma más activa en el mundo laboral y, en parte como resultado de ello, cada vez tenía más movilidad, aumentó la demanda práctica de bolsos. Así, aparecieron maletas de cuero para el trabajo; los bolsos de paseo y de visita elaborados en cuero o plástico se llevaban durante el día, por la noche se lucían bolsos de elegantes brillos y minaudières y, para asistir al teatro, se utilizaban las bolsas para la ópera.

Fue en el siglo XX cuando los nombres de marca comenzaron a desempeñar un papel destacado. Hermès, Louis Vuitton, Gucci y Prada son ejemplos de marcas que han adquirido fama mundial por sus exclusivos bolsos y otros artículos de cuero. Pero actualmente el bolso de mano también es un accesorio de moda importante para empresas y diseñadores como Chanel, Dior, Yves Saint-Laurent, Versace, Donna Karan y Dolce & Gabbana. A diferencia de lo que ocurría en siglos anteriores, en los que un mismo modelo se mantenía inalterado durante décadas, hoy en día el bolso es un capricho que cambia cada temporada.

500 anni di borse e borsette

1500 - 1800, borse e borsellini da cintura

Sin dal più remoto passato, le borse per contenere effetti personali sono state accessori utilissimi sia per le donne, sia per gli uomini. Poiché gli indumenti non avevano ancora tasche interne, per trasportare monete e altri piccoli oggetti personali si utilizzavano borse e borsellini; l'aspetto di questi contenitori del passato si può osservare ammirando gli esemplari conservati nei musei e le loro raffigurazioni nei dipinti, stampe e tappeti dell'epoca.

A seconda della loro funzione, borse e borsellini assumevano le forme più disparate: borse con cerniera, scarselle di pelle, sacchetti appesi a lunghi cordoni. Le borse erano appese in vita, alla cintura o alla fascia, tranne alcune che pendevano dalle spalle. La borsa per uomo cadde gradualmente in disuso con l'avvento delle tasche negli indumenti maschili, alla fine del XVI secolo e nel XVII secolo. Ad eccezione dei carnieri e delle valigette portadocumenti, nei secoli successivi la borsetta divenne così un accessorio esclusivamente femminile.

Dal XVI secolo in poi, le donne portavano piccole borsette appese a una châtelaine: un gancio metallico da cui si dipartivano molte catenelle cui venivano appesi diversi accessori come chiavi, guaine per coltelli e il necessario per il cucito. Per la preziosità dei materiali utilizzati, la châtelaine, oltre che un accessorio pratico, era anche un ornamento che indicava la posizione sociale della sua proprietaria. Nel corso dei secoli, la forma delle châtelaine e gli accessori che vi si appendevano subirono molte variazioni, ma fu solo all'inizio del XX secolo che questo oggetto venne soppiantato definitivamente dalla borsetta.

Nel XVII, XVIII e per buona parte del XIX secolo, gli abiti femminili erano tanto voluminosi che si potevano portare senza difficoltà una o due borse piatte nascoste sotto la gonna. Di solito, queste borsette o tasche erano in coppia, e ricadevano ciascuna lungo un fianco. Rimasero in voga fino a buona parte del XIX secolo.

Italiano

1800 - 1900, nuova era, nuove borsette

Durante il XVIII secolo, in parte a causa della scoperta di Pompei, tutto ciò che aveva a che fare con gli antichi Greci e Romani conobbe grande popolarità. Alla fine del secolo, l'influenza della classicità modificò profondamente la moda: gli abiti femminili adottarono linee più semplici e un punto vita più alto. Sotto questi indumenti leggeri non vi era più posto per le tasche piatte appese alla cintura, i cui contenuti vennero trasferiti nelle cosiddette reticule. La novità era che la *reticule* veniva portata in mano o al braccio, appesa a un nastro o a una catenella; nei primi decenni del XIX secolo, divenne di moda portare le borse a mano. Vi erano *reticule* di ogni tipo di tessuto, spesso confezionate dalle loro stesse proprietarie.

Con l'avvento di nuovi metodi di produzione nell'era della Rivoluzione Industriale, anche per la confezione di borse e borsette si iniziò a usare nuovi materiali come papier-mâché, ferro e acciaio tagliato. La combinazione tra questi materiali innovativi e le nuove tecnologie di produzione diede origine a nuovi tipi di borse e borsette. Con l'intensificarsi dei viaggi, nacquero nuove borse per il viaggiatore moderno. Il bagaglio usato per i viaggi ferroviari divenne precursore della borsa a mano, utilizzata non solo per i lunghi tragitti ma anche come borsa da passeggio per recarsi in visita e a fare acquisti.

1900 - oggi, la borsetta

Nel XX secolo, la borsetta cambiò ancora, sotto l'influenza di una rapida successione di diverse correnti artistiche e di nuovi materiali, anche se il maggiore fattore di cambiamento fu senz'altro l'emancipazione femminile. Il crescente coinvolgimento delle donne nel mondo del lavoro e la loro maggiore mobilità, che ne fu in parte la conseguenza, fecero sì che alla borsetta si richiedesse soprattutto funzionalità. Apparvero così i portadocumenti in cuoio per il lavoro, pratiche borse da giorno in pelle o plastica per passeggiare e far visita ai conoscenti, borsette da sera e *minaudières* eleganti e scintillanti, e borsette da teatro per recarsi all'opera.

Nel XX secolo, le grandi marche di pelletteria cominciarono a svolgere un ruolo importante. Tra le firme diventate famose in tutto il mondo per le loro borsette e i loro accessori di pelletteria eleganti ed esclusivi vi sono Hermès, Louis Vuitton, Gucci e Prada. Ma oggi la borsetta è anche un accessorio moda importante per gli stilisti e le case di moda come Chanel, Dior, Yves Saint Laurent, Versace, Donna Karan e Dolce & Gabbana. Mentre nei secoli precedenti alcuni modelli di borsetta restavano in voga per decenni, oggi la borsetta è diventata una moda passeggera che cambia ad ogni stagione.

Italiano

Italiano

500 Jahre Taschen

1500 - 1800 Gewandtaschen und Beutel

In frühester Zeit bereits galt die Tasche als hilfreiches Utensil, sowohl für Frauen als auch für Männer. Da die Kleider früher keine Innentaschen hatten, wurden Taschen und Beutel für die Aufbewahrung von Geld und persönlichen Gegenständen benutzt. Wie so eine Tasche früher ausgesehen hat, können wir an Beispielen aus Museen sowie anhand einiger Illustrationen, Gemälde und einiger Wandteppiche sehen.

Je nach ihrem Verwendungszweck gab es Taschen und Beutel in allen Formen und Farben: Bügeltaschen, Ledertaschen und Beuteltaschen an langen Trageriemen. Mit Ausnahme einiger weniger Taschen, die von der Schulter hingen, wurden Taschen am Gürtel oder Bund getragen. Bei den Männern kam die Tasche nach und nach außer Gebrauch, als man gegen Ende des 16. Jahrhunderts und im 17. Jahrhundert damit anfing, Innentaschen in die Männerkleider zu nähen. So wurde die Tasche, mit Ausnahme von Jagdtaschen oder Aktentaschen, für die folgenden Jahrhunderte zu einer exklusiv weiblichen Angelegenheit.

Seit dem 16. Jahrhundert trugen die Frauen die Beutel auch an einer Kette, Chatelaine genannt, die einen Haken hatte, an der verschiedene Gegenstände befestigt werden konnten, wie zum Beispiel Schlüssel, Messerscheiden oder Nähzeug. Durch die kostbaren Materialen, aus denen die Kette gefertigt wurde, war die Chatelaine nicht nur ein praktisches Utensil, sondern vor allem auch ein Statussymbol. Im Laufe der Jahrhunderte veränderte sich die Form der Ketten und die der an ihr befestigten Objekte ständig, aber erst zu Beginn des 20. Jahrhunderts wurde die Chatelaine vollständig durch die Handtasche ersetzt.

Während des 17., 18. und des größten Teils des 19. Jahrhunderts waren die üblichen Frauenkleider so weit und voluminös, dass man unter den Gewändern problemlos einen oder zwei Untertaschen verbergen konnte. Die meisten dieser Untertaschen trug man als Paar, an jeder Seite der Hüfte baumelte eine. Diese Gewandtaschen waren bis ins fortgeschrittene 19. Jahrhundert sehr beliebt.

deutsch

1800 – 1900: Neue Zeiten, neue Taschen

Im Laufe des 18. Jahrhunderts, zum Teil beeinflusst durch die Entdeckungen von Pompeji, wurde alles Mode, was mit den alten Griechen und Römern zu tun hatte. Dies wirkte sich gegen Ende des Jahrhunderts auch auf die Mode aus. Die Kleider wurden eng und schmal, die Taille rutschte nach oben. Da war nun kein Platz mehr für Gewandtaschen. Also wurden die notwendigen Utensilien von nun an in einer sogenannten Retikül befördert. Neu war, dass man diese neuen Taschen in der Hand an einer Kordel oder einer Kette trug. In den ersten Jahrzehnten des 19. Jahrhunderts war es Mode, die Tasche einfach in der Hand zu tragen. Die Retiküle wurden aus den unterschiedlichsten Textilien gefertigt und oft von ihren Trägerinnen selbst hergestellt. Mit dem Aufkommen neuer Produktionsverfahren als Folge der industriellen Revolution wurden Taschen auch aus Pappmaschee, Eisen und poliertem Stahl hergestellt. Die Kombination dieser Materialien mit neuen Technologien führte zum Entstehen neuer Taschentypen. Reisen wurde immer beliebter, und es gab neue Taschen für den modernen Reisenden. Das Handgepäck für die Zugfahrt wurde zum Vorläufer der heutigen Handtasche. Diese neue Taschenform wurde dann nicht nur auf Reisen, sondern auch für Besuche oder Einkäufe verwendet.

1900 – Gegenwart: Die Handtasche

Unter dem Einfluss schnell aufeinanderfolgender neuer Strömungen in der Kunst, vieler neuer Materialien, aber vor allem auch durch die Emanzipation der Frauen veränderte sich im 20. Jahrhundert die Handtasche stetig weiter. Da Frauen nun immer häufiger im außerhäuslichen Arbeitsleben mitwirkten, nahm auch ihre Mobilität zu, und als Folge dessen musste die Tasche immer mehr praktische Funktionen erfüllen. Lederbrieftaschen für das Büro kamen auf, handliche Taschen aus Leder oder Kunststoff für Spaziergänge und Besuche tagsüber, elegant glänzende Modelle und sogenannte Minaudières für das Ausgehen am Abend und Operntäschchen für den Theater- oder Opernbesuch erwei-

terten die Palette der bereits bestehenden Taschentypen. Markennamen spielten ab dem 20. Jahrhundert eine große Rolle. Zu den Marken, die für ihre exklusiven Handtaschen und Lederartikel weltberühmt wurden, gehören Hermès, Louis Vuitton, Gucci und Prada. Handtaschen wurden aber gleichzeitig auch zu einem wichtigen Mode-Accessoire für Modehäuser und Designer wie Chanel, Dior, Yves Saint-Laurent, Versace, Donna Karan und Dolce & Gabbana. Im Unterschied zu vergangen Jahrhunderten, in denen sich einige Taschentypyen über Jahrzehnte überhaupt nicht veränderten, wurde die Tasche nun zum Accessoire, das in jeder Saison eine neue Form annimmt.

deutsch

deutsch

500 年のバッグ史

1500 年 〜 1800 年 ― ぶら下げ式バッグ、パース

最も早い時期からバッグ類は女性にとっても男性にとっても便利な道具でした。その当時の洋服には内ポケットがなく、お金やほかの手回り品を携帯するときにバッグやパースを利用しました。過去のバッグ類は、博物館の展示物、絵画や印刷物の図解、カーペットの絵柄などからその外見を察することができます。

機能に合わせて、さまざまな種類のバッグやパース―口金付きのバッグ、レザーのパースやポーチに似た長い持ちひも付きパースなどがありました。 肩から下げるようになっている例外的なものもいくつかありますが、当時バッグは全てベルト、またはウエストバンドに取り付けて持ち歩くものでした。紳士用バッグは 16 世紀末から 17 世紀にかけて紳士服にポケットが取り付けられ始めたことから、徐々に使用されなくなっていきました。ゲーム用バッグとブリーフケースは例外的に使用され続けましたが、バッグ類は以降婦人専用領域になります。

16 世紀以降、女性はパースをシャトレーンと呼ばれるチェーン付きの留金に取り付けて持ち歩くようになりました。シャトレーンとは鍵、ナイフ鞘、裁縫道具などを取り付けるためのものです。高価な素材を用いて作られていたため、シャトレーンは実用的なアクセサリーであると同時に持ち主の地位を象徴する装飾品でもありました。時代の流れの中で、シャトレーンとそれに取り付けられる装身具は常に変わりましたが、そのシャトレーンがついにハンドバッグに座を奪われたのは 20 世紀の初めになってからでした。

17 世紀、18 世紀、さらに 19 世紀の大部分において、婦人服は大変かさばっていたため取り外しのできるポケットのひとつやふたつは簡単にスカートの下に取り付けて隠すことができました。大抵、これらのポケットは対で持ち歩き、腰の両側にひとつずつ下げていました。このような結びポケットは 19 世紀になってもしばらくの間愛用され続けました。

1800 年 〜 1900 年 ― 新たな時代、新たなバッグ

18 世紀の流れの中で、ポンペイの発見も加わって、古代ギリシャ人やローマ人に関わるもの全般に対する関心が高まりました。その影響を受けて、ファッションの本質が 18 世紀末に変わります。ドレスが簡素化され、ウエストの位置が高くなります。このような薄手

日本語

の衣服ではもはや結びポケットの場所などなく、ポケットに入れていたものはレティキュール（婦人用小型ハンドバッグ）に入れるようになりました。斬新だったのは、レティキュールはひもまたはチェーンが付いていて、その部分を手に握って持つようになっていた点でした。19世紀に突入してから数十年間はレティキュールを手からぶら下げて持ち歩くことが流行しました。レティキュールにはいろいろな生地が使用され、女性自身による手作りのものもよくありました。

新たな製造方式が産業革命の到来によってもたらされ、張子や鉄、カットスチール、ビーズなどの新素材がバッグ類の製造に使用されるようになります。これらの素材の組み合わせと新技術とが相まって新種のバッグ誕生につながります。

旅行の機会が増えてモダンな旅行者向けに新たなバッグ登場します。列車で旅をするときの手荷物用鞄がハンドバッグの先駆けとして現れ、鞄は、旅行時はもちろん訪問時や買い物時にも持ち歩かれました。

1900年 〜 現在ーハンドバッグ

20世紀になって、バッグ類は芸術の流れと素材の急速な移り変わりの影響を受け変化していきますが、女性解放の動きはバッグにさらに大きな影響をもたらします。女性の社会進出が増加したことで女性が出かける機会も増え、バッグ類に対する実用面での需要が伸びました。通勤にはレザー製ブリーフケースが登場し、日中は便利なレザー・プラスチック製の外出用、訪問用バッグ、夜の外出にはエレガントで光沢のあるイブニングバッグやミノディエール、劇場へはオペラバッグが使われました。

ブランド名も20世紀では重要な役割を持ち始めました。専売のハンドバッグで世界的に有名になったブランドにはエルメス、ルイヴィトン、グッチ、プラダなどが挙げられます。しかし、ハンドバッグは今日では重要なファッション・アクセサリーとして、シャネル、ディオール、イヴサンローラン、ヴェルサーチ、ドナキャラン、ドルチェ＆ガバナなどのデザイナーやデザイナーズ店でも取り扱われています。何十年間も型が変わらなかった以前の世紀とは対照的に、バッグ類は現代においてシーズンごとに変化する流行ものに生まれ変わりました。

日本語　　　　　　　　　　　　　　　　　日本語

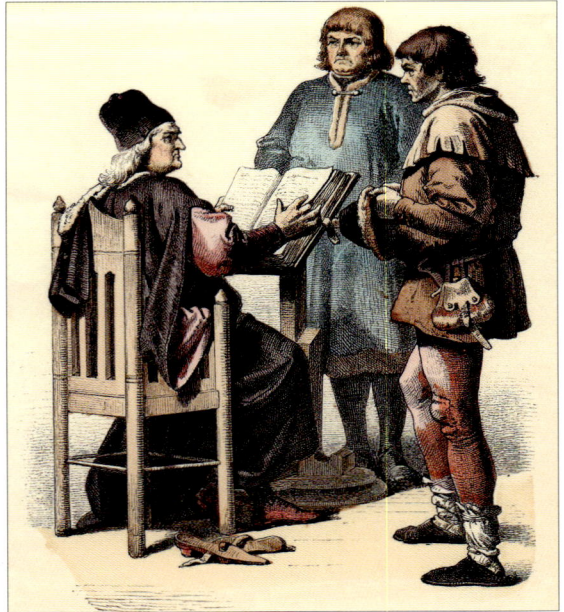

▲ 'Der Beutler' by Jost Amman Frankfurt, Germany, 1568.
▼ Fashion plate from 'La Belle Assemblée' France, 1815.

▲ Judge, Citizen and Farmer, from 'Geschichte der Costüme'
Germany, 15th century.
▼ 'Zuidbevelandse Boerin' from 'Kabinet van Mode en Smaak',
Haarlem, 1791. Reproduction: Koninklijke Bibliotheek, The Hague,
The Netherlands.

▲ 'Familie Thoe Schwartzenberg en Hohenlansberg Ulson de Saint Maurice' (detail), by Rienk Keijert, 1743. Collection: Fries Museum, Leeuwarden, The Netherlands.
▼ 'The Chatelaine; a really useful Present', from 'Punch', 1849. Reproduction: Koninklijke Bibliotheek, The Hague, The Netherlands.

▲ 'Tight Lacing, or Fashion before Ease', by John Collet, England, 1770-1780. Collection: The Colonial Williamsburg Foundation, USA.
▼ Fashion plate from 'La Mode illustrée' France, 1882.

▲ Fashion plate from 'Gazette du Bon Ton', France, 1912-1913.
Reproduction: Public library, Amsterdam, The Netherlands.
▼ Fashion plate 1951.

▲ Woman carrying pochette, from the catalogue of Maison Rugemer
Belgium, 1913-1914.
▼ Image from the catalogue of Werber, Paris France, 1950s.

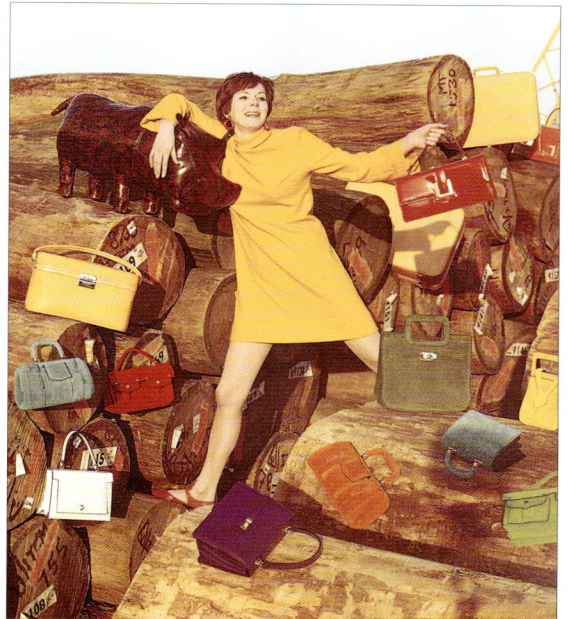

▲ Les idées nouvelles France, 1920s.
▼ Woman holding shoulder bag 1960s.

▲ Woman holding a handbag The Netherlands, ca. 1916
▼ Advertisement for Zumpolle, leathergoods store, Amsterdam and Laren The Netherlands, 1967.

Early bags and purses

Premiers sacs et bourses

Vroege tassen en beurzen

Los primeros bolsos y monederos

Prime borse e borsellini

Frühe Taschen und Beutel

初期のバッグとパース

From the late Middle Ages until the seventeenth century, men and women used bags and purses to store and carry around their coins, papers, alms, bibles and holy relics. These bags and purses were worn on a strap or belt and were often made from unadorned leather or cloth. But there were also more luxurious models made from costly materials with beautiful embroidery in silk, gold and silver thread. The oldest bag in the Bag Museum is a sixteenth-century goat leather man's pouch with decorative buttons and a metal frame. Eighteen pockets are concealed behind the mostly secret clasps. In addition to wearing them on their belts, women wore their bags and purses on chatelaines.

Small pouches and bags could serve as luxury packaging for money or fragrant flower petals. In England and France, these purses were given at the New Year. Purses containing flower petals or perfumed powder were laid or hung as sweet bags between clothing. It was also the tradition in various European countries to give a purse containing money as a wedding present. In the French city of Limoges, special bridal bags were produced between 1690 and 1760: little flat oval purses made of silk with enamel depictions of the bride and groom, or sometimes of saints, on both sides. Other wedding purses were made from minuscule glass beads (sablé beads), tiny beads as small as grains of sand strung on a silk thread. A horse's hair was used as a needle for this, because the beads were so small that no normal needle could go through them. Purses with other uses include gaming purses and alms purses. Card players kept their coins or gambling chips in these gaming purses, which had a stiff round bottom so that they could stand upright on the table. Sometimes the bottom was decorated with a family crest so that there could be no doubt as to the owner. A beaded purse with the inscription 'Remember the Pore 1630' hints at alms purses, or aumônières, which were used from the thirteenth to the fifteenth century.

English

De la fin du Moyen Âge au dix-septième siècle, hommes et femmes ont utilisé des sacs et des bourses pour ranger et transporter leurs pièces, papiers, aumônes, bibles et reliques saintes. Ces accessoires se portaient à une courroie ou ceinture et étaient souvent en simple cuir ou toile. Cependant, il existait aussi des modèles plus sophistiqués en tissus précieux et richement brodés de soie ou de filaments d'or et d'argent. Le sac le plus ancien du Musée des sacs est une bourse d'homme du seizième siècle en chevreau ornée de boutons décoratifs et dotée d'un fermoir métallique : dix-huit poches sont dissimulées par les différentes boucles, la plupart secrètes. Les femmes portaient quant à elles les sacs et porte-monnaie à la ceinture, mais aussi accrochés à des châtelaines.

Les bourses et sacs de petit format pouvaient aussi servir de récipients de luxe pour de l'argent ou des pétales de fleurs. En Angleterre et en France, ils sont offerts au Nouvel an, alors que des sacs remplis de pétales de fleurs ou de poudres parfumées sont posés ou suspendus entre les vêtements. Dans plusieurs pays européens, la tradition était d'offrir une bourse d'argent en cadeau de mariage, des bourses de mariage ayant été fabriquées à cet effet dans la ville de Limoges entre 1690 et 1760 : de petites bourses plates et ovales en soie portant des deux côtés la représentation émaillée des époux ou parfois de saints. D'autres sont faits de minuscules perles de verre, aussi petites que des grains de sable, enfilées sur un fil de soie (pour cela on utilisait un crin de cheval, aucune aiguille ne pouvant passer à travers ces perles). Parmi d'autres usages connus, on trouve les bourses de jeu et les bourses à aumônes. Les joueurs de cartes conservaient leurs pièces ou jetons dans les premières, qui avaient un fond rond et dur afin de tenir debout sur la table. Le fond était parfois orné des armoiries familiales pour écarter tout doute quant au propriétaire. Un sac en perles portant l'inscription « Remember the Pore » (« *N'oubliez pas les pauvres* ») de 1630, quant à lui, rappelle les bourses à aumônes, ou aumônières, utilisées du treizième au quinzième siècle.

Vanaf de late middeleeuwen tot in de zeventiende eeuw hebben mannen en vrouwen tassen en beurzen gebruikt voor het bewaren en meenemen van muntgeld, documenten, brieven, aalmoezen, bijbels en relikwieën. Deze tassen en beurzen werden gedragen aan een riem of gordel en waren veelal gemaakt van onversierd leer of textiel. Er waren echter ook luxere uitvoeringen van kostbare stoffen met fraai borduurwerk in zijde-, goud- en zilverdraad. De oudste tas uit het Tassenmuseum is een zestiende-eeuwse geitenleren mannentas met sierlijke knopen en een metalen beugel. Achter de veelal geheime sluitingen gaan achttien vakken schuil. Vrouwen droegen hun tassen en beurzen behalve aan de riem ook aan de chatelaine.

Kleine beursjes en tasjes konden dienen als luxe verpakking voor geld of lekker ruikende bloemblaadjes. In Engeland en Frankrijk werden met nieuwjaar beurzen met geld aan de koning geschonken. De beurzen met bloemblaadjes of geparfumeerd poeder werden als reuktasjes tussen kleding gelegd of gehangen. Ook was het in diverse Europese landen traditie om bij een huwelijk een beurs met geld cadeau te geven. In de Franse stad Limoges werden tussen 1690 en 1760 speciale bruidsbeurzen gemaakt: kleine platte eivormige beurzen van zijde, met aan weerszijden emaillen afbeeldingen van bruid en bruidegom, of soms van heiligen. Andere huwelijksbeurzen werden gemaakt van zeer fijne glaskralen (sablékralen): kraaltjes zo klein als zandkorrels die aan een zijdedraad werden geregen. Een paardenhaar werd daarbij als naald gebruikt, omdat de kralen zo klein waren, dat er geen gewone naald doorheen kon.

Beurzen met weer andere toepassingen zijn speelbeurzen en aalmoezenbeurzen. Kaartspelers bewaarden hun geld of fiches in deze speelbeurzen die een stijve ronde bodem hadden, waardoor ze op tafel konden blijven staan. Soms was die bodem voorzien van een familiewapen, zodat er geen twijfel kon ontstaan over de eigenaar. Een kralenbeurs met het opschrift 'Remember the Pore 1630' doet denken aan aalmoezenbeurzen, *aumônières*, uit de dertiende tot en met vijftiende eeuw.

français

nederlands

Desde finales de la Edad Media hasta el siglo XVII, hombres y mujeres se servían de bolsas y monederos para almacenar y transportar monedas, papeles, limosnas, Biblias y reliquias religiosas. Estos recipientes pendían de una cinta o cinturón y a menudo estaban elaborados con cuero o tela no decoradas. Existían, asimismo, modelos más lujosos confeccionados con materiales más costosos y decorados con hermosos bordados realizados con hilos de seda, oro y plata. El exponente más antiguo con que cuenta el museo es un morral masculino elaborado en cuero de cabra que data del siglo XVI y que presenta botones decorativos y una boquilla metálica. Tras unos cierres, en su mayoría secretos, se esconden dieciocho bolsillos. Además de en el cinturón, las mujeres también llevaban las bolsas y los monederos colgados de *chatelaines*.

Los morrales y bolsos de menor tamaño resultaban un envoltorio de lujo para el dinero o los pétalos de flores perfumados. En Inglaterra y en Francia, los portamonedas se regalaban con la llegada de un nuevo año. Los que contenían pétalos de flores o polvos perfumados se disponían o colgaban como bolsas perfumadas entre las prendas de ropa. En diversos países europeos también era tradición ofrecer un monedero lleno de dinero como regalo de bodas. En la ciudad francesa de Limoges, entre los años 1690 y 1760 se produjeron bolsos especiales para las bodas. Se trataba de pequeños monederos planos y ovalados confeccionados en seda con una representación de los novios en esmalte a cada lado, o bien de santos. También se realizaban monederos nupciales con delicadísimos abalorios de cristal (*sablé*), diminutas cuentas del tamaño de un grano de arena ensartadas en un hilo de seda. Para ello se empleaba una cerda de caballo a modo de aguja, ya que las cuentas eran tan pequeñas que una aguja normal no podía atravesarlas. Había monederos con otros usos, como los monederos de juego y las limosneras. Los jugadores de cartas guardaban el dinero o las fichas para las apuestas en estos monederos de juego, cuyo fondo era redondo y rígido para que pudieran sostenerse de pie sobre la mesa. Algunas veces el fondo se decoraba con el escudo familiar para que no hubiera dudas sobre la identidad de su propietario.

Dal tardo medioevo al XVII secolo, sia gli uomini sia le donne usavano borse e borsellini per riporre e trasportare monete, carte, elemosine, bibbie e reliquie sacre. Queste borse, che venivano appese al collo o alla cintura, erano spesso fatte di pelle o tessuto privi di decorazioni. Tuttavia ne esistevano anche modelli più sfarzosi, confezionati con materiali pregiati e ornati da splendidi ricami di seta o in filo d'oro e d'argento. La borsa più antica conservata al Museo della Borsetta è una saccoccia da uomo in pelle di capra del XVI secolo, ornata da bottoni decorativi e munita di una cerniera metallica. I fermagli di chiusura, per lo più nascosti, danno accesso a ben diciotto scomparti. Oltre che appenderle alla cintura, le donne portavano le borse anche agganciate a una châtelaine.

Le borse e i sacchetti più piccoli potevano servire anche come eleganti contenitori per le monete o per petali di fiori profumati. In Inghilterra e in Francia, era usanza regalare questo tipo di borse in occasione del Capodanno. I sacchetti contenenti petali di fiori o polvere profumata venivano posati o appesi tra i vestiti per profumarli. In diversi paesi europei vi era anche la tradizione di regalare una borsa contenente monete in occasione di un matrimonio. Tra il 1690 e il 1760, nella città francese di Limoges si fabbricavano speciali borse da matrimonio: si trattava di piccole borsette ovali e piatte in seta, decorate in smalto sui due lati con l'effigie degli sposi o, a volte, quella di santi. Altre borse da matrimonio venivano confezionate con finissime perline di vetro *sablé*, non più grandi di granelli di sabbia e intessute con filo di seta. Poiché queste perline erano troppo piccole per gli aghi normali, per infilarle si utilizzava un crine di cavallo. Altri tipi di borsa venivano usati per il gioco delle carte e per le elemosine. I giocatori di carte tenevano il denaro o i gettoni da gioco in speciali borse il cui fondo rotondo e rigido consentiva di posarle comodamente sul tavolo. A volte queste borse erano istoriate con lo stemma di famiglia, in modo che non vi fossero dubbi su chi ne era il proprietario. Una borsa ricamata in perline che porta la scritta 'Remember the Pore 1630' ("ricorda i poveri") rappresenta un esempio delle elemosiniere o *aumônières*, che erano diffuse tra il XIII e il XV secolo.

Español

Italiano

Vom späten Mittelalter an bis ins 17. Jahrhundert benutzten Männer und Frauen Taschen, um Münzen, Papiere, Bibeln, Almosen oder heilige Reliquien mit sich zu führen. Die Taschen und Beutel wurden an einem Band oder Riemen getragen, waren meist undekoriert und aus Leder oder Stoff gearbeitet. Es gab aber auch luxuriösere Modelle aus wertvollen Materialien, mit Stickereien aus Seide oder Silber- und Golddrähten. Die älteste Tasche im Museum ist eine Herrentasche aus Ziegenleder aus dem 16. Jahrhundert mit hübschen Knöpfen und Metallbügel. Hinter den meist versteckten Schnallen verbergen sich 18 Innentaschen. Frauen trugen die Taschen und Beutel am Gürtel oder an einer Kette (Chatelaines). Kleine Beutel und Täschchen dienten zur Aufbewahrung von Geld oder wohlriechenden Blütenblättern. In England und Frankreich verschenkte man die Taschen zu Neujahr. Täschchen mit Blütenblättern oder parfümierten Pudern wurden als Räuchertäschchen zwischen die Kleidung gehängt.

In vielen europäischen Ländern war es auch Mode, zu einer Hochzeit kleinere Beutel mit Geld zu verschenken. In der französischen Stadt Limoges wurden zwischen 1690 and 1760 ganz besondere Brauttäschchen hergestellt: Kleine, flache, ovale Beutel aus Seide mit Email-Darstellungen der Braut und des Bräutigams auf beiden Seiten, manchmal wurden auch Heiligenfiguren auf den Taschen abgebildet. Andere Hochzeitstäschchen wurden aus feinen Glasperlen angefertigt, den sogenannten Sandperlen. Das waren Perlen, so klein wie Sandkörner, die auf feine Seidendrähte aufgereiht wurden. Als Nadel diente Pferdehaar, denn die Perlen waren so klein, dass man sie mit einer gewöhnlichen Nadel nicht hätte fassen können. Taschen und Beutel mit anderem Verwendungszweck galten der Aufbewahrung von Spielgeld oder auch von Almosen. Kartenspieler hatten ihre Spielmarken und ihr Spielgeld in einem solchen Beutel dabei. Dieser Taschentyp hatte immer einen steifen runden Boden, so dass man ihn auf den Tisch stellen konnte. Manchmal war der Taschenboden mit dem Familienwappen geschmückt, damit kein Zweifel über den Eigentümer entstehen konnte.

中世後期から 17 世紀まで、男性も女性もバッグやパース（小物入れ）を携帯し、中に小銭、紙、施し物、聖書、お守りなどを入れて持ち歩きました。これらのバッグやパースなどは簡素なレザーや布で作られ、バンドまたはベルトに留めて身に着けました。しかし、中には高価な素材や絹糸、金糸、銀糸を用いて美しい刺繍を施した豪華なものも存在しました。バッグ博物館にあるバッグの中で最古のものは 16 世紀の紳士用ポーチで、ヤギの皮で作られ装飾のためのボタンと金属の口金が取り付けられています。18 個のポケットは、ほとんどが隠し留金になった留金に留められて見えないようになっています。ベルトに取り付けるほか、女性はバッグやパースをシャトレーヌに留めて身に着けていました。

小型のポーチやバッグは金銭や香りの良い花びらなどを入れる贅沢な小袋としての利用価値もありました。イギリスやフランスではパースは新年の贈り物でした。花びらや香りのついた粉などを中に詰めたパースをにおい袋として衣服の上に置いたり、衣服の間につるしたりしました。また、欧州の国々には結婚祝いに金銭をパースに詰めて送るという伝統的な習慣もありました。フランスのリモージュ市では、1690 年から 1760 年までの間特製婚礼用バッグが作られていました。小さめの平らなだ円形のパースで素材には絹が使われ、両面にはエナメルで花嫁と花婿の、時には聖人の肖像が施されたものです。そのほかの婚礼用パースには非常に小さなガラスのビーズで作られたものもありました。このビーズはサブレビーズと呼ばれ砂粒ほどの極小ビーズを絹糸に通して連ねます。このとき通常の針では太すぎて小さなビーズの穴に通るものが無かったため代わりに馬の毛を針代わりにしていました。パースにはほかにもゲーム用パース、施し物パースとしての利用法などがありました。カードを楽しむ人たちは小銭やギャンブル用のチップなどをこれらのゲーム用パースに入れていました。ゲーム用パースの底は円形で硬いため、テーブルの上に立てて置くことができます。時によってはパースの底に家紋が施され、持ち主がはっきりとわかるような工夫を凝らしていました。ビーズのパースには「Remember the Pore 1630（1630 年貧民を忘れるなかれ）」という文字が刻まれたものがあり、このことから施し物パース、またはオモニエール（aumônières：巾着袋）だったと察しがつきます。これらは 13 世紀から 15 世紀にかけて使用されていました。

deutsch   日本語

◄◄ Goat leather belt pouch with iron frame and with 18 pockets, some behind secret closures European, 16th c.
◄ Silk bridal bag with decoration in silver and gold thread
Italy, ca. 1700.

▲ Velvet purse with silver thread cord and silver balls and key
The Netherlands, 1600-1650.

▲ Velvet bag with chamois lining and copper frame
The Netherlands, late 17th c.
▼ A beadwork purse with inscription: "REMEMBER THE PORE 1630"
England, 1630.

▲ Leather coin-purse European, 17th c.
▼ Leather pouch covered with velvet and with gold thread and
sequin embroidery England, 17th c.

▲ Bag worked in green silk and silver and gold thread with crown
and initials P.C.S. Scotland, ca. 1745.
▼ Velvet bag (to hang from belt) with gold thread trim and tassels
The Netherlands, 17th c.

▲ Bag embroidered with thistles and initials J.R.8 for James VIII,
The Old Pretender Scotland, early 18th c.
▼ Crocheted drawstring purse with silver thread trim
France, 17th c.

▲ Silk purse embroidered with gilt thread, drawstring of plaited silk with large tassels France, ca. 1600.
▼ Velvet bag with silver thread embroidery European, 17th c.

▲ Sweetbag embroidered with silk on silver thread, lady amidst flowers and insects England, ca. 1630-1640.
▼ A sweetbag worked in silks on a ground of silver thread with text woven in drawstring England, 1620-1630.

▲ Sablé-beaded drawstring purse and sablé-beaded bridal drawstring purse France, 18th c.
▼ Leather coin purse with iron cover plate The Netherlands, 16th c.

▲ Drawstring purse woven with silk and gilt thread France, early 18th c.
▼ Silver and parcel-gilt belt pouch (for gun-powder?) with picture of goddess Victoria Europe, early 17th c.

▲ Velvet gaming purse embroidered with silver thread and silk gaming purse embroidered with coloured silks France, 18th c.
▼ Shield shaped purse with silk and gilt thread embroidery France, 1700-1730.

▲ Velvet gaming purse embroidered with gilt thread; coat of arms on bottom France, 18th c.
▼ Silk purse embroidered with gilt and silver thread and gilt thread tassels France, 18th c.

▲ Silk bridal bag with bride (Princess Maria Lesczynska, the bride of King Louis XV) in enamel on copper, Limoges France, 1725.
◄ Silk bridal bag with Martha and Mary Magdalene in enamel on copper, Limoges France, 1690-1730.

▲ Silk bridal bag with groom (the French king Louis XV) in enamel on copper, Limoges France, 1725.
▼ Silk bridal bag with gold lace and bride and groom in enamel on copper, Limoges France, 1690-1715.

Letter cases and wallets

Pochettes et portefeuilles

Portefeuilles

Portadocumentos y carteras

Portafogli

Brieftaschen und Geldbörsen

レターケースと札入れ

From the seventeenth century on, both men and women kept their letters and valuable papers in letter cases or wallets. They stowed their coins in purses.

There were many different varieties of letter cases, and materials such as leather, silk, glass beads and straw were popular.

Many letter cases were made from coloured leather, with one or more compartments which were sometimes lined with marbled paper. Letter cases could serve as a gift or souvenir. An example is the brown leather letter case with the embroidered inscription 'Constantinopoli 1732' on the obverse side and the name of the owner under the flap. Letter cases like these were often made in Constantinople in the late seventeenth and in the eighteenth century. It is clear that this city had long specialised in the production of this kind of leather letter case, which were embroidered with name and date on request.

Silk letter cases were embroidered with silk or metal thread, sequins and/or foil. They were also embroidered or pasted with straw and hair or painted with Indian ink. The eighteenth-century letter cases with sablé beads are highly unique.

Many of the illustrations and motifs on letter cases were related to love and loyalty: cupids, hearts with and without flames, the love god Venus, two dogs (a symbol of faithfulness), two birds (betrothal) and an anchor (hope). Letter cases with such motifs were very probably given at engagements and weddings. A rare example is a letter case in green leather embroidered with silver gilt thread and set off with a gilt border, with a minute painted portrait of a young woman and an embroidered love poem for her beau inside.

English

À partir du dix-septième siècle, hommes et femmes conservent leur lettres et papiers importants dans des porte-lettres ou portefeuilles et transportent leurs pièces de monnaie dans des bourses.

Il existe de multiples variétés de portefeuilles et divers matériaux comme le cuir, la soie, les perles de verre et la paille.

Beaucoup de portefeuilles sont en cuir teint avec un ou plusieurs compartiments parfois doublés de papier marbré. Ils servent également de présent ou de souvenir, comme par exemple la pochette de cuir brun portant l'inscription brodée « Constantinopoli 1732 » au recto et le nom de son propriétaire sous le rabat. À la fin du dix-septième et au dix-huitième siècle, ces pochettes venaient souvent de Constantinople, qui s'était spécialisée dans leur production en cuir brodé sur demande du nom et de la date.

Les portefeuilles en soie sont brodés de fils de soie ou métalliques, de sequins et/ou de feuille métallique. Ils sont parfois aussi brodés ou collés de paille et de cheveux, ou encore peints à l'encre de Chine. Les portefeuilles sablés en perles du dix-huitième siècle sont des pièces absolument uniques.

Probablement offerts lors de fiançailles ou de mariages, les portefeuilles sont souvent ornés d'illustrations et de motifs ayant trait à l'amour et à la fidélité : amours, cœurs avec et sans flammes, Vénus déesse de l'amour, deux chiens (symbole de loyauté), deux oiseaux (fiançailles) ou une ancre (espérance). Parmi les exemplaires rares, un portefeuille de cuir vert brodé de fils d'argent et rehaussé d'une bordure dorée, renfermant le portrait miniature d'une jeune femme et un poème d'amour brodé pour son galant.

Zowel mannen als vrouwen bewaarden vanaf de zeventiende eeuw hun brieven en waardepapieren in portefeuilles. Hun muntgeld stopten ze in beurzen.

De portefeuilles laten een gevarieerd beeld zien: materialen als leer, zijde, glaskralen en stro waren populair. Veel portefeuilles werden vervaardigd van gekleurd leer, voorzien van een of meerdere vakken die soms met gemarmerd papier beplakt werden. Portefeuilles konden dienen als geschenk of souvenir. Een voorbeeld hiervan is de bruine leren portefeuille met het geborduurde opschrift 'Constantinopoli 1732' op de achterzijde en de naam van de eigenaar onder de flap.

Portefeuilles als deze werden aan het eind van de zeventiende en in de achttiende eeuw veelal gemaakt in Constantinopel. Deze stad was kennelijk langere tijd gespecialiseerd in de vervaardiging van dit soort leren portefeuilles, die in opdracht van naam en datum werden voorzien.

Zijden portefeuilles werden geborduurd met zijde- of metaaldraad, met pailletten en/of folie. Ook werden ze geborduurd of beplakt met stro en haar, of beschilderd met Oost-Indische inkt. Bijzonder zijn de achttiende-eeuwse portefeuilles met sablékralen.

Veel van de afbeeldingen en motieven op portefeuilles hadden betrekking op liefde en trouw: cupido's, harten met en zonder vlammen, de liefdesgodin Venus, twee honden (symbool voor trouw), twee vogels (trouwbelofte) en een anker (hoop). Portefeuilles met dergelijke motieven waren hoogstwaarschijnlijk geschenken bij verlovingen en huwelijken. Een zeldzaam exemplaar is een portefeuille van groen leer, geborduurd met verguld zilverdraad en afgezet met een verguld montuur, met aan de binnenzijde een minutieus geschilderd portret van een jonge vrouw en een geborduurd liefdesgedicht voor haar man.

français

nederlands

A partir del siglo XVII, tanto los hombres como las mujeres empleaban portadocumentos para conservar cartas y documentos de valor. Las monedas se guardaban en monederos.

Estos estuches forman un conjunto variopinto: entre los materiales más utilizados figuran el cuero, la seda, los abalorios de cristal y la paja.

Muchas de estas carpetas se confeccionaban con cuero teñido y disponían de uno o más compartimentos, que a veces se forraban con papel jaspeado. Los portadocumentos podían servir de regalo o de recuerdo de viaje. Como ejemplo de ello encontramos uno de cuero marrón que lleva bordada la inscripción "Constantinopoli 1732" en la parte exterior y el nombre del propietario bajo la solapa. Este tipo de estuches se confeccionaban en Constantinopla a finales del siglo XVII y durante el siglo XVIII. Queda patente que durante mucho tiempo la ciudad estuvo especializada en la producción de este tipo de carteras de piel, en las que se bordaba el nombre y la fecha a petición del comprador.

Los portadocumentos de seda se bordaban con hilo de seda o de metal, con lentejuelas y/o láminas metálicas. También se bordaban o se les pegaba paja y pelo, o se pintaban con tinta china. Son exponentes únicos los que datan del siglo XVIII y presentan cuentas *sablé*. Muchas de las ilustraciones y motivos representados en ellos se inspiran en el amor y la lealtad: cupidos, corazones con y sin llamas, Venus (diosa del amor), dos perros (símbolo de la fidelidad), dos pájaros (desposorios) y un ancla (esperanza). Es muy probable que las carpetas decoradas con estos motivos se regalaran en ceremonias de pedida de mano y en bodas. Constituye un raro ejemplo un portadocumentos elaborado en cuero verde, bordado con hilo de plata dorada y resaltado con un reborde dorado, que en el interior presenta el minucioso retrato de una joven y un poema de amor bordado para su pretendiente.

A partire dal XVII secolo, sia gli uomini che le donne utilizzavano portafogli di varie fogge per conservare lettere e carte preziose, mentre tenevano le monete in appositi borsellini.

I portafogli venivano prodotti in una grande varietà e con diversi materiali come la pelle, la seta, le perline e la paglia.

Molti portafogli erano confezionati in pelle colorata e avevano uno o più scomparti, a volte rivestiti di carta marmorizzata. Questi oggetti potevano diventare regali o souvenir, come testimoniato da un portafogli di pelle marrone che porta ricamata la scritta 'Constantinopoli 1732' sulla parte anteriore e il nome del proprietario sotto la pattina. Alla fine del XVII secolo e all'inizio del XVIII, molti portafogli di questo tipo venivano fabbricati a Costantinopoli. Infatti questa città si era specializzata da tempo nella manifattura di portafogli di pelle, che potevano essere ricamati con nomi e date su richiesta.

I portafogli in seta erano ricamati con filo di seta o metallico, lustrini e/o foglie di metallo. Potevano anche essere decorati con fili di paglia o crini, che venivano ricamati o incollati sulla superficie, oppure dipinti con inchiostro di china. Particolarmente preziosi i portafogli in perline sablé del XVIII secolo.

Spesso i portafogli recavano illustrazioni e motivi decorativi ispirati all'amore e alla lealtà: cupidi, cuoricini con o senza fiammelle, effigi della dea dell'amore Venere, due cani (simbolo di fedeltà), due uccelli (fidanzamento) o un'áncora (speranza). È probabile che portafogli con queste decorazioni venissero regalati in occasione di fidanzamenti o matrimoni. Un esemplare raro è un portafogli in pelle verde ricamato con filo d'argento dorato e rifinito con una cerniera dorata, al cui interno si trovano il minuscolo ritratto dipinto di una giovane donna e una poesia d'amore ricamata dedicata al suo amato.

Español

Italiano

Ab dem 17. Jahrhundert bewahrten sowohl Männer als auch Frauen ihre Briefe und wichtige Papiere in Brieftaschen auf. Das Münzgeld trugen sie in Geldbörsen mit sich. Brieftaschen gab es in den verschiedensten Ausführungen: Sie wurden aus Leder, Seide, Glasperlen oder Stroh gefertigt.

Viele der Brieftaschen wurden aus gefärbtem Leder hergestellt, hatten ein oder zwei Fächer, die manchmal mit Marmorpapier eingefasst waren. Brieftaschen waren ein beliebtes Geschenk oder Souvenir. Ein Beispiel hierfür ist die braune Lederbrieftasche mit der gestickten Inschrift „Constantinopoli 1732" auf der Vorderseite und dem Namen des Eigentümers unter der Lasche. Brieftaschen wie diese wurden in Konstantinopel gegen Ende des 17. und im 18. Jahrhundert viel hergestellt. Offensichtlich hatte man sich in dieser Stadt über lange Jahre hinweg auf die Produktion derartiger Taschen spezialisiert, in die auf Wunsch des Kunden auch Datum und Namen des Trägers eingestickt wurden.

Seidene Brieftaschen wurden mit Seide oder Metalldraht bestickt und mit Pailletten und/oder spiegelnden Folien verziert. Manche wurden auch mit Stroh oder Haar bestickt, oder mit Tusche bemalt. Die Brieftaschen mit Stickerei aus Sablé-Perlen aus dem 18. Jahrhundert sind ausgesprochen seltene Stücke.

Viele der Darstellungen und Verzierungen auf den Brieftaschen hatten die beliebten Themen Liebe und Treue zum Thema: So gab es Illustrationen des Liebesgottes Amor, Darstellungen von (manchmal flammenden) Herzen, Bilder der Liebesgöttin Venus, Abbildungen zweier Hunde (Symbol der Treue), zweier Vögel (Verlobung) oder eines Ankers (Hoffnung). Brieftaschen mit derlei Verzierungen waren häufig Geschenke zu Verlobungen oder Hochzeiten. Ein seltenes Beispiel hierfür ist eine Brieftasche aus grünem Leder, mit Silberdraht bestickt und abgesetzt mit einem vergoldeten Rand. Besonders schön ist das exakt gezeichnete Portrait einer jungen Frau und das eingestickte Liebesgedicht für ihren Schatz.

17 世紀以降は男性も女性も手紙や貴重な文書をレターケースや札入れに入れて保管するようになります。小銭はパースにしまっていました。

レターケースは多種多様で、なかでもレザー、絹、ガラスビーズ、麦わら製のものがよく愛用されていました。

レターケースの多くは着色を施したレザーでできていて、ひとつまたはふたつ以上に仕切られ、場合によっては底に大理石柄の下敷き紙が敷かれていました。レターケースは贈り物や記念品としても使われていました。絹製レターケースは絹、金属糸、スパンコール、金属箔の、またはそれらを組み合わせた刺繍が施されていました。また、麦わらや毛髪を刺繍、糊付けしたもの、または墨で模様を描いたものなどもありました。18 世紀のサブレビーズ製レターケースは非常に独特です。

レターケースの絵柄やモチーフの多くは愛や忠誠に関連したものが多く、キューピッド、炎を添えたハートまたはハートのみ、愛の女神ヴィーナス、２匹の犬（忠実さの象徴）、つがいの鳥（結納）、いかり（希望）などがあります。そのようなモチーフをあしらったレターケースはほぼ間違いなく婚約や結婚の時に贈られたものでしょう。珍しいレターケースの例を紹介しますと、それは緑のレザー製のもので、銀メッキの糸で刺繍をし、メッキで口金を強調、内側には非常に小さな若い女性の肖像画が描かれ、肖像画には彼女の恋人に捧げる愛の詩の刺繍が添えられています。

deutsch

日本語

▲ Leather lettercase with pictures of Amsterdam city hall
Germany, 1800-1830.
▼ Leather lettercase embroidered with gold thread and text
'Constantinopoli 1732' Turkey, 1732.

▲ Envelope style silk lettercase with ink paintings England,
late 18th c.
▼ Leather wallet with letter dated 1811 France, 1811.

▲ Silk lettercase with gold thread embroidery and long, tender text
France, late 18th c.
▼ Leather lettercase with fine beaded pictures and copper closure
Russia, early 19th c.

▲ Sablé-beaded envelope-model lettercase, Tudor roses
France, ca. 1725.
▼ Silk lettercase with sequins and text 'il brûle pour vous'
and 'il est toujours fidèle' France, ca. 1800.

Que de mon Amour pour Vous.
Ce portrait soit le gage & l'assurance
Mais mon cœur en avoir jaloux
S'il Vous consolait de l'absence.

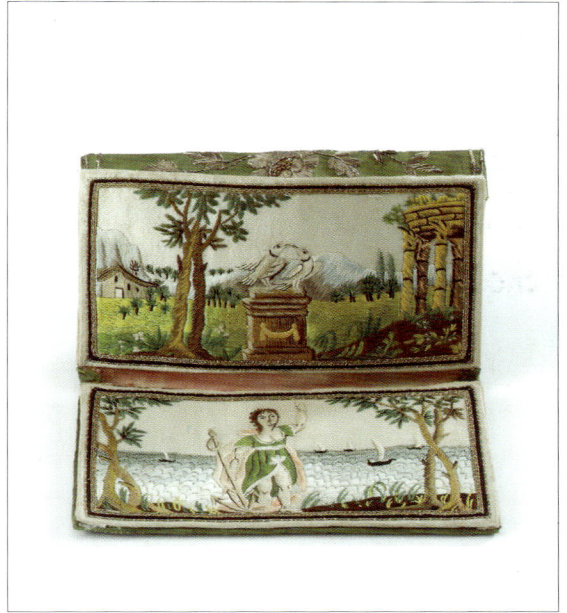

▲ Finely embroidered silk lettercase France, ca. 1800.
▼ Linen lettercase embroidered with silk and trimmed with silver lace, initials P.L. France, 17th c.
◄ Leather and silk lettercase with embroidery, poem and miniature by Favorin Lerebour France, 1806.

▲ Silk lettercase embroidered with silk, silver thread and sequins France, early 19th c.
▼ Silk lettercase embroidered with straw and hair The Netherlands, 19th c.

Chatelaines

Châtelaines

Chatelaines

Chatelaines

Châtelaine

Chatelaines

シャトレーン

The symbol of power for the medieval lady of the manor was the keys she wore on chains on her waistband or belt. These long chains, which hung together on a hook from the belt or skirt waistband, were also called chatelaines (after the French châtelaine, lady of the manor, or château), a term that incidentally only came into use in 1828. Before that time they were called equipages. Chatelaines were worn for centuries, although their form and use were always changing.

In the sixteenth and seventeenth centuries, women hung their purse, bible, keys, fan, pomander and knife sheath on ankle-length chains. In the eighteenth century, the chains became shorter and more sewing equipment was hung on them, as were a smelling box, seals for documents and a watch. In the meantime, the chatelaine had become common among greater strata of the population. In addition to versions in silver and gold, they were now also available in pinchbeck, enamel, mother of pearl and cut steel.

The chatelaine underwent a revival in the nineteenth century. All kinds of new types of chatelaines appeared with spectacle holders, devices for holding up the skirt, key holders, umbrellas and notebooks. There also appeared chatelaines for the evening with a dance card, mirror, perfume bottle and fan holder, and chatelaines with a little bag, called chatelaine bags. The chatelaines were constructed from gold, gilt or silvered metal, silver and cut steel and were often decorated with carnelian, porcelain and enamel. Cheaper chatelaines were available in leather, and instructions for making cloth chatelaines were published in needlework magazines. The chatelaine went out of fashion in the first decade of the twentieth century due to the arrival of the handbag.

English

Le symbole du pouvoir pour les châtelaines dans leurs manoirs sont les clés qu'elles portaient à des chaînes pendant de leur ceinture. Ces longues chaînes, fixées à la ceinture par une agrafe, étaient appelées châtelaines, du nom de leurs principales utilisatrices, même si ce terme n'est vraiment utilisé que depuis 1828. Avant cette date, on parlait simplement d'équipages. Les châtelaines ont été portées pendant des siècles mais leur forme et leurs usages n'ont cessé de changer. Aux seizième et dix-septième siècles, les femmes suspendent bourse, bible, clés, éventail, parfum et couteau dans sa gaine à des chaînes qui leur pendent jusqu'aux chevilles. Au dix-huitième siècle, les chaînes raccourcissent et retiennent surtout des ustensiles de couture, ainsi que des sels, des sceaux à cacheter et une montre. À cette époque, la châtelaine a gagné les autres couches de la société et, outre les versions en or et argent, il s'en fabrique en chrysocale, en émail, en nacre et en acier.

La châtelaine connaîtra un renouveau au dix-neuvième siècle, avec porte-lunettes, dispositifs pour relever les jupes, porte-clés, ombrelles et bloc-notes. Sans compter les châtelaines du soir, avec carnet de bal, miroir, flacon de parfum et porte éventail, ou les châtelaines assorties d'un petit sac, appelées sacs-châtelaines. Elles sont en or, métal doré ou argenté, argent ou acier coupé, et sont souvent ornées de cornaline, porcelaine ou émail. Les moins chères sont en cuir et les magazines de couture expliquent comment en fabriquer en toile. La châtelaine passera de mode dans la première décennie du vingtième siècle avec l'arrivée du sac à main.

Het symbool van de macht van de middeleeuwse kasteelvrouwe waren de sleutels die zij aan kettingen aan haar riem of gordel droeg. Deze lange kettingen die samen aan een haak aan de gordel of rokband hingen, worden dan ook chatelaines (naar het Franse *châteleine*, kasteelvrouwe) genoemd, een naam die overigens pas in 1828 in gebruik is gekomen. Voor die tijd werden ze tuigjes genoemd. Chatelaines zijn eeuwenlang gedragen, hoewel vorm en gebruik steeds veranderden.

In de zestiende en zeventiende eeuw hingen vrouwen hun beurs, bijbel, sleutels, waaier, reukbal en messenkoker aan enkellange kettingen. In de achttiende eeuw werden de kettingen korter en werd er meer naaigerei aan gehangen, maar ook lodereindoosjes, signetten en een horloge. De chatelaine was inmiddels in grotere lagen van de bevolking gemeengoed geworden. Naast uitvoeringen in zilver en goud waren ze nu ook in pinchbeck, email, parelmoer en geslepen staal verkrijgbaar.

In de negentiende eeuw werd de chatelaine opnieuw populair. Er ontstonden allerlei nieuwe soorten: chatelaines met brillenhouders, rokophouders, sleutelhouders, paraplu's en notitieboekjes; chatelaines voor de avond met balboekje, spiegel, parfumflesje en waaierhouder, en chatelaines met een tasje, die chatelainetassen werden genoemd. De chatelaines werden in goud, verguld of verzilverd metaal, zilver en geslepen staal uitgevoerd en vaak gedecoreerd met kornalijn, porselein en email. Goedkopere chatelaines waren verkrijgbaar in leer, en in handwerkbladen stonden aanwijzingen voor het maken van stoffen chatelaines. In het eerste decennium van de twintigste eeuw raakte de chatelaine uit de mode door de opkomst van de handtas.

français

nederlands

El símbolo de poder de las damas medievales de las casas feudales eran las llaves que llevaba colgadas con cadenas de la pretina o cinturón. Estas largas cadenas, que pendían juntas del gancho del cinturón o de la pretina de la falda, también se denominaban *chatelaines* (palabra procedente del francés *châtelaine*, dama del castillo o *château*), un término que comenzó a emplearse de manera accidental a partir de 1828. Si bien las *chatelaines* se utilizaron durante varios siglos, su forma y uso cambiaban constantemente.

En los siglos XVI y XVII, la mujer colgaba el monedero, la Biblia, las llaves, el abanico, un recipiente de porcelana con hierbas perfumadas y la funda para la navaja en cadenas largas hasta el tobillo. En el siglo XVIII las cadenas se acortaron y de ellas pendía más material de costura, así como una cajita aromática, sellos para documentos y un reloj. En esta época, la *chatelaine* ya era un elemento habitual para amplios sectores de la población. Además de las versiones confeccionadas en oro y plata, entonces también se creaban modelos en similor, esmalte, madreperla y acero cortado.

La *chatelaine* volvió a cobrar popularidad en el siglo XIX. Surgió entonces todo un abanico de *chatelaines* con soportes para lentes, aparatos para sostener la falda, llaveros, sombrillas y blocs de notas. Aparecieron también *chatelaines* para la noche con un soporte para la tarjeta de baile, el espejo, el frasco de perfume y el abanico, además de *chatelaines* con una pequeña bolsa denominada escarcela. Las *chatelaines* se elaboraban con oro, metal plateado o dorado, plata y acero cortado, y a menudo se decoraban con cornalina, porcelana y esmalte. Las versiones más económicas se realizaban en cuero y las revistas especializadas en costura explicaban cómo confeccionar *chatelaines* de tela. En la primera década del siglo XX, la *chatelaine* pasó de moda debido a la llegada del bolso de mano.

In epoca medievale, il potere della castellana era simboleggiato dalle chiavi che portava appese a catenelle fissate alla cintura. Queste lunghe catenine, raccolte tutte insieme in un gancio fissato alla cintola, erano chiamate così dal francese *châtelaine*, ossia castellana, un termine che tuttavia si è affermato nel vocabolario internazionale solo nel 1828. Pur modificandosi continuamente nella forma e nella funzione, le châtelaine sono rimaste in uso per secoli.

Nel XVI e nel XVII secolo, le donne si servivano di catenine lunghe fino alla caviglia per appendervi borse per le monete, bibbia, chiavi, ventaglio, pomander e guaina per il coltello. Nel XVIII secolo le catenine si accorciarono; tra gli oggetti che vi venivano appesi apparvero accessori per il cucito, ma anche astucci per essenze, sigilli per documenti e orologi. Nel frattempo, la châtelaine era diventata un oggetto d'uso comune per strati più ampi della popolazione. Oltre che nelle versioni originali in argento e oro, erano diffuse anche châtelaine in similoro, smalto, madreperla e acciaio tagliato.

Nel XIX secolo la châtelaine visse un revival di popolarità. Apparve così tutta una gamma di nuovi tipi di châtelaine, con portaocchiali, fermagli per tenere sollevato l'orlo della gonna, portachiavi, ombrelli e taccuini; c'erano châtelaine da sera con carnet di ballo, portaspecchio, boccette di profumo e portaventaglio, e châtelaine munite di un borsellino. Le châtelaine potevano essere fatte d'oro, di metallo dorato o argentato, d'argento e di acciaio tagliato, e spesso erano decorate con corniole, porcellana e smalto. Tuttavia se ne trovavano anche modelli più economici in pelle, e le riviste di ricamo fornivano istruzioni su come confezionarne di stoffa. Fu solo nel primo decennio del XX secolo che la châtelaine andò fuori moda, a causa dell'avvento della borsetta.

Español

Italiano

Das Machtsymbol der Dame eines ritterlichen Anwesens waren im Mittelalter die Schlüssel, die an Ketten getragen wurden, die wiederum an der Taille an einem Band oder Gurt befestigt waren. Diese langen Ketten, die zusammen an einem Haken am Gürtel oder dem Taillenband des Gewandes hingen, nannte man auch Chatelaines (nach dem französischen Begriff Châtelaine, Herrin eines Ritterguts oder Schlosses). Diese Bezeichnung kam ab 1828 in Verwendung, davor nannte man sie auf Französisch und Englisch „Equipages". Chatelaines wurden über Jahrhunderte hinweg getragen, auch wenn sich sowohl die Form als auch der Verwendungszweck stetig veränderten.

Im 16. und 17. Jahrhundert hängten die Frauen Gegenstände aller Art an diese Ketten, die bis zu den Knöcheln reichten: Bibeln, Schlüssel, Fächer, Pomander (Duftfläschchen) und Messerscheiden. Im 18. Jahrhundert wurden die Ketten kürzer, man trug jetzt vor allem Nähutensilien daran, sowie Duftdöschen, Siegel für Dokumente und eine Uhr. Die Chatelaine war mittlerweile zum alltägliche Gebrauchsgegenstand breiter Teile der Bevölkerung geworden. Zusätzlich zu den Versionen in Silber und Gold waren nun auch Modelle aus Tombak (einer Kupferlegierung), Email, Perlmutt oder poliertem Stahl erhältlich.

Im 19. Jahrhundert erlebt die Chatelaine ihre zweite Blüte. Viele neue Arten kamen auf den Markt. So gab es Ketten für Augengläser, Ketten um den Rock zu raffen, Schlüsselhalter, Ketten für Regenschirme oder Notizbücher. Es gab die typischen Chatelaines für den Abend mit Halterung für Tanzheftchen, Spiegel, Parfümflakons und Fächer. Es gab auch Chatelaines mit einem kleinen Täschchen, die sogenannten Chatelaine-Täschchen. Die Ketten waren aus Gold oder aus versilbertem oder vergoldetem Metall oder aus poliertem Stahl gearbeitet und oft mit Karneol, Porzellan oder Email dekoriert. Billigere Versionen gab es in Leder. In Handarbeitszeitschriften gab es Anleitungen zur Anfertigung von Modellen aus Stoff oder Wolle. Im ersten Jahrzehnt des 20. Jahrhunderts kam die Chatelaine schließlich außer Mode und wurde von der Handtasche abgelöst.

中世の女主人にとって権力の象徴は、ウエストバンドまたはベルトから下がるチェーンに取り付けられた鍵でした。これらの留金が付いている、ベルトまたはスカートのウエストバンドから鍵とともに垂れ下がる長いチェーンもまた同様にみなされていました。シャトレーンは何世紀もの間身に付けられてきたものですが、その形や利用法は常に変化していました。

16、17 世紀では、女性は足首まで届くチェーンにパース、聖書、鍵、扇子、におい玉、ナイフ鞘などを下げていました。18 世紀になってチェーンは短くなり下げるものとしては裁縫道具が多くなり、ほかは香り箱、文書の封印具、時計などでした。その間、シャトレーンはさまざまな階級層に広がります。さらに、銀製や金製のもののほか、合金、エナメル、真珠層、カットスチールでできたものが出回りました。

19 世紀になってシャトレーンは起死回生を遂げます。さまざまな種類の目新しいシャトレーンが、メガネホルダー、スカート吊り具、キーホルダー、傘や帳面とともに登場しました。またイブニング用のシャトレーンも、ダンスカード、香水瓶、扇子ホルダーとともに登場します。さらに、シャトレーン・バッグと呼ばれるシャトレーンに小ぶりのバッグが付いたものも登場しました。シャトレーンは金、金メッキまたは銀メッキの施された金属、銀、カットスチールなどから作られ、装飾としてカーネリアン、陶石、エナメルなどをあしらったものです。安価なシャトレーンにはレザーでできたものがあり、布製シャトレーンの作り方が手芸雑誌に載りました。シャトレーンは 20 世紀に突入して最初の 10 年で時代遅れになり、ハンドバッグの登場という出来事がその背景にありました。

deutsch　　　　　　　　　日本語

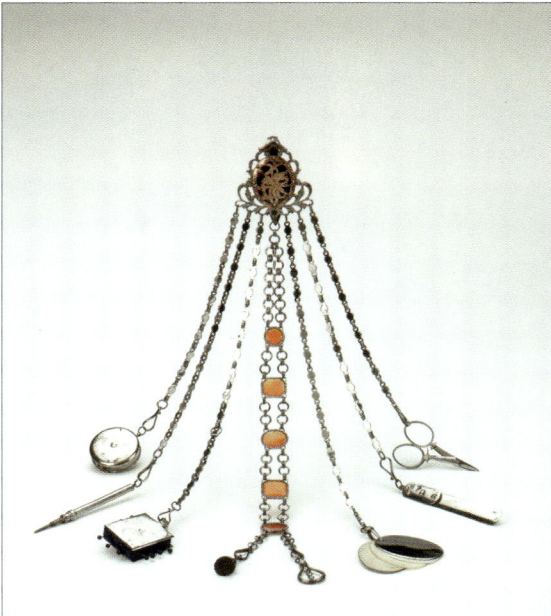

▲ Silver chatelaine with filigrane decoration on hook; Willem Rosier, Amsterdam The Netherlands, ca. 1740.
▼ Cut steel chatelaine with carnelian and gold decoration on hook England, late 19th c.
◀ Gilded chatelaine with Diana on hook England, ca. 1740.

▲ Silver chatelaine; Roelof Snoek, Leeuwarden The Netherlands, 1775-1800.
▼ Cut steel chatelaine, W. Thornhill England, late 19th c.

▲ Velvet bag with silver closure and hook England, 1903.
▼ Velvet chatelaine bag with silver frame, chain and hook and
matching silver belt Germany, 1870-1890.

▲ Velvet chatelaine bag with brass decoration and hook
France, 1874.
▼ Velvet chatelaine bag with brass decoration and hook
France, 1874.
▶ Leather chatelaine England, 1902.

Framed bags

Sacs à fermoir

Beugeltassen

Bolsos de boquilla

Borse con cerniera

Bügeltaschen

口金式バッグ

Bags with silver frames came into fashion among Dutch women starting in the last quarter of the seventeenth century. The bag with a frame was traditionally worn under the apron with a hook on the belt or skirt waistband. The bags usually had a silver frame but could also be made from other metals. Because silver was costly, the frame was often handed down from mother to daughter. There is a wide variety in the form and decoration of bags with frames. In line with the prevailing fashion, a new bag made of velvet, damask, silk or leather could be attached to the silver frame. The silver frame with a knitted beaded bag, still seen quite frequently today, is a version that first appeared shortly after 1800.

When the handbag finally became an indispensable part of the wardrobe at the beginning of the twentieth century, many old bags with frames were altered, with the hook disappearing and the bag being supplied with a little chain as a handle. At that time, bags with frames were so sought after that the old silver frames were imitated and then furnished with a chain and modern snap fastening. In addition to bag frames, from the eighteenth century onward there were also smaller frames for money purses.

English

Chez les Néerlandaises, la mode du sac à fermoir en argent commence dès le dernier quart du dix-septième siècle. Il est alors traditionnellement porté sous le tablier, fixé par un crochet à la ceinture de la robe. Les fermoirs étaient généralement en argent mais pouvaient aussi être faits d'un autre métal ; en raison du coût de l'argent, le fermoir se transmettait de mère à fille. Les formes et ornements des sacs à fermoir sont extrêmement variés. Selon la mode du moment, un nouveau sac de velours, soie damassée, soie ou cuir se fixait au fermoir d'argent. La version avec sac de perles tricoté, encore d'actualité, est apparue pour la première fois peu après 1800. Au début du vingtième siècle, lorsque le sac à main devient définitivement un accessoire indispensable de la garde-robe, de nombreux sacs à fermoir anciens sont adaptés en éliminant le crochet et en le remplaçant par une petite chaîne tenant lieu de poignée. Les anciens sacs à fermoir d'argent sont alors si recherchés que des imitations sont faites avec une chaîne et un fermoir moderne. Outre les fermoirs pour sacs, il existe depuis le dix-huitième siècle des fermoirs plus petits pour bourses.

Tassen met zilveren beugels raakten bij Nederlandse vrouwen in de mode vanaf het laatste kwart van de zeventiende eeuw. De beugeltas werd op traditionele wijze met een haak aan gordel of rokband onder het schort gedragen. De tassen hadden meestal een zilveren beugel, maar werden ook van andere metalen gemaakt. Omdat zilver kostbaar was, werd de beugel vaak van moeder op dochter doorgegeven. De beugel-tassen laten een grote verscheidenheid aan vorm en versiering zien. In stijl met de heersende mode werd aan de zilveren beugel een nieuwe tas van fluweel, damast, zijde of leer gezet. De zilveren beugel met gebreide kralentas, zoals die nu nog veel voorkomt, is een uitvoering die pas kort na 1800 ontstond. Toen in het begin van de twintigste eeuw de handtas definitief een onmisbaar onderdeel van de garderobe was geworden, werden veel oude beugeltassen ver-maakt, waarbij de haak verdween en de tas voorzien werd van een kettinkje als handvat. De beugeltassen waren toen zo gewild, dat de oude zilveren beugels werden nagemaakt, maar dan wel voorzien van een ketting en moderne knipsluiting. Naast de tasbeugels kende men vanaf de achttiende eeuw ook kleinere beugels voor geldbeurzen.

français

nederlands

Los bolsos con boquilla de plata se pusieron de moda entre las mujeres holandesas a partir del último cuarto del siglo XVII. Tradicionalmente, el bolso de boquilla se llevaba bajo el delantal, con un gancho que colgaba del cinturón o de la pretina de la falda. Por regla general la boquilla era de plata, pero también podía ser de otro metal. La plata era un metal caro, por lo que la boquilla solía pasar de madres a hijas. Los bolsos de boquilla presentan una amplia variedad de formas y de motivos decorativos. Según la moda imperante, a la boquilla de plata podía unirse una bolsa de terciopelo, damasco, seda o cuero. El bolso de boquilla de plata tejido con abalorios, aún en uso hoy en día, es una versión que apareció poco después del año 1800. Cuando el bolso de mano se convirtió definitivamente en parte indispensable de la indumentaria a comienzos del siglo XX, muchos bolsos de boquilla se modificaron: el gancho desapareció y a la bolsa se le añadió una pequeña cadena a modo de asa. Los bolsos de boquilla eran tan buscados que se imitaba la antigua boquilla de plata pero se les dotaba de una cadena y un broche a presión moderno. Además de los bolsos de boquilla, a partir del siglo XVIII aparecieron boquillas de menor tamaño para los monederos.

Le borse con cerniera d'argento entrarono in voga tra le donne olandesi a partire dagli ultimi venticinque anni del XVII secolo. Tradizionalmente, la borsa con cerniera veniva portata sotto il grembiule, fissata con un gancio alla cintura di pelle o di stoffa. Di solito le cerniere erano d'argento, ma a volte anche di altri metalli. Poiché l'argento era costoso, spesso la cerniera passava di madre in figlia. Le borsette con cerniera presentano una grande varietà di forme e motivi ornamentali. A seconda della moda in vigore, si poteva riutilizzare la cerniera d'argento per appendervi una nuova borsa di velluto, di damasco, di seta o di pelle. La borsa in maglia e perline con cerniera d'argento, ancor oggi piuttosto diffusa, è un modello apparso per la prima volta poco dopo il 1800.
All'inizio del XX secolo, quando la borsetta con manico si affermò definitivamente come parte indispensabile del guardaroba femminile, molte vecchie borsette con cerniera vennero modificate, sostituendo il gancio con una catenina che serviva da manico. All'epoca, le borsette con cerniera erano tanto ricercate che circolavano imitazioni delle vecchie cerniere d'argento munite di catenella e di una moderna chiusura a scatto. Oltre alle più grandi cerniere per borsetta, a partire dal XVIII secolo si diffusero anche cerniere più piccole per borsellini e portamonete.

Español

Italiano

Ab dem letzten Viertel des 17. Jahrhunderts kamen in Holland für Frauen Taschen mit Silberbügel in Mode. Die Bügeltasche wurde für gewöhnlich unter der Schürze mit einem Haken am Gürtel oder Rockband befestigt. Gewöhnlich hatten diese Taschen einen Bügel aus Silber oder evtl. auch aus einem anderen Material. Da Silber sehr teuer war, wurden die Bügel oft von der Mutter an die Tochter weitervererbt. Die Bügeltaschen waren sehr vielfältig in Form und Ausführung. Je nach Mode wurden die Taschen aus Samt, Damast, Seide oder Leder an den silbernen Bügel genäht. Die gestrickte Perlentasche mit Silberbügel, die man bis heute noch sehr häufig finden kann, ist ein Modell, das kurz nach 1800 entstand.

Als schließlich zu Beginn des 20. Jahrhunderts die Handtasche zum unentbehrlichen Bestandteil der Damengarderobe avancierte, wurden viele der alten Bügeltaschen verändert. Der Haken verschwand und wurde durch eine zierliche kurze Kette, die auch als Henkel diente, ersetzt. Die Bügeltaschen waren mittlerweile so begehrt, dass die alten Silberbügel imitiert wurden. Hinzu kam nun das neue kurze Kettchen sowie ein moderner Schnappverschluss. So wie es Bügeltaschen in Handtaschengröße gab, kamen seit dem 18. Jahrhundert auch kleinere Bügeltaschen für Geldbörsen in Mode.

口金の付いたバッグは従来、ベルトやスカートのウエストバンドに留金をかけてエプロンの下に身に付けるものでした。バッグには通常銀の口金が付いていましたが、他の金属を口金に使用したものもありました。当時銀は高価だったので、しばしば銀口金は母から娘へと譲り渡されていました。口金式バッグはその型も装飾も種類が非常に豊富でした。一般的な流行に合わせてベルベット、ダマスク織、絹、レザーなどで作成されたバッグに銀の口金を取り付けました。銀の口金が付いた編みこみのビーズバッグは今日にいたっても頻繁に見受けられ、この様式は1800年直後に初めて登場したものです。

ついにハンドバッグが洋服ダンスの必須アイテムに加わった20世紀初期、多くのハンドバッグは様相が変化します。留金が姿を消し、代わりに小さなチェーンが持ち手としてバッグに取り付けられました。当時、口金式バッグを求める人が非常に多かったため、銀の口金の代わりにイミテーションが使用され、チェーンと開き口を閉じるゲンコツも取り付けられました。口金に加え、18世紀以降はがま口用の小型口金も出回っていました。

deutsch

日本語

▲ Velvet bag with silver frame and hook, maker: Van Gelderen, Schoonhoven The Netherlands, 1773.
▼ Silk bag with gilded frame and fringe; net of gold thread and Fer de Berlin beads France, 19th c.

▲ Velvet bag with beaded fringe and silver frame and hook, maker: Oosterloo, Franeker The Netherlands, ca. 1810.
▼ Gold ring-mesh bag with gold empire frame, maker: Straaten, Amsterdam The Netherlands, 1817.

▲ Velvet bag with 'the horn of plenty' in steel beads; silver frame, maker: Reitsma, Heereveen The Netherlands, 1866.
▼ Beaded bag with silver frame, hook and chain, maker: Van Wijk, Amsterdam (bag and chain, 19th c.) The Netherlands, 1771.

▲ Woven silk bag with silver frame The Netherlands, 1919.
▼ Beaded bag with silver frame and chain, maker: Fliringa, Leeuwarden The Netherlands, 1843.
▶ Beaded bag with gold Empire frame, maker: Moot, Utrecht The Netherlands, ca. 1820.

Tie pockets

Poches

Dijzakken

Los bolsillos exteriores

Borse piatte a tasca

Gewandtaschen

結びポケット

As skirts became more capacious in the seventeenth and eighteenth centuries, tie pockets became popular. Women used them to carry their personal belongings, such as their money purse, letter case, sewing materials, snuffbox, perfume bottle, handkerchief and keys.
The tie pocket is a long rectangular or pear-shaped bag that is tied round the middle with a ribbon. Most were made from sturdy linen or cotton, and they were often decorated with embroidery. In the front centre there was a vertical opening. The tie pocket was worn (often two at a time) over the upper petticoat and was reached through a slit in the side of the dress or skirt. Thus, because tie pockets were hidden from view, illustrations of them are rare in paintings and prints. Although during the nineteenth century women's clothing gradually came to have more inside pockets, tie pockets remained in use until the twentieth century. In women's magazines they were recommended as travel purses. The same magazines published patterns for making them at home, but shops also carried tie pockets made of cloth or leather.

◀ 1194 Brocade bag with gold frame, maker: Netelenbosch, **Amsterdam** The Netherlands, 1823.

English

Aux dix-septième et dix-huitième siècles, les jupes se faisant de plus en plus volumineuses, les poches deviennent très populaires. Les femmes y mettent leurs objets personnels – porte-monnaie, pochette, ustensiles de couture, tabatière, flacon de parfum, mouchoir et clés.

La poche à nouer est un long sac rectangulaire ou en forme de poire noué autour de la taille par un ruban. Le plus souvent en lin ou coton résistant, elles sont souvent ornées de broderies. Elles portent sur l'avant une ouverture verticale au centre, se portent (souvent par paire) sur le jupon du dessus et sont accessibles par une fente pratiquée sur le côté de la robe ou de la jupe. Cachées des regards, les représentations de ces poches sont rares dans les peintures et les gravures. Au dix-neuvième siècle, les poches intérieures gagnent de plus en plus les vêtements féminins, mais les poches à nouer demeurent jusqu'au vingtième siècle. Les magazines féminins conseillaient leur usage comme porte-monnaie de voyage et proposaient des patrons pour les réaliser soi-même, tandis que les boutiques en proposaient en toile ou en cuir.

Met het wijder worden van de rokken werden in de loop van de zeventiende en in de achttiende eeuw dijzakken populair. Vrouwen bewaarden daarin hun persoonlijke bezittingen, zoals hun beurs, portefeuille, naaigerei, snuifdoos, parfumfles, zakdoek en sleutels. De dijzak is een lange rechthoekige of peervormige zak, die met een lint om het middel werd gebonden. De meeste werden gemaakt van stevig linnen of katoen, en vaak werden ze versierd met borduurwerk. Middenvoor zat een verticale opening. De dijzak werd (vaak als paar) op de bovenste onderrok gedragen en was bereikbaar door een split in de zijkant van de japon of rok. Doordat dijzakken dus aan het oog ont-trokken waren, zijn afbeeldingen ervan op schilderijen en prenten zeldzaam.

Hoewel vrouwenkleding in de loop van de negentiende eeuw steeds meer van binnenzakken werd voorzien, bleven dijzakken tot in de twintigste eeuw in gebruik. In damesbladen werden ze aangeraden als reisbeurs. Diezelfde bladen publiceerden daarvoor zelfmaakpatronen, maar ook winkels boden dijzakken te koop aan, uitgevoerd in stof of leer.

français

nederlands

En el transcurso de los siglos XVII y XVIII, a medida que la falda se hacía más ampulosa se fueron popularizando los bolsillos exteriores. Las mujeres los utilizaban para transportar pertenencias tales como el monedero, el portadocumentos, el material de costura, la tabaquera, el frasco de perfume, el pañuelo y las llaves.

El bolsillo exterior es una bolsa en forma de pera o de rectángulo alargado, que se ata por el medio con un lazo. La mayoría estaban realizados en algodón o lino resistente y a menudo se decoraban con bordados. La parte anterior presentaba una abertura vertical en el centro. Estos bolsillos (generalmente eran dos) se llevaban sobre la parte superior de las enaguas y se accedía a ellos a través de un orificio practicado en el lateral del vestido o la falda. Puesto que los bolsillos exteriores se ocultaban a la vista, raramente pueden apreciarse en cuadros y láminas.

A pesar de que a lo largo del siglo XIX las prendas femeninas cada vez se proveían de más bolsillos interiores, los bolsillos exteriores siguieron utilizándose hasta el siglo XX. Las revistas femeninas recomendaban su uso como monederos de viaje. Estas mismas revistas publicaban patrones para poder confeccionarlos, aunque en las tiendas también podían adquirirse modelos realizados en tela o cuero.

Nel XVII e XVIII secolo, quando le gonne divennero più voluminose, si diffusero borse piatte da appendere alla vita. Le donne le utilizzavano per riporvi i propri effetti personali, come borsellino, portafogli, materiali per il cucito, tabacchiera, boccetta di profumo, fazzoletto e chiavi.

Si trattava di borse lunghe e piatte, di forma rettango- lare o a goccia, che venivano legate alla vita con un nastro. La maggior parte era confezionata in lino o cotone robusti, spesso decorati con ricami. L'apertura si trovava al centro della parte anteriore. Queste borse venivano indossate (spesso a coppie) tra la gonna e la sottana superiore, e vi si accedeva infilando la mano in un taglio praticato sul lato del vestito o della gonna. Dato che erano nascoste sotto gli abiti, è raro trovarle raffigurate nei dipinti e nelle stampe dell'epoca.

Anche se, nel corso del XIX secolo, gli indumenti femminili acquisirono un maggior numero di tasche interne, questo tipo di borse restò in uso fino al XX secolo. Le riviste femminili le raccomandavano per chi si recava in viaggio e pubblicavano modelli per confezionarle da sé; tuttavia, le borse piatte da legare in vita, in stoffa o in pelle, si trovavano in vendita anche nei negozi.

Español

Italiano

Als im Verlauf des 17. und 18. Jahrhunderts die Röcke weiter wurden, wurden die sogenannten Gewandtaschen populär. Die Frauen bewahrten in ihnen ihre persönlichen Habseligkeiten auf, so zum Beispiel Geldbeutel, Brieftasche, Nähzeug, das Riechsalzdöschen, Parfümflakons, Taschentücher und Schlüssel. Die Gewandtasche ist eine längliche, rechteckige oder birnenförmige Tasche, die an ein Band um die Taille gebunden wurde. Meist wurde sie aus grobem Leinen oder Baumwolle hergestellt und mit Stickereien verziert. In der Mitte auf der Vorderseite verfügen sie über eine vertikale Öffnung. Diese Gewandtaschen wurden (häufig als Paar) über dem oberen Unterrock getragen, man erreichte sie durch einen Schlitz an der Seite des Kleides oder Rockes. Daher gibt es leider von diesem Taschentyp nur wenig Abbildungen auf Gemälden oder Drucken, denn die Taschen waren ja unter dem Rock nicht zu sehen.

Auch wenn die Frauenkleider im Laufe des 19. Jahrhunderts immer mehr mit Innentaschen versehen wurde, blieben die Gewandtaschen bis ins 20. Jahrhundert weiterhin in Gebrauch. In Frauenmagazinen wurden sie für Reisen empfohlen und es wurden Schnittanleitungen zum Selbermachen veröffentlicht. Auch in den Geschäften konnte man Gewandtaschen aus Leder oder Stoff kaufen.

スカートがさらに大きく広がっていた 17、18 世紀、結びポケットの人気が高まります。女性は小銭入れ、レターケース、裁縫道具、嗅ぎ煙草入れ、香水瓶、ハンカチーフ、鍵など身の回り品を入れていました。

結びポケットは長い長方形、または洋ナシ形の袋で中央部をリボンで結びます。そのほとんどはしっかりした麻、または綿素材で作られ、しばしば装飾として刺繍があしらわれていました。表側の中央にたての開き口があります。結びポケットは（一度に 2 つ装着することが良くあり）一番外側のペチコートの上に身に付け、ドレスまたはスカート側面にあるスリットから手をいれて中のものを取り出しました。このように結びポケットは外から見えなかったため、絵画や印刷物などに描かれていることはまれです。

19 世紀中に婦人服にも徐々に内ポケットが取り付けられるようになりましたが、結びポケットは 20 世紀まで使用され続けました。婦人雑誌には結びポケットを旅行用パースとして推奨しました。同誌は家庭で手作りできるよう型紙を出版していましたが、店頭にも布製や皮製の結びポケットは並んでいました。

deutsch

日本語

▲ Pair of linen tie pockets false-quilted in yellow silk
England, 1725-1750.
◄ Linen tie pocket embroidered in coloured silks
England, 1725-1750.

▲ Pair of linen tie pockets embroidered in flame-stitch with date and
initials England, 1766.
▼ Cotton tie pocket as still being used in Dutch national costume
The Netherlands, ca. 1995.

Reticules and workbags

Réticules et sacs à ouvrage

Reticules en handwerktassen

Retículas y bolsas de labores

Reticule e borse da lavoro

Retiküle und Handarbeitsbeutel

レティキュールと作業バッグ

Partly influenced by the discovery of Pompeii and the revived interest in the Greek temples, in the course of the eighteenth century everything related to classical antiquity became popular. For fashion, this meant that at the end of the century monumental, capacious dresses gave way to simply-cut dresses made of thin fabrics with a higher waist. There was no longer space for heavy tie pockets under these gossamer-thin garments, and a new place had to be found for their contents. They moved to the already-existing workbag and to the fashionable new reticule, the first real forerunner of the handbag.

The reticule, made of cloth or other materials, always had a cord or chain with which the bag could be drawn shut and carried. The French term *réticule* probably comes from the Latin *reticulum*, which refers to the small ladies' net bags from Roman times. Despite the return of ample skirts after 1825, the reticule remained in use until the early decades of the twentieth century. At a time when every well-bred woman was expected to spend her leisure time on fine needlework, the workbag was an indispensable accessory. Both needle-work and sewing materials were stowed away in it. The workbag was often taken on visits. From the 1770s on, the most popular workbag was a flat rectangular bag that was closed at the top with a drawstring. These workbags were mostly made of white satin and were embroidered and decorated with ribbons, foil and sequins. In many cases, women most likely made their reticules and workbags themselves.

English

Au dix-huitième siècle, en partie sous l'influence de la découverte de Pompéi et de l'intérêt accru pour les temples grecs, tout ce qui a trait à l'antiquité classique connaît un grand succès. Dans la mode, les robes imposantes et volumineuses font place à la fin du siècle à d'autres de coupe simple en tissus fins et à la taille plus haute. Ces vêtements, souvent aussi fins que la gaze, ne laissent plus d'espace à de lourdes poches nouées par-dessous. Leur contenu doit alors être transféré ailleurs. On choisit pour cela le sac à ouvrage, qui existe déjà, et surtout le réticule, nouveau et très chic, premier véritable précurseur du sac à main.

En toile ou autre matière, le réticule était toujours muni d'une chaîne ou d'un cordon pour le fermer et le porter. Le terme vient sans doute du latin *reticulum* qui désignait les petits sacs en filet des dames de l'époque romaine. Il continuera d'être utilisé jusqu'aux premières décennies du vingtième siècle – malgré le retour des jupes amples après 1825.

À une époque où toute femme de bonne famille est supposée passer son temps libre à de délicats travaux d'aiguille, le sac à ouvrage est un accessoire indispensable. On y range lesdits travaux et les ustensiles de couture et on l'emmène souvent avec soi en visite.

À partir des années 1770, le sac à ouvrage le plus populaire est un sac plat et rectangulaire fermé en haut par un cordon. Le plus souvent en satin blanc, il peut être brodé et décoré de rubans, feuilles métalliques et sequins. La plupart des réticules et sacs à ouvrage ont très probablement été réalisés par leurs utilisatrices.

Mede onder invloed van de ontdekking van Pompeii en de herwaardering voor de Griekse tempels werd in de loop van de achttiende eeuw alles populair wat met de klassieke oudheid te maken had. Voor de mode betekende dit dat monumentale, wijde japonnen aan het eind van die eeuw plaatsmaakten voor sluike japonnen van dunne stof met een verhoogde taillenaad. Voor zware dijzakken was onder deze ragfijne kleding geen plaats meer en voor de inhoud ervan moest een nieuwe plek worden gevonden. Die verhuisde naar de al bestaande handwerktas en naar de modieuze nieuwe reticule, de eerste echte voorloper van de handtas.

De reticule van textiel of ander materiaal had altijd een koord of ketting waarmee de tas dichtgetrokken en gedragen kon worden. De Franse term *réticule* komt waarschijnlijk van het Latijnse *reticulum*, dat verwijst naar de kleine damestassen van netwerk uit de Romeinse tijd. Ondanks de terugkeer van de wijde japonnen na 1825 bleef de reticule tot in de eerste decennia van de twintigste eeuw in gebruik.

In een tijdperk waarin van iedere beschaafde vrouw werd verwacht dat ze haar vrije uren doorbracht met fijn handwerk, was de handwerktas een onmisbaar attribuut. Zowel het handwerk als het naaigerei werd erin opgeborgen. Niet zelden werd de handwerktas meegenomen bij het afleggen van visites.

Vanaf de jaren zeventig van de achttiende eeuw was de populairste handwerktas een rechthoekige platte tas die bovenaan met een draagkoord werd gesloten. Deze handwerktassen waren veelal van wit satijn, geborduurd en versierd met lint, folie en lovertjes. In veel gevallen zullen vrouwen zelf hun reticules en handwerktassen hebben gemaakt.

En parte influidos por los descubrimientos de Pompeya y el revivido interés por los templos griegos, durante el siglo XVIII se popularizó todo lo relacionado con la Antigüedad clásica. En la esfera de la moda esto significó que, a finales de siglo, los vestidos monumentales y ampulosos dieron paso a vestidos de corte sencillo, confeccionados con telas ligeras y con una cintura más alta. Bajo estas finísimas prendas ya no quedaba espacio para los pesados bolsillos exteriores, por lo que era preciso encontrar un nuevo recipiente donde guardar su contenido. Éste se trasladó a la bolsa de labores, ya existente, y a la moderna retícula, el primer precedente real del bolso de mano.

La retícula, confeccionada en tela u otro material, siempre estaba provista de una cuerda o cadena con la que la bolsa podía cerrarse y asirse. El término francés réticule probablemente procede del latín reticulum, que se refiere a las pequeñas bolsas de tejido similar a una red que utilizaban las mujeres de la época romana. A pesar del retorno de las faldas anchas después de 1825, la retícula siguió utilizándose hasta las primeras décadas del siglo XX.

En una época en la cual se esperaba que las mujeres de educación refinada dedicaran su tiempo libre a realizar labores, la bolsa de labores era un accesorio indispensable. En ella se guardaban tanto las labores como el material de costura. Cuando se realizaban visitas era frecuente llevar consigo la bolsa de labores. A partir de 1770, la bolsa de labores más extendida era plana y rectangular, cerrada en la parte superior con un cordón. La mayoría de estas bolsas estaban confeccionadas en satén blanco, y se bordaban y decoraban con lazos, láminas metálicas y lentejuelas. Es probable que en muchos casos fueran las propias mujeres quienes confeccionaran sus retículas y bolsas de labores.

Anche a causa della scoperta di Pompei e del nuovo interesse per gli antichi templi greci, durante il XVIII secolo divenne di moda tutto ciò che si ispirava all'antichità classica. Nella moda femminile, ciò significò che alla fine di questo secolo gli ampi e voluminosi vestiti femminili lasciarono il passo ad abiti di taglio più semplice, fatti di tessuti più sottili e con punto vita più alto. Sotto la leggerissima stoffa di questi abiti non c'era più spazio per le pesanti borse piatte legate in vita: si impose quindi la necessità di trovare un modo nuovo di trasportare i loro contenuti. I sostituti furono la preesistente borsa da lavoro e le nuove reticule, le prime vere antesignane della moderna borsetta.

La reticule, fatta di stoffa o di altri materiali, era sempre provvista di un cordone o di una catenella con cui chiuderla e trasportarla. Probabilmente il termine francese réticule deriva dal latino reticulum, che si riferiva alle piccole borse di rete delle donne romane. Anche dopo il ritorno delle gonne ampie, dal 1825 in poi, la reticule restò di moda fino ai primi decenni del XX secolo.

In un'epoca in cui si dava per scontato che ogni donna perbene trascorresse il suo tempo libero a ricamare, la borsa da lavoro era un accessorio indispensabile. Vi si conservavano sia i ricami sia i materiali per il cucito. Spesso, le signore la portavano con sé anche quando andavano a far visita a conoscenti. Dagli anni Settanta del XVIII secolo in poi, il modello più diffuso di borsa da lavoro era quello piatto e rettangolare, chiuso nella parte superiore da un nastro scorrevole inserito in appositi passanti. La maggior parte di queste borse da lavoro era di satin bianco, ricamato e decorato con nastri, lamine di metallo e lustrini. Spesso, le donne confezionavano con le proprie mani reticule e borse da lavoro.

Español

Italiano

Teilweise unter dem Einfluss der Entdeckung von Pompeji und dem auflebenden Interesse für griechische Tempel wurde im Laufe des 18. Jahrhunderts alles modern, was mit der Antike zu tun hatte. In der Kleidung kamen weit geschnittene, ausladende Modelle nach und nach außer Mode, und neue, leichtere, schmaler geschnittenere Gewänder nahmen deren Platz ein. Die Taille wurde nach oben geschoben. Da war nun kein Platz mehr für die schweren Gewandtaschen. Es musste eine neue Lösung für den Transport persönlicher Gegenstände gefunden werden. Zunächst trug man seine Habseligkeiten in dem bereits existierenden Handarbeitsbeutel, dann in dem neuen schicken Retikül, dem ersten richtigen Vorgänger unserer heutigen Handtasche. Das Retikül aus Stoff oder anderen Materialien hatte immer eine Kordel oder eine Kette, mit der die Tasche verschlossen transportiert werden konnte. Der Begriff kommt vom französischen „Réticule", das sich wahrscheinlich aus dem lateinischen Wort *reticulum* ableitet, mit dem bei cen Römern die kleinen, von Damen getragenen Netztaschen bezeichnet wurden. Auch wenn später, ab 1825, wieder weitere Röcke in Mode kamen, tauchte das Retikül noch bis ins beginnende 20. Jahrhundert häufig auf.

Zu einer Zeit, in der von jeder Dame aus gutem Hause erwartet wurde, dass sie ihre Zeit zu Hause stickend oder strickend mit Handarbeiten verbrachte, galt der Handarbeitsbeutel als unverzichtbares, tägliches Accessoire. Näh- und Strickzeug wurde in diesen Taschen verstaut und konnten so problemlos überallhin mitgenommen werden. Oft wurde der Beutel bei Besuchen mitgenommen. Ab 1770 waren flache, rechteckige Beutel, die oben mit einer Zugschnur verschlossen wurden, besonders modern. Meist waren diese Handarbeitstaschen aus weißem Satin gearbeitet, mit Bändern verziert oder bestickt oder mit Metallfolie und Pailletten dekoriert. In vielen Fällen stellten die Frauen ihre Retiküle und Handarbeitsbeutel auch selbst her.

ポンペイの発見やギリシャ神殿への興味が復活したことが一因し、18世紀の流れの中では古典的なアンティークに関連するもの全ての人気が高まります。ファッションに関していうと、このことは記念すべき世紀終幕において、広く膨らんだ今までのドレスは、薄い生地を用い簡素に裁断された高ウエスト位置のドレスに取って代わられます。極薄生地のドレスでは、もはや重い結びポケットを下げる場所などありません。ポケットに入れていたものを持ち歩くため別のしまい場所を見つける必要が生じたわけです。身の回り品は、すでに存在していた作業バッグに入れるようになり、その後新たに登場したファッショナブルなレティキュール—最初の本格的なハンドバッグの先駆け—に入れました。

レティキュールは布または他の素材で作られ、常に紐またはチェーンが付いていてそれを引っ張って口を閉じ、またそれが持ち手にもなりました。1825年以降に広がりの大きなスカートが復活したにもかかわらず、レティキュールは20世紀の初期の何十年間かまで愛用され続けました。

良家の女性は余暇にすばらしい手芸作品を作ることが常識とされていた時代、作業バッグは無くてはならない持ち物でした。手芸作品と手芸道具の両方を作業バッグに入れていました。作業バッグはしばしば訪問時にも持ち歩かれました。1770年代以降、もっとも人気の高かった作業バッグは、平らな長方形のバッグで上部に引き紐があり、それで口を閉じるようになっています。これらの作業バッグは大抵白のサテンで作られ刺繍を施し、リボン、金属箔、スパンコールなどで装飾されていました。多くの場合、レティキュールや作業バッグは自分たちで手作りしたに違いないでしょう。

deutsch

日本語

▲ Silk working bag with gold stitchery, sequins, glass and gold-braid
France, late 18th c.
▼ Silk working bag with appliqué of felt, sequins and beads;
needlework tools England, ca. 1830.

▲ Silk working bag embroidered with silk, wire and sequins
. England, late 18th c.
▼ Silk working bag embroidered with coloured silk late 18th c.
▶ Fabric reticule embroidered with gilt thread England, 1850-1870.

▲ Satin reticule with emboidery and lace border France, early 19th c.
▼ Fabric reticule with embroidery and cut steel beads
France, 1850-1870.

▲ Silk reticule embroidered with ribbon and silk England, ca. 1840.
▼ Reticule decorated with embroidery and beads, chenille tassels
France, 1850-1870.

▲ Satin reticule embroidered with silk, felt and beads, beaded fringe
England, 1850s
▼ Fabric and velvet reticule embroidered with gilt thread
England, 1850-1870.

▲ Two identical fabric reticules with silk embroidery France,
early 19th c.
▼ Velvet reticule embroidered with pearls and turquoise
France, 1850-1870.

▲ Reticule in Berlin woolwork, chenille tassels England, 1840-1870.

▲ Silk reticule with Berlin woolwork embroidery, chenille tassels
England, 1840-1870.
▼ Reticule in Berlin woolwork, chenille tassels England, 1840-1870.

▲ Reticule in Berlin woolwork England, 1850-1900.
▼ Silk reticule with scene of town on river Germany, 19th c.

Coin purses

Bourses

Beurzen

Portamonedas

Borse per monete

Geldbeutel

コインパース

A strikingly long purse that became popular in the last quarter of the eighteenth century is the stocking purse (also called the long purse, ring purse or gentlemen's purse). The stocking purse is a long crocheted or knitted sheath which is closed at both ends and carried in the middle. In that same middle of the purse was the opening, through which money could be dropped toward one of the two sides. The two ends were often different, so that one could easily distinguish what was kept on which side. Two rings around the middle were moved towards the ends in order to close off the contents. The stocking purse remained in use until the 1920s, although its popularity decreased rapidly with the arrival of paper money at the beginning of the century.

Variations on the stocking purse were the 'à la reine Elisabeth' (the Queen Elizabeth) and the 'en diable' purse (the Devil's purse). The latter was so christened because it was so difficult to open and close. A typical French purse was the 'bourse à Louis', a little purse made of gilt metal or gold named after the Louis d'Or, the French gold coin.

English

Une bourse d'une longueur étonnante a connu un grand succès dans le dernier quart du dix-huitième siècle : la bourse chaussette (également appelée longue bourse, bourse à anneau ou bourse de gentleman), un long fourreau crocheté ou tricoté fermé aux deux extrémités et porté par le milieu, où se trouve l'ouverture par laquelle l'argent pouvait être déposé d'un côté ou de l'autre. Les deux bouts étaient souvent différents pour permettre de distinguer facilement ce que chacun contenait et deux anneaux au milieu pouvaient être glissés vers les extrémités pour en enfermer le contenu. La bourse chaussette a été utilisée jusqu'aux années 1920, pour perdre ensuite rapidement sa popularité avec l'introduction du papier monnaie au début du siècle.

Parmi les variantes de bourses chaussette, on trouve les bourses « à la reine Elisabeth » et « en diable » (ainsi nommée parce qu'elle était si difficile à ouvrir et fermer). Typiquement française, la « bourse à louis » était quant à elle une petite bourse de métal doré ou d'or qui doit son nom au louis d'or.

Een opvallende lange beurs die in het laatste kwart van de achttiende eeuw populair werd, is de kousenbeurs (ook wel lange beurs of wel herenbeurs genoemd). De kousenbeurs is een aan beide uiteinden gesloten lange koker van haak- of breiwerk, die in het midden gedragen werd. In datzelfde midden van de beurs zat de opening, waardoor men het geld naar een van beide kanten kon laten vallen. Vaak waren de uiteinden verschillend van vorm, zodat makkelijk te onthouden was wat aan welke kant bewaard werd. Twee ringen om het midden werden naar de uiteinden geschoven om de inhoud af te sluiten. De kousenbeurs is tot in de jaren twintig van de twintigste eeuw in gebruik gebleven, hoewel zijn populariteit met de komst van het papiergeld in het begin van die eeuw snel afnam.

Varianten op de kousenbeurs waren de beurs 'à la reine Elisabeth' en de beurs 'en diable'. De laatste werd zo genoemd omdat het zo lastig was hem open en dicht te krijgen. Een typische Franse beurs was de 'bourse à Louis', een beursje van verguld metaal of goud, genoemd naar de Louis d'Or, de Franse gouden munt.

français

nederlands

La bolsa de media es un bolso sorprendentemente largo que se popularizó en el último cuarto del siglo XVIII. También recibe el nombre de bolsa larga, bolsa de aro o bolsa de caballero. Se trata de una funda larga de punto o ganchillo cerrada en ambos extremos, que se ase por el medio. Justo aquí es donde se hallaba la abertura a través de la cual el dinero podía meterse hacia uno u otro lado. Por lo general, cada uno de los extremos era diferente a fin de poder distinguir fácilmente qué se guardaba en cada lado. En el medio había dos aros que se desplazaban hacia los extremos para evitar que saliera el contenido. La bolsa de media siguió en uso hasta la década de 1920, si bien su popularidad disminuyó rápidamente con la llegada del papel moneda, a principios de siglo.

La bolsa de media tenía variantes como la bolsa "à la reine Elisabeth" (de la reina Isabel) y la bolsa "en diable" (del diablo). Ésta última se bautizó así porque resultaba muy complicado abrirla y cerrarla. Típicamente francesa era la "'bourse à Louis", pequeña y elaborada con metal dorado u oro y que toma su nombre del *louis d'or*, la moneda de oro francesa.

Nell'ultimo quarto del XVIII secolo divenne popolare una borsa portamonete di forma molto allungata, la borsa lunga o tubolare. Si trattava di un lungo involucro lavorato a maglia o a uncinetto, chiuso ad entrambe le estremità e portato piegato a metà sulla cintura. Nella parte centrale della borsa si trovava anche l'apertura, che consentiva di infilare le monete in una delle due estremità. Spesso, le due estremità erano diverse tra loro, per distinguerle l'una dall'altra con facilità. Al centro di questo contenitore tubolare si trovavano anche due anelli che si potevano fare scivolare verso le estremità per impedire che il contenuto fuoriuscisse. La borsa tubolare per monete restò in uso fino agli anni Venti del XX secolo, anche se la sua popolarità diminuì rapidamente con l'avvento delle banconote all'inizio del secolo.

Altre varianti della borsa per monete erano quella detta "à la reine Elisabeth" (alla regina Elisabetta) e quella 'en diable' (del diavolo), il cui nome bizzarro era dovuto al fatto che era molto difficile da aprire e chiudere. Un modello tipicamente francese era la 'bourse à Louis', un piccolo borsellino d'oro o di metallo dorato così chiamato in omaggio al 'Louis d'Or', la moneta d'oro francese.

Español   Italiano

Gegen Ende des 18. Jahrhunderts kam ein besonders langer Geldbeutel in Mode, der Geldstrumpf. Der Geldstrumpf ist ein langer gehäkelter oder gestrickter Beutel, der an beiden Enden geschlossen war und in der Mitte gehalten wurde. Der Beutel öffnete sich in der Mitte, und man konnte in eine der beiden Seiten des Strumpfs Geld hineinlegen. Häufig waren die beiden Enden unterschiedlich gestaltet, damit der Träger leicht unterscheiden konnte, was er in der einen oder anderen Seite verstaut hatte. Zwei Ringe um das Mittelstück werden zu den beiden Enden auseinandergeschoben und schließen so den jeweiligen Inhalt auf jeder Seite ab. Bis in die 20er Jahre des 20. Jahrhunderts blieb dieser Geldbeuteltyp in Gebrauch, verschwand dann aber rasch durch die Verbreitung des Papiergelds. Variationen des Geldstrumpfs waren zum Beispiel die der Geldbeutel „à la reine Elisabeth" (nach der Königin Elisabeth) oder die Geldbörse „en diable" (Teufelsbörse), die so genannt wurde, weil sie nur sehr schwer zu öffnen war. Eine typisch französische Geldbörse war die „Bourse à Louis", eine kleine Börse aus Gold oder vergoldetem Metall, das nach der französischen Goldmünze Louis d'Or benannt wurde.

驚くほど長いパースが 18 世紀の最後の 25 年間に人気が出ます。これはストッキングパース（またはロングパース、リングパース、紳士用パース）というものです。ストッキングパースは長いレース網または編み込みシースで、両方のバッグ部分を閉じて真ん中を持ちます。パースの中心部には開き口があり、金銭をそこからどちらか一方に落とすことができるようになっています。両バッグ部分はそれぞれ異なっているため、何をどちら側にしまってあるか容易に区別できます。2 個のリングが取り付けられ、それを端へ動かして中身が出ないよう口を閉じます。ストッキングパースは 1920 年代まで使用され続けましたが、世紀の始めに紙幣が登場したことで急速に人気が下がりました。

ストッキングパースが変形したものに「ア・ラ・レーヌ・エリザベート（à la reine Elisabeth: エリザベス女王）や「エン・ディアブル（en diable: 悪魔のパース）などがあります。後者にそのような名前が付いたのは、開け閉めが大変困難だったことに由来します。典型的なフランス製パースは「ボース・ア・ルイ（bourse à Louis）」で、メッキ加工の金属や金でできた小型パースです。これはフランスの金貨、ルイ・ドールにちなんで名づけられました。

▲ Gilded coin-purse 'Louis d'Or' France, ca. 1830.
◄ Long purse of white glass beads and gold-coloured metal beads,
gilt rings France, 19th c.
◄◄ Crocheted coin purse in shape of jug Germany, ca. 1865 and
crocheted coin purse with perfume-bottle on top France, ca. 1855.

▲ Long purse of coral pink, the base worked with circles of gold and
silver thread England, late 18th c.
▼ Crocheted coin purse in the so called 'en diable'-execution
France, 19th c.

▲ Two long purses and one 'en diable' coin purse France, 1800-1850.
▼ Two long crocheted purses with cut steel beads, one with text:
'A token of gratitude' England, 1850-1900 and 1886.

▲ Crocheted long purse France, late 19th c.
▼ Coin purse with special closure, decorated with steel beads
France, ca. 1880.

Souvenirs

Souvenirs

Souvenirs

Recuerdos de viajes

Souvenir

Souvenirs

土産品

With the increase in travel, the demand for souvenirs increased. In France, special little purses and bags showing pictures of Paris were sold as souvenirs. Souvenir purses in different forms made from cloth, gilt metal, silver, gold, mother of pearl, ivory, tortoiseshell or celluloid were purchased by travellers to take home as a memento of their trip. The front of many nineteenth-century souvenir purses had a picture of a church, castle or other well-known building or monument from the city visited.

A handbag with wooden cover sheets showing pictures of Fontainebleau and a little wooden money box showing the house where the Scottish poet Robbie Burns was born are typical examples of Mauchline Ware: small implements (needle cases, letter openers, little boxes, bags and purses) with pictures of tourist attractions produced in the nineteenth century in the Scottish town of Mauchline, amongst other places. The pictures were initially applied by hand, but towards the middle of the nineteenth century they were printed with the aid of transfer plates.

Some souvenirs are mementos of historical events, such as the beaded coin purse from circa 1826 showing a picture of Zarafa, the first giraffe in France, and the beaded reticule showing the Sirius, the first steamship to cross the Atlantic Ocean in 1838.

A special set of leather handbags and clutches with coloured relief decorations of Japanese and Egyptian scenes strongly hint at being souvenirs. These bags were probably made in the Far East for the European market. Comparable bags were sold in around 1930 at Liberty & Co in London under the name of Japanese leatherwork. They are evidence of Europe's interest in the Far East at that time. Simple versions in dark green or brown leather were for sale in the bazaar in Port Said in Egypt from the thirties to the early fifties.

English

Avec le développement des voyages, la demande de souvenirs s'accroît. En France, on vend à cet effet des petits sacs et porte-monnaie avec des images de Paris, et les voyageurs achètent des porte-monnaie souvenir de différentes formes en tissu, métal doré, argent, or, nacre, ivoire, écaille ou celluloïd en souvenir de leur voyage. Beaucoup de ces porte-monnaie souvenir du dix-neuvième siècle portent par devant l'image d'une église, d'un château ou de tout bâtiment ou monument célèbre de la ville visitée.

Un sac à main dont la feuille de couverture en bois illustre Fontainebleau et la petite tirelire en bois avec l'image de la maison où le poète écossais Robert Burns est né sont des exemplaires typiques de la production de Mauchline : petits ustensiles (porte-aiguilles, coupe-papier, petites boîtes, sacs ou porte-monnaie) ornés de représentations de lieux touristiques et fabriqués au dix-neuvième siècle dans la ville écossaise de Mauchline, entre autres. Les images étaient au départ appliquées à la main ; à partir du milieu du dix-neuvième siècle, elles commencent à être imprimées à l'aide de plaques de transfert.

Certains de ces souvenirs rappellent des événements historiques, comme la bourse en perles de 1826 environ qui montre Zarafa, la première girafe arrivée en France, ou le réticule de perles illustré du Sirius, premier paquebot à traverser l'océan Atlantique en 1838.

Une série spéciale de sacs à main et de pochettes en cuir aux décorations en relief colorées représentent des scènes japonaises et égyptiennes et sont visiblement des souvenirs : ils ont sans doute été fabriqués en Extrême-Orient pour le marché européen. Des modèles comparables étaient vendus vers 1930 chez Liberty & Co, à Londres, sous le nom de maroquinerie japonaise et témoignent de l'intérêt de l'Europe pour l'Extrême-Orient à cette époque. Des versions plus simples en cuir vert ou brun foncé ont été vendues dans le bazar de Port-Saïd, en Égypte, des années trente au début des années cinquante.

Met het toenemende reisverkeer steeg de vraag naar souvenirs. In Frankrijk werden speciale beursjes en tasjes met taferelen van Parijs als souvenir verkocht. Souvenirbeursjes in aparte vormen gemaakt van textiel, verguld metaal, zilver, goud, parelmoer, ivoor, schildpad of celluloid werden door de reiziger gekocht om mee te nemen naar huis als herinnering aan een mooie reis. Veel negentiende-eeuwse souvenirbeursjes hadden op de voorkant een afbeelding van een kerk, kasteel of een ander bekend gebouw of monument uit de bezochte stad.

Een handtas met houten dekbladen met afbeeldingen van Fontainebleau en een houten beursje met het geboortehuis van de Schotse dichter Robert Burns zijn typische voorbeelden van *Mauchline Ware*: kleine gebruiksvoorwerpen (naaldenkokers, briefopeners, doosjes, tassen en beursjes) met afbeeldingen van toeristische attracties, die in de negentiende eeuw werden onder andere geproduceerd in het Schotse Mauchline. De afbeeldingen werden aanvankelijk met de hand aangebracht, maar tegen het midden van de negentiende eeuw gebeurde dat met behulp van gedrukte transferplaatjes.

Sommige souvenirs herinneren aan een historische gebeurtenis, zoals de kralenbeurs van rond 1826 met een afbeelding van Zarafa, de eerste giraf in Frankrijk, en de kralenreticule met de Sirius, het eerste stoomschip dat in 1838 de Atlantische Oceaan overstak.

Een bijzondere serie leren hand- en enveloptassen met kleurige reliëfdecoraties van Japanse en Egyptische taferelen doet sterk denken aan souvenirs. Deze tassen werden waarschijnlijk in het Verre Oosten gemaakt voor de Europese markt. Vergelijkbare tassen waren rond 1930 onder de benaming Japans leerwerk te koop bij Liberty & Co in Londen. Zij tonen de belangstelling voor het Verre Oosten die er in die jaren in Europa bestond. Eenvoudige uitvoeringen in donkergroen of bruin leer werden van de jaren dertig tot begin jaren vijftig te koop aangeboden op de bazaar van de Egyptische haven-stad Port Said.

français   nederlands

Con el aumento de los viajes, aumentó también la demanda de recuerdos. En Francia se confeccionaban especialmente pequeños portamonedas y bolsas que mostraban imágenes de París y que se vendían como recuerdos de viaje. El viajero se llevaba consigo bolsas de distintas formas realizadas con tela, metal dorado, plata, oro, madreperla, marfil, carey o celuloide para rememorar el viaje. En el siglo XIX, la parte anterior de muchas de estas bolsas presentaba la imagen de una iglesia, un castillo u otro edificio o monumento célebre de la ciudad visitada.

Típicas de la ciudad escocesa de Mauchline son un bolso de mano con cubiertas de madera que muestra imágenes de Fontainebleau y una cajita de madera para monedas que lleva pintada la casa donde nació el poeta escocés Robbie Burns. Durante el siglo XIX, en esta localidad y en algunas otras se realizaban pequeños complementos (recipientes para agujas, abrecartas, pequeñas cajas, bolsos y portamonedas) con imágenes de atracciones turísticas. En su origen, las imágenes se pintaban a mano, pero hacia mediados de siglo comenzaron a imprimirse con la ayuda de planchas.

Algunos recuerdos de viajes rememoran acontecimientos históricos como es el caso del monedero con abalorios que data de 1826 aproximadamente y que presenta una imagen de Zarafa, la primera jirafa que hubo en Francia, así como la retícula con abalorios que muestra el *Sirius*, el primer barco de vapor que cruzó el océano Atlántico en 1838.

Existe un conjunto especial de *clutches* y bolsos de mano de cuero con decoraciones de colores en relieve que muestran escenas japonesas y egipcias que hacen sospechar de que se trate de recuerdos de viaje. Es probable que estas bolsas se confeccionaran en el Lejano Oriente para el mercado europeo. Hacia 1930 en la tienda Liberty & Co de Londres se comercializaban bolsas parecidas a éstas bajo la denominación de "marroquinería japonesa", lo cual constituye una muestra del interés que Europa sentía por los países orientales en aquellos momentos.

Con il diffondersi dei viaggi di piacere, aumentò anche la richiesta di souvenir. In Francia, si vendevano speciali borsellini e borsette ricordo decorati con vedute di Parigi. I viaggiatori acquistavano borsellini e astucci souvenir di forma diversa fatti di stoffa, metallo dorato, argento, oro, madreperla, avorio, tartaruga o celluloide, che portavano a casa come ricordo del proprio viaggio. Sulla parte anteriore di molti borsellini souvenir del XIX secolo appaiono una chiesa, un castello o un altro edificio o monumento famoso della città visitata.

Una borsetta rivestita di fogli di legno che raffigura Fontainebleau, e un piccolo astuccio portamonete che mostra la casa in cui nacque il poeta scozzese Robbie Burns sono tipici esempi di *Mauchline Ware*, oggettini (agorai, tagliacarte, astucci, borse e borsellini) decorati con immagini di attrazioni turistiche che venivano prodotti nel XIX secolo nella cittadina scozzese di Mauchline, tra le altre. Inizialmente le immagini erano dipinte a mano, ma verso la metà del XIX secolo si iniziò a produrne anche di stampate.

Alcuni souvenir ricordano avvenimenti storici: è questo il caso del portamonete di perline del 1826 circa che raffigura Zarafa, la prima giraffa apparsa in Francia, e della *reticule* in perline che commemora la Sirius, la prima nave a vapore ad attraversare l'Atlantico nel 1838. È molto probabile che fossero souvenir una speciale serie di borsette e pochette con variopinte immagini in rilievo che raffigurano scene di ambientazione giapponese ed egiziana. Probabilmente queste borsette venivano confezionate in Estremo Oriente per il mercato europeo. Intorno al 1930, borsette di questo tipo erano in vendita presso il grande magazzino Liberty & Co di Londra sotto nome di "pelletteria giapponese". Questi oggetti testimoniano il forte interesse per l'Estremo Oriente che si nutriva nell'Europa dell'epoca. Modelli più semplici, in pelle verde scuro o marrone, si trovavano in vendita al bazar di Port Said, in Egitto, dagli anni Trenta ai primi anni Cinquanta.

Español

Italiano

Mit der Zunahme der Reisetätigkeit stieg auch die Nachfrage nach Souvenirs. In Paris wurden besonders angefertigte kleine Geldbörsen und Täschchen verkauft, die ein Motiv der Stadt trugen. Die Souvenirbörsen waren aus den verschiedensten Materialien gearbeitet. Börsen aus Stoff, aus vergoldetem Metall oder sogar aus Silber und Gold, aus Perlmutt, Elfenbein, Schildpatt oder Zelluloid wurden von den Reisenden als Erinnerung gekauft. Souvenirbörsen und Taschen aus dem 19. Jahrhundert trugen das Motiv einer Kirche, eines Schlosses oder eines anderen berühmten Gebäudes der Stadt. Eine Handtasche mit hölzerner Deckklappe zeigt das Schloss Fontainebleau. Ein kleines Portemonnaie, ebenfalls aus Holz, zeigt das Haus, in dem der schottische Poet Robert Burns geboren wurde und ist eines der typischen Beispiele der Mauchline-Produktion: Kleine Gegenstände (Nähkästchen, Brieföffner, Etuis, Taschen und Geldbörsen) mit Bildern von Sehenswürdigkeiten, die im 19.Jahrhudert in der schottischen Stadt Mauchline und anderorts hergestellt wurden. Die Bilder wurden zu Beginn von Hand aufgetragen, aber bereits gegen Mitte des 19. Jahrhunderts wurden die Darstellungen mit Hilfe einer Druckplatte aufgedruckt.

Manche Souvenirs erinnern an ein historisches Ereignis, wie zum Beispiel das perlengeschmückte Portemonnaie aus der Zeit um 1826 mit einem Bild von Zarafa, der ersten Giraffe in Frankreich. Oder das Perlenretikül mit einem Bild von Sirius, dem ersten Dampfschiff, das im Jahre 1838 den Atlantik überquerte.

Ein spezielles Set von Lederhandtaschen und Unterarmtaschen mit einem kolorierten Relief und Darstellungen japanischer oder ägyptischer Szenen war eindeutig für den Verkauf als Souvenir bestimmt. Die Taschen wurden höchstwahrscheinlich im fernen Osten für den europäischen Markt hergestellt. Vergleichbare Taschen gab es um 1930 bei Liberty & Co. in London unter dem Namen Japanese Leatherwork (japanische Lederarbeiten) zu kaufen. Man erkennt bereits das große Interesse Europas an dem fernen Osten der damaligen Zeit. Einfache Versionen in dunkelgrünem oder dunkelbraunen Leder gab es im Bazar in Port Said in Ägypten von den 30ern an bis in die frühen 50er Jahre.

旅行の機会が増えるにつれ、土産品に対する需要も増加しました。フランスでは特製の小さいパースやバッグにパリの絵が描かれたものが土産用として売り出されました。土産用パースは種類も豊富で布、メッキ加工金属、銀、金、真珠層、象牙、べっ甲、セルロイドなどの素材からできたものが出回り、旅の記念にと旅行者が購入しました。19世紀の土産用パースの正面には、訪れた土地の教会や城、または有名な建物や記念碑などが描かれていました。

表面を木板で覆いフォンテーヌブロー城の風景画が描かれたハンドバッグや、小さな木製の銭箱に家の絵を描いたものなどは、典型的なモークリン・ウェア（Mauchline Ware）の例です。小道具（針箱、ペーパーナイフ、小箱、バッグ、パース）に観光名所の絵をあしらったものは、19世紀にスコットランドのモークリンほか各地で製作されました。絵柄は当初手書きで行われていましたが、19世紀中頃に近づいた頃から転写プレートを用いるようになります。

土産品の中には歴史的な出来事の描写を絵柄にしたものもあります。1826年頃のビーズ製コインパースにはフランスに初めてやってきたキリン、ザラファの絵が描かれ、ビーズ製レティキュールには1838年に初めて大西洋を横断した初の蒸気船、シリウス（Sirius）の絵が描かれています。

特殊なレザー製ハンドバッグとクラッチバッグのセットで日本やエジプトの風景を色彩豊かにレリーフしたものなどは、土産品として作製されたことが強くうかがえます。これらのバッグはおそらく欧州市場に向けて極東で製作されたものでしょう。類似のバッグが1930年頃ロンドンのリバティー（Liberty & Co）で日本のレザー製品という形で販売されていました。その当時極東に対する関心が欧州に広がっていたことを裏付けています。深緑または茶のレザーを使った簡素な様式のものが1930年代から50年代始めにかけてエジプト、ポートサイドのバザーで売られていました。

deutsch

日本語

▲ Beaded reticule 'Souvenir De Venice' Italy, 1825-1850.
◄ Crocheted reticule with medallions showing Paris' buildings
France, 1855.

▲ Beaded reticule showing the 'Sirius', the first steamship crossing
the ocean European, 1838.
▼ Beaded coin-purse showing the arrival of the first giraffe in
France France, 1827.

▲ Tortoise-shell coin purse with picture of the Trocadéro, World's Fair in Paris France, 1878.

▼ Tortoise-shell coin purse with Venetian scene Italy, late 19th c.

▲ Leather handbag with cover in Mauchline ware showing Fontainebleau Scotland, 1880s.

▼ Mauchline ware coin purse showing Burns' Cottage Scotland, late 19th c.

▲ Tortoise-shell coin purse inlaid with Eiffel Tower in silver, World's Fair in Paris France, 1889.
▼ Crocheted reticule with medallions showing Paris' buildings France, 1855.

▲ Two Tam O'Shanter coin purses with steel beaded crocheted bottom and embossed England, 1903.
▼ Two souvenirs: Notebook and card holder in mother-of-pearl, silver and gilt France, early 19th c.

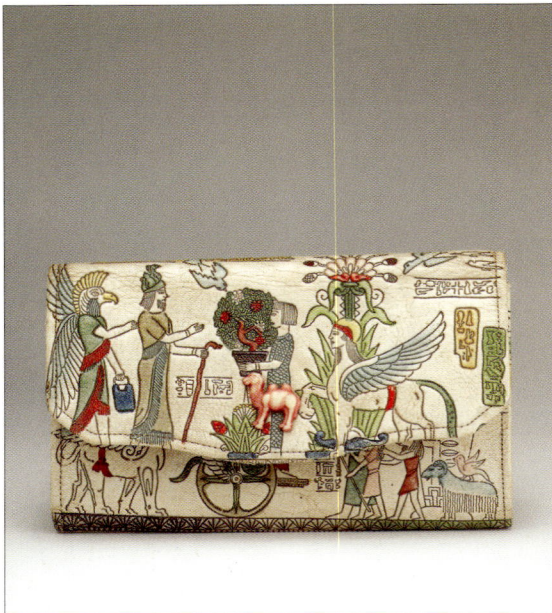

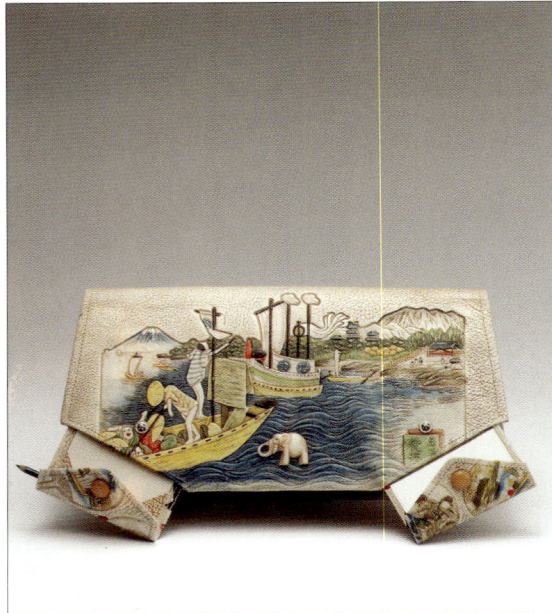

▲ Leather pochette with embossed Egyptian decoration
Egypt, 1925-1935.
▼ Leather pochette with embossed Japanese decoration
Japan, 1925-1935.

▲ Leather pochette with embossed Oriental decoration
Japan, 1925-1935.
▼ Leather pochette with embossed Oriental decoration
Japan, 1925-1935.

◄ Suede cloth handbag with decoration of Mount Fuji and silver cover, matching wallet Japan, 1920s.

▲ Handbag with embossed Egyptian decoration Egypt, 1950-1955.
▼ Leather pochette with embossed Egyptian decoration Egypt, 1936.

Suitcases and travel bags

Valises et sacs de voyage

Koffers en reistassen

Maletas y bolsas de viaje

Valigeria e borse da viaggio

Koffer und Reisetaschen

スーツケースと旅行鞄

In the nineteenth century, steam trains and steamships made travelling more comfortable, faster and cheaper. Because people were travelling more often, the range of suitcases, shoe- and hatboxes and dressing cases changed. Trunks with spherical lids, which could be easily transported on top of a horse-drawn carriage, were increasingly replaced by flat leather suitcases that could be stacked and easily carried by hand. Dressing cases containing brushes, manicure sets, little bottles and boxes made of silver, crystal, ivory and mother of pearl were the forerunners of today's beauty-case. The travel bag was also an indispensable article for travelling. Suitcases, travel bags, dressing cases, shoe- and hat-boxes were mostly made of leather; however, in around 1826, the Frenchman Pierre Godillot made a travelling bag out of canvas which became extraordinarily popular in the second half of the nineteenth century. The canvas travelling bag was also very suitable for being embroidered in Berlin woolwork. Many women embroidered their bags themselves and then had the local saddler add leather hooks, handles and a metal frame. For shorter journeys, Gladstone bags, city bags and baskets were used. The oblong leather doctor's bag with a metal frame and leather handle was mostly used by men for work. From 1870 on, the wickerwork rail-basket with flaps became popular for holding shopping, lunch or needlework. Until the early decades of the twentieth century, many different versions of these little baskets could be seen. For a trip to the countryside, there was the leather picnic set or hamper, neatly filled with plates, cutlery, teacups, sugar bowl, biscuit tin, thermos flask and in some cases even a spirit burner.

English

Au dix-neuvième siècle, les trains à vapeur et les paquebots rendent les voyages plus agréables, plus rapides et meilleur marché. Les gens se mettent à voyager plus souvent et le choix de valises, boîtes à chaussures, cartons à chapeaux et nécessaires de toilette évolue. Les malles à couvercle bombé, faciles à transporter sur le toit d'une voiture à chevaux, sont peu à peu remplacées par des valises plates en cuir, empilables et faciles à porter à la main. Les nécessaires de toilette contenant des brosses, kits de manucure, flacons et boîtes en argent, cristal, ivoire et nacre, sont quant à eux les précurseurs des vanity-cases actuels. Le sac de voyage est lui aussi indispensable : comme les valises, nécessaires de toilette, boîtes à chaussures et cartons à chapeaux, il est alors le plus souvent en cuir. Cependant, vers 1826, le Français Pierre Godillot fabrique un sac de voyage en tapisserie qui connaîtra un succès extraordinaire dans la deuxième moitié du dix-neuvième siècle. Il se prête également très bien à la broderie de laine et de nombreuses femmes broderont elles-mêmes leurs sacs avant d'y faire ajouter par leur sellier des crochets et poignées en cuir, ainsi qu'un fermoir en métal. Pour les voyages courts, on préfère des port-habits, sacs de ville et paniers. La trousse de médecin oblongue en cuir avec un fermoir métallique et une poignée en cuir est principalement utilisée par les hommes pour le travail. À partir de 1870, le panier en osier à rabats s'impose comme sac à provisions, panier-repas ou pour les travaux d'aiguilles. On en verra de multiples versions jusqu'aux premières décennies du vingtième siècle. Enfin, pour les excursions à la campagne, on remplit soigneusement un panier de pique-nique avec assiettes, couverts, tasses, sucrier, boîte à biscuits, bouteille thermos et parfois même un réchaud à gaz.

In de negentiende eeuw maakten stoomtreinen en stoomboten het reizen comfortabeler, sneller en goedkoper. Doordat er meer en anders gereisd werd, veranderde het aanbod aan koffers, schoenen- en hoedentassen en reisnecessaires. Reiskisten met bolvormige deksels, die eenvoudig bovenop een koets vervoerd konden worden, werden steeds meer vervangen door leren, platte stapelbare koffers, die ook makkelijk in de hand gedragen konden worden. Reisnecessaires met borstels, manicuresets, flesjes en dozen van zilver, kristal, ivoor en parelmoer waren de voorlopers van de huidige beautycase. Daarnaast werd de reistas tijdens het reizen een onmisbare attribuut.
Koffers, reistassen, reisnecessaires, schoenen- en hoedentassen waren meestal van leer. Rond 1826 had de Fransman Pierre Godillot een reistas gemaakt van canvas. Deze werd in de tweede helft van de negentiende eeuw buitengewoon populair. De reistas van canvas was bovendien heel geschikt om geborduurd te worden in Berlijnse wol. Veel vrouwen borduurden hun tassen zelf, om er daarna bij de plaatselijke zadelmaker leren hoeken, handvatten en een metalen beugel aan te laten maken. Voor de kortere reizen werden *Gladstone bags*, *city bags* en manden gebruikt. De langwerpige leren dokterstas met metalen beugel en leren handgreep werd veelal door mannen gebruikt als werktas. Vanaf 1870 werd het rieten spoormandje met kleppen populair voor het meenemen van boodschappen, lunch of handwerk. Tot in de eerste decennia van de twintigste eeuw zag men deze mandjes in allerlei uitvoeringen. Voor een uitje in de vrije natuur had men de picknick-koffer of -mand, op efficiënte wijze gevuld met borden, bestek, theekopjes, suikerpot, koektrommel, thermoskan en in sommige gevallen zelfs een spiritusstel.

français

nederlands

En el siglo XIX, los trenes y barcos de vapor hicieron de viajar una actividad más cómoda, rápida y económica. Puesto que cada vez se viajaba con más frecuencia, la gama de maletas, cajas para zapatos, sombrereras y neceseres se fue modificando. Los baúles de tapa esférica que se podían transportar fácilmente sobre el techo de un carruaje tirado por caballos se fueron sustituyendo paulatinamente por maletas planas de cuero que podían apilarse y transportarse a mano sin dificultad. Los antiguos neceseres, que contenían cepillos, utensilios de manicura, pequeños frascos y cajitas de plata, cristal, marfil y madreperla fueron los precursores de los neceseres actuales. La bolsa de viaje también constituía un artículo indispensable para viajar. Las maletas, bolsas de viaje, neceseres, cajas para zapatos y sombrereras se elaboraban principalmente en cuero. Sin embargo, hacia 1826, el francés Pierre Godillot confeccionó una bolsa de viaje con lona, que tuvo una gran aceptación en la segunda mitad del siglo XIX. Esta bolsa también resultaba muy adecuada para ser bordada al estilo de Berlín. Muchas mujeres bordaban ellas mismas las bolsas y luego las llevaban al guarnicionero del barrio para que añadiera los ganchos de cuero, las asas y una boquilla de metal. En los trayectos cortos se empleaban maletines, así como cestos y bolsas de ciudad. El maletín rectangular de médico con una boquilla metálica y un asa de cuero era utilizado principalmente por los hombres para trabajar. A partir de 1870, se difundió el uso del cesto de mimbre con tapas para transportar la compra, la comida o las labores. Hasta las primeras décadas del siglo XX podían verse distintas versiones de estos cestos de pequeñas dimensiones. Si se hacía una excursión al campo, se utilizaba una maleta o cesta de picnic en cuero con platos, cubiertos, tazas de té, azucarera, caja de galletas, termo e, incluso, un quemador de alcohol, y todo bien ordenado.

Nel XIX secolo, l'avvento dei treni e delle navi a vapore rese il viaggiare più comodo, più veloce e più economico. Poiché si viaggiava più spesso, la gamma di valigie, scarpiere, cappelliere e bauli si modificò. I bauli dal coperchio bombato, che si caricavano con facilità sul portabagagli di una carrozza a cavalli, vennero gradualmente sostituiti da valigie di cuoio piatte, che si potevano sovrapporre e trasportare agevolmente a mano. Si diffusero anche i progenitori dell'odierno beauty case, bauletti che contenevano spazzole, il necessario per la manicure, boccette e astucci d'argento, cristallo, avorio e madreperla. Anche la borsa da viaggio divenne un articolo indispensabile per il viaggiatore. Di solito valigie, borse da viaggio, bauletti, scarpiere e cappelliere erano in cuoio o pelle; tuttavia, intorno al 1826 il francese Pierre Godillot fabbricò una borsa da viaggio in tela pesante che godette di una straordinaria popolarità nella seconda metà del XIX secolo. La borsa da viaggio di tela presentava anche il vantaggio di prestarsi molto bene ad essere ricamata a piccolo punto con la tecnica del ricamo berlinese o *Berlin work*. Molte donne eseguivano il ricamo con le proprie mani e chiedevano al sellaio locale di rifinire la borsa applicandovi le parti in cuoio, i manici e la cerniera di metallo. Per i viaggi più brevi si utilizzavano valigie a doppio scomparto chiamate *Gladstone bags*, city bags e cestini. La valigetta da medico di forma allungata, con cerniera di metallo e manici di cuoio, veniva usata per lo più dagli uomini per recarsi al lavoro. A partire dal 1870, il "cestino da viaggio" in vimini con ribaltina si diffuse come contenitore per gli acquisti, il pranzo o i lavori di ricamo. Fino ai primi decenni del XX secolo, erano diffuse diverse versioni di questi piccoli cesti. Per le gite in campagna, c'erano appositi set in pelle e panieri, riempiti in bell'ordine con piatti, posate, servizi da tè, zuccheriera, scatola per biscotti, thermos e, in alcuni casi, persino un fornello a spirito.

Español

Italiano

Durch die Erfindung der Lokomotive und der Dampf-schifffahrt wurde das Reisen im 19. Jahrhundert un-komplizierter und komfortabler, schneller und auch billiger. Man reiste mehr als früher, und die Auswahl an Koffern, Schuh- und Hutschachteln sowie Reisenecessaires nahm jeden Tag zu. Die zuvor üblichen Truhen mit gewölbtem Deckel, die man in einer Kutsche gut befördern konnte, wurden jetzt zunehmend durch flache Lederkoffer ersetzt, die man sowohl stapeln als auch leicht in der Hand tragen konnte. Reisenecessaires enthielten Bürsten, Maniküre-Sets, kleinere Fläschchen und Schachteln aus Silber, Glas, Elfenbein oder Perlmutt. Sie waren die Vorläufer unserer heutigen Reisenecessaires und Beauty-Cases. Die Reisetasche wurde zum unentbehrlichen Gepäckstück auf Reisen. Koffer, Reisetaschen, Reisenecessaires, Schuh- und Hutschachteln waren zumeist aus Leder. Um das Jahr 1826 fertigte jedoch der Franzose Pierre Godillot eine Reisetasche aus Leintuch. Diese wurde in der zweiten Hälfte des 19. Jahr-hunderts ausgesprochen beliebt. Die Leinentaschen eigneten sich außerdem hervorragend für Verzierungen mit Berliner Wollstickereien. Viele Frauen bestickten ihre Taschen selbst, dann brachten sie diese zum heimischen Sattler und der versah die Taschen dann mit Haken, Griffen und einem Metallbügel. Für kürzere Reisen benutzte man Gladstone-Taschen, Stadttaschen und Körbe. Die typische längliche Doktorentasche aus Leder mit Metallbügel wurde vor allem von Männern für die Arbeit benutzt. Ab dem Jahre 1870 kommt der Hand-korb mit Deckel aus Weidenruten in Mode. Er wird oft zum Einkauf, für das Lunchpaket oder zur Aufbewahrung von Nähzeug benutzt. Anfang des 20. Jahrhunderts sind diese Körbe in allen Versionen und Größen in Gebrauch. Für einen Ausflug aufs Land gab es den Picknickkoffer oder Esskorb, der mit Tellern, Teetassen, Besteck, Zuckerdose, Keksdosen, Thermosflaschen und manchmal sogar einem kleinen Spiritusbrenner gefüllt war.

19世紀、蒸気機関車や蒸気船によって旅行がより快適でより速く、より低額な旅行が可能になります。人々が以前と比べて頻繁に旅行をするようになり、一連のスーツケース、靴箱、帽子箱、化粧道具入れなどに変化が訪れました。馬車の屋根に積むことが用意な球状のふたが付きトランクは、次第に積み重ねと持ち運びが容易な平たいレザー製スーツケースに座を奪われていきます。ブラシ、マニキュアセット、小瓶、銀製や象牙製、真珠層製の小箱を詰めた化粧道具入れは今日のビューティー・ケースの先駆けです。旅行鞄もまた旅行に欠くことのできないものでした。スーツケース、旅行鞄、化粧道具入れ、靴箱、帽子箱はほとんどがレザー製だったなか、1826年頃、フランス人のピエール・ゴディローはキャンバス地の旅行鞄を作成し、これが19世紀後半に爆発的に流行しました。多くの女性がバッグに自分で刺繍を施し、地元の馬具店で皮の留金、取っ手、金属口金の取り付けを依頼していました。近場への旅行にはシティーバッグやバスケットを利用しました。長だ円形の、金属口金と皮の取っ手が付いたドクターバッグは大抵男性が通勤用に愛用していました。1870年以降、籐細工の開きぶた付きレールバスケットが買い物、お弁当、手芸道具入れとして愛用されました。20世紀に入っても最初の数十年間は、このようないろいろな様式の小型バスケットが出回っていました。地方への小旅行には皿、ナイフ・フォーク類、ティーカップ、砂糖入れ、ビスケット缶、魔法瓶、時によってはアルコールバーナーなどがきちんと収納できるレザー製のピクニックセットまたは詰めかごがありました。

deutsch

日本語

▲ Leather hatbox with gentleman's hat England, late 19th c.

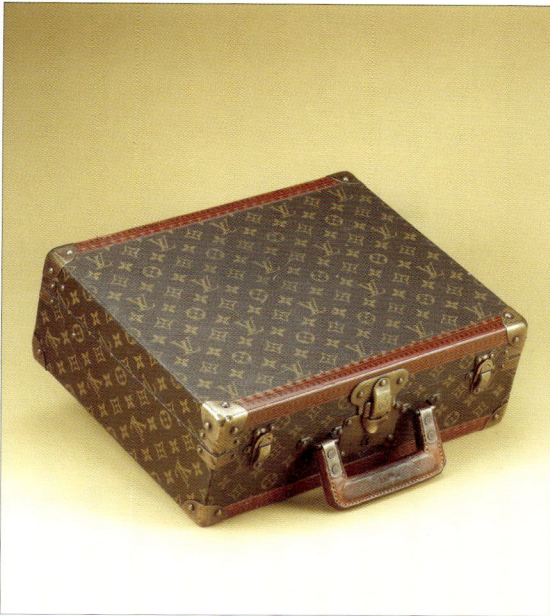

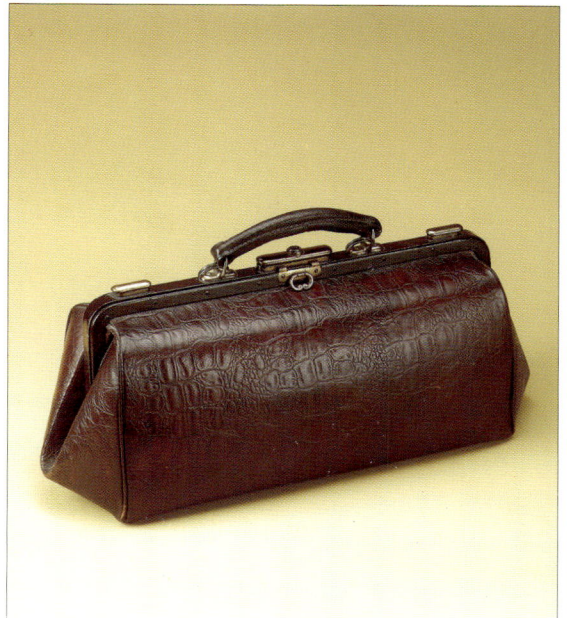

▲ Suitcase, canvas and leather, Louis Vuitton France, ca. 1920.
▼ Two 'rail'-baskets of straw, wood and leather. With metal and leather handle Germany, 1880-1930.

▲ Berlin woolwork and beaded travelling bag with brass frame Germany, mid 19th c.
▼ Alligator print leather brief bag England, early 20th c.

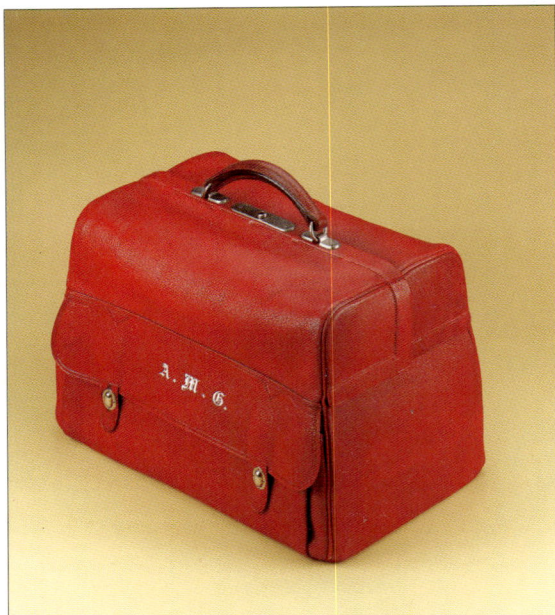

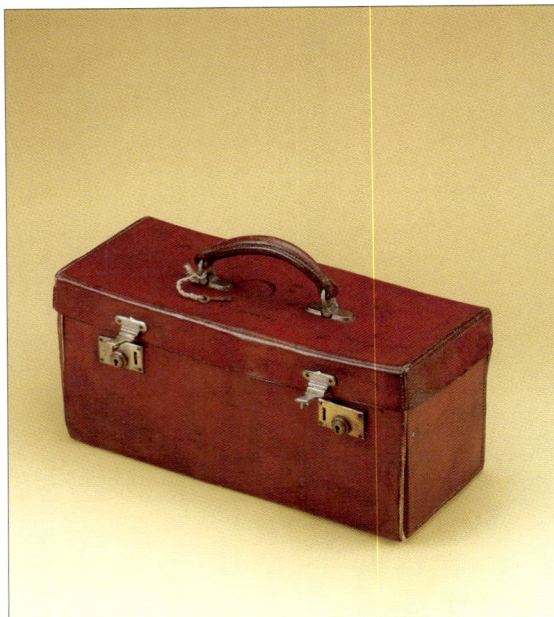

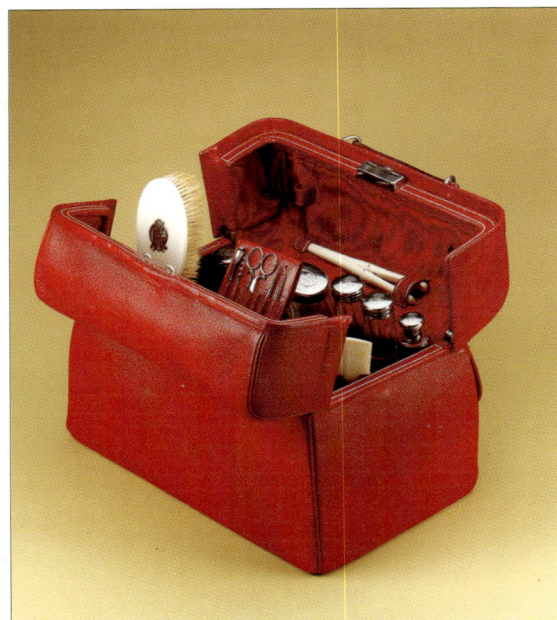

▲▼ Leather ladies' dressing case with silver and ivory necessaries England, 1896.

▲▶ Leather picnic case for two, chromium and porcelain, Asprey England, 1920s.
▼ Leather gentleman's dressing case with glass, silver and ivory necessaries, J.W. Benson England, 1910.

Handbags

Sacs à main

Handtassen

El bolso de mano

Borsette

Handtaschen

ハンドバッグ

The real breakthrough for the leather handbag came during the nineteenth century with the arrival of railway travel. Rail travellers needed bags that were less delicate. Initially, small leather bags were worn as chatelaine bags on the belt or skirt waistband. In the course of the nineteenth century, it became more and more usual to carry bags in one's hands. Bags made of cloth took on yet another function: whereas leather bags served for travelling or visits, cloth bags were used indoors and with formal dress. In the first decade of the twentieth century, the handbag finally took over the function of the chatelaine and chatelaine bag.

A rich variety of handbags emerged in the twentieth century. Some were specially made as visiting bags or vanity bags with a mirror, powder puff, scent bottle and coin purse. For theatre outings, there were opera bags with compartments for opera glasses, fan, mirror, powder puff, coin purse and ticket. Even today, the handbag has a variety of forms and uses, such as the clutch, which is carried under the arm or in the hands.

English

Le sac à main en cuir doit sa percée aux voyages en chemin de fer du dix-neuvième siècle qui demandaient des sacs moins fragiles. De petits sacs en cuir seront d'abord portés en châtelaines accrochés à la ceinture avant que, au dix-neuvième siècle, la tendance soit de porter de plus en plus ses sacs à la main. Les sacs en tissu, eux aussi, changent de fonction, utilisés pour l'intérieur et les tenues de cérémonie, tandis que les sacs en cuir servent en voyage ou en visite. Enfin, dans les années 1910, le sac à main finit par remplacer la châtelaine et son sac.

Le vingtième siècle verra émerger toute une variété de sacs à main. Certains ont été spécialement conçus pour les visites ou les produits de toilette avec un miroir, une houppe à poudre, un flacon à parfum et un porte-monnaie ; pour les sorties au théâtre, les sacs d'opéra comptent plusieurs compartiments pour les jumelles, l'éventail, le miroir, la houppe à poudre, le porte-monnaie et l'entrée au spectacle. Aujourd'hui encore, le sac à main présente de multiples formes et usages, comme par exemple la pochette, portée sous le bras ou dans la main.

De echte doorbraak van de leren handtas kwam in de loop van de negentiende eeuw met de opkomst van het reizen per trein. Treinreizigers hadden behoefte aan minder kwetsbare tassen. Aanvankelijk werden de kleine leren tasjes als chatelainetas aan riem of rokband gedragen. In de loop van de negentiende eeuw werd het steeds gebruikelijker om de tas in de hand te dragen. Tassen van textiel kregen een andere functie: terwijl leren tassen dienden voor op reis en op visite, waren tassen van textiel voor gebruik binnenshuis en bij de formele japon. In het eerste decennium van de twintigste eeuw nam de handtas definitief de functie van de chatelaine en chatelainetas over.

In de twintigste eeuw ontstond een rijke variatie aan handtassen. Sommige werden speciaal gemaakt als visitetasje of make-uptasje met een spiegel, een poederdons, een reukflesje en een beurs. Voor theaterbezoek waren er operatasjes met vakjes voor toneelkijker, waaier, spiegel, poederdons, beurs en entreekaartje. Tot op heden kent de handtas diverse vormen en toepassingen, zoals de enveloptas, die onder de arm of in de hand wordt gedragen.

français

nederlands

La llegada de los viajes en ferrocarril durante el siglo XIX fue el factor decisivo para que se fabricaran bolsos de mano en piel, pues los viajeros necesitaban bolsas que fueran menos delicadas. Al principio, en el cinturón o pretina de la falda se llevaban pequeñas bolsas de cuero a modo de escarcela. En el transcurso del siglo XIX, cada vez era más frecuente llevar bolsas en la mano. Se trataba de bolsas confeccionadas con tela y adquirieron una función distinta: mientras que las de cuero se utilizaban para los viajes o las visitas, las bolsas de tela se empleaban dentro de casa y con vestidos formales. En la primera década del siglo XX, el bolso de mano finalmente adoptó la función de la *chatelaine* y de la escarcela.

En este siglo surgió un amplio espectro de bolsos de mano. Algunos de ellos se realizaban especialmente como bolsas de visita o neceseres, con un espejo, una esponjita para aplicar los polvos, un frasco de perfume y un monedero. En las salidas al teatro se llevaban las bolsas para la ópera con compartimentos para los binóculos, el abanico, un espejo, una esponjita para aplicar los polvos, un monedero y el billete de entrada. Incluso en la actualidad, el bolso de mano cuenta con gran variedad de formas y usos, como es el caso del *clutch*, que se lleva bajo el brazo o en la mano.

Per la borsetta di pelle, la svolta arrivò nel XIX secolo, con l'avvento dei viaggi in ferrovia: infatti le viaggiatrici cominciarono a richiedere borsette meno delicate. Inizialmente, si usava indossare borsette di pelle appese alla cintura con una châtelaine. Durante il XIX secolo, tuttavia, si diffuse sempre più l'abitudine di portare a mano le borsette. Le borse di tessuto assunsero così una nuova funzione: mentre quelle di pelle erano adibite ai viaggi o usate come borse da passeggio, quelle di tessuto venivano indossate in casa e con l'abbigliamento formale. Nel primo decennio del XX secolo, infine, la borsetta a mano o a tracolla rimpiazzò definitivamente la châtelaine e le borsette da cintura. Nel XX secolo, si affermò una gran varietà di borsette. Alcune erano adibite a impieghi particolari, come le borsette da visita o le trousse per il trucco, che erano fornite di specchietto, piumino da cipria, boccetta di profumo e portamonete. C'erano speciali borsette da teatro, dotate di comparti per il binocolo, il ventaglio, lo specchio, il piumino, il portamonete e il biglietto. Ancor oggi, la borsetta presenta una gran varietà di modelli e di utilizzi, come la pochette da portare sotto il braccio o in mano.

Español

Italiano

Den eigentlichen Durchbruch erlebten die typischen ledernen Handtaschen im 19. Jahrundert mit dem Aufkommen der Zugreisen. Bahnreisende brauchten robusteres Reisegepäck. Anfangs trug man kleinere Ledertaschen an einer Chatelaine-Kette, die am Gürtel oder am Rockband befestigt wurde. Im Laufe des 19. Jahrhunderts begann man mehr und mehr, die Taschen in der Hand zu tragen. Taschen aus Stoff bekamen eine neue Funktion. Während man Ledertaschen für die Reise benutzte, trug man Stofftaschen für die Arbeit passend zur formellen Kleidung. In den ersten Jahren des 20. Jahrhunderts ersetzte schließlich die Handtasche die bis dahin übliche Chatelaine-Kette bzw. Chatelaine-Tasche.

Im 20. Jahrhunderts kamen unzählige neue Handtaschentypen auf den Markt. Manche wurden speziell als Besuchertaschen oder Make-Up-Täschchen angefertigt. Dann enthielten sie einen Spiegel, Puderdose, Parfümflakon und das Portemonnaie. Für den Theaterbesuch gab es feingearbeitete Operntäschchen mit speziellen Fächern für Operngläser, den Fächer, Spiegel, Puderdose, Portemonnaie und Eintrittskarten. Bis in die heutige Zeit gibt es Handtaschen in verschiedensten Formen und für die verschiedensten Anwendungsbereiche, so zum Beispiel die Unterarmtasche, die unter dem Arm oder in der Hand getragen wird.

事実的なハンドバッグの躍進は 19 世紀中に、鉄道による旅行とともに起こります。鉄道旅行者はより丈夫なバッグを希望しました。はじめは小型のレザーバッグをシャトレーン・バッグとして身に付け、ベルトまたはスカートのウエストバンドに取り付けていました。19 世紀の流れの中で、バッグを手に持地歩くことが徐々に一般化します。布製のバッグにはもうひとつの新機能が加わります。レザーバッグが旅行や訪問時に利用されたのに対し、布製バッグは室内やフォーマルドレス着用時に利用されました。20 世紀最初の 10 年間で、ハンドバッグはついにシャトレーンとシャトレーン・バッグの両方の機能を兼ね備えるようになったのです。

豊富な種類のハンドバッグが 20 世紀に登場します。中には鏡、パウダーパフ、芳香瓶、コインパースが備わった訪問用バッグまたは化粧バッグとして特別に製作されたものもありました。劇場へ出かけるときは、オペラグラス、扇子、鏡、パウダーパフ、コインパース、チケットなどの収納仕切りが付いたオペラバッグがありました。現在でもハンドバッグは形、利用法など種類が多岐にわたり、小脇に抱える、または手で持つクラッチバッグなどがその例に当たります。

deutsch

日本語

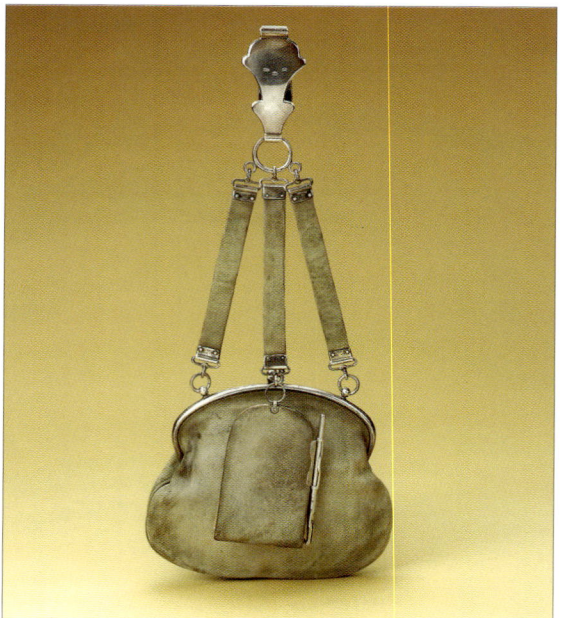

▲ Leather hand- and wrist bag Germany, 1880s.
▼ Leather handbag England, 1870s.

▲ Leather hand- and wrist bag with angel decoration and metal frame and ring Germany, 1880s.
▼ Suede and silver chatelaine bag with notebook and pencil Germany, ca. 1900.

▲ Leather chatelaine bag with brass decoration in Art Nouveau style France, ca. 1900.
▼ Leather handbag early 20th c.

▲ Embossed leather hand- and wrist bag with metal frame and ring Germany, 1880s.
▼ Embossed leather belt with two embossed leather bags Germany, 1890s.

▲ Leather opera bag fitted with opera glasses, notebook and folding fan England, ca. 1906.

▼ Leather handbag with plastic grip and brass decoration England, 1930s.

▲ Two leather handbags with chrome frame and plastic handle/decoration England, 1930s.

▶ Embossed leather handbag, 1880-1900.

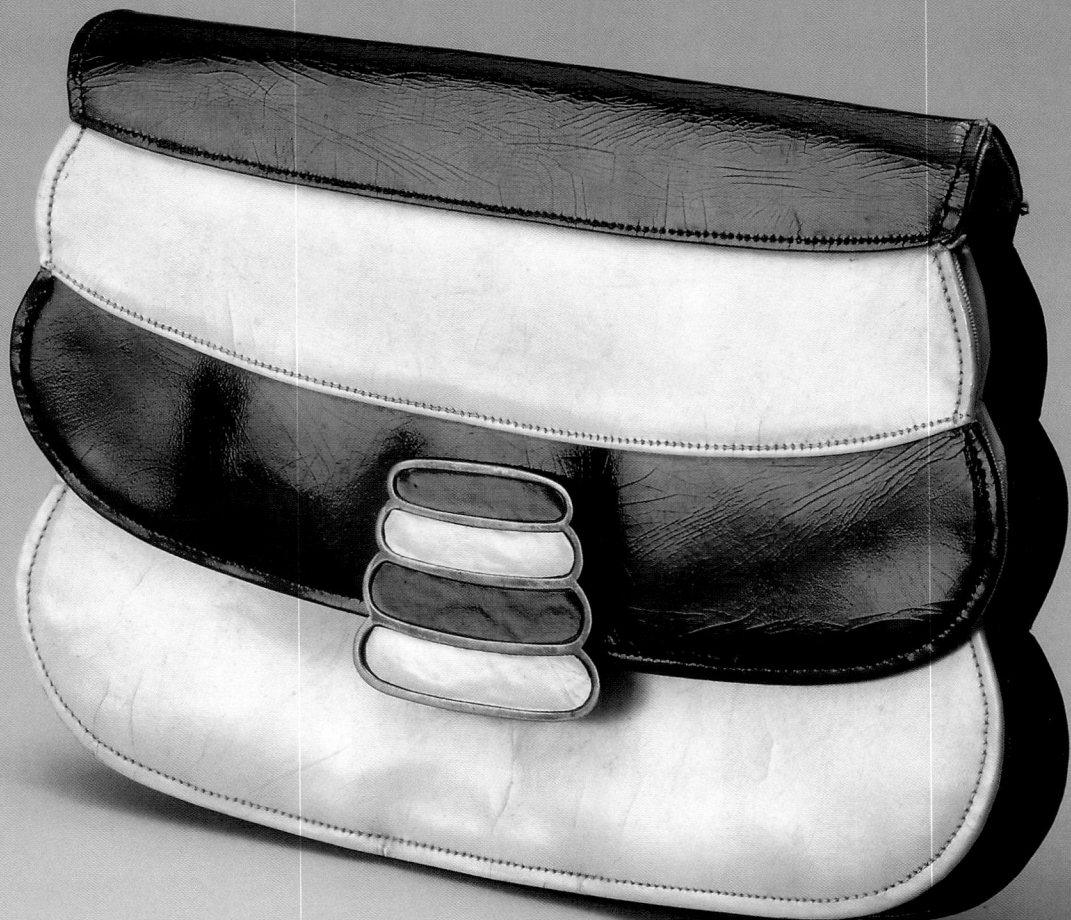

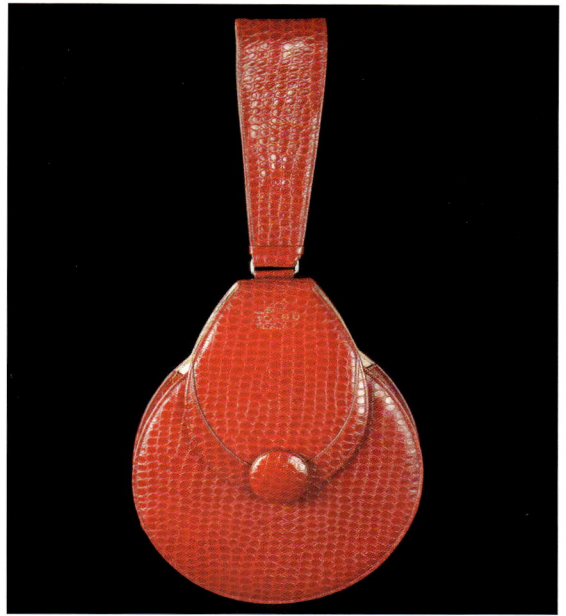

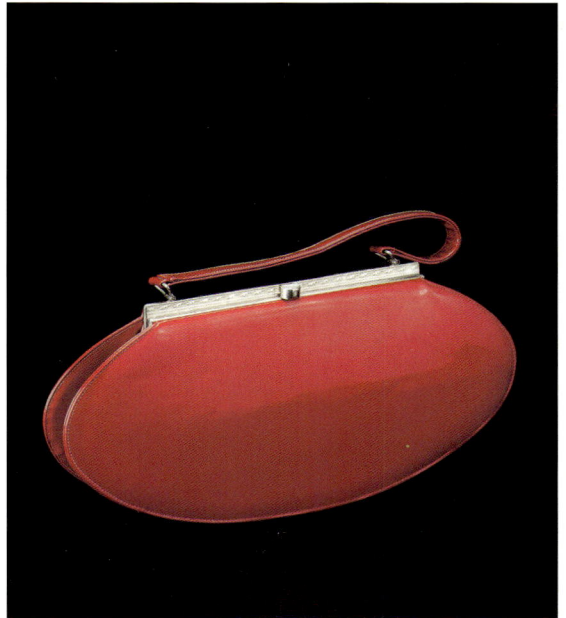

▲ Leather pochette with chrome frame England, 1930-1935.
▼ Leather pochette with chrome frame England, 1930-1935.
◄ Leather pochette France, 1930s.

▲ Leather wrist bag England, 1940s.
▼ Patent leather handbag with chrome frame Belgium, ca. 1962.

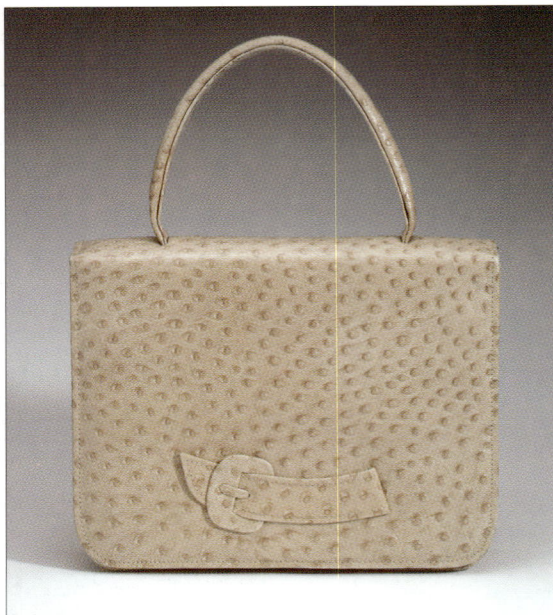

▲ Imitation ostrich leather handbag, Strass Switzerland, 1950.
▼ Leather handbag with printed decoration Belgium, 1960s.

▲ Leather handbag with plastic front decorated with strass
France, 1920s.
▼ Patent leather 'Dutch flag' handbag with brass lock
The Netherlands, 1970s.
▶ Imitation suede wrist bag France, 1940s.

▲ Leather handbag with double lock France, 1948.

▲ Synthetic leather handbag The Netherlands, 1968.

Decoration

Décoration

Sierkunst

Motivos decorativos

Decorazioni

Dekoration

装 飾

The applied arts were flourishing in the late nineteenth and first few decades of the twentieth centuries. Various styles succeeded one another, and their influence on the bags from the time can be clearly seen.

Under the influence of movements such as Arts & Crafts (1874-1910) in England, the Roycrafters (1895-1938) in the United States and the Wiener Werkstaette (1903-1932) in Austria, much attention was paid by bag makers to hand-crafted leather. The leather was worked and decorated so that the beauty of the material itself was especially highlighted.

From 1906 to 1932, the Wiener Werkstaette made port-folios, wallets and bags mostly in dark leather with gold-tooled patterns. The designs often had linear motifs, but after 1915 the leatherwork had more stylised flower and plant motifs. Various kinds or colours of leather were also combined, such as in the orange leather handbag decorated with narrow coloured stripe inserts.

Art Deco, an international applied arts movement that emerged in around 1910 and was popular well into the twenties and thirties, furnished Cubist and geometric forms, new materials and bright primary colours. In this period, handbags were created in chrome, aluminium and in the colours red, blue, black and silver.

In the twenties, batik on leather and cloth bags was in vogue. Examples are the velvet bag by the designer Agathe Wegerif and the leather bag by decorative artist Cris Agterberg.

English

À la fin du dix-neuvième et au début du vingtième siècle, les arts appliqués fleurissent. Les styles variés se succèdent et leur influence sur les sacs à main de l'époque est flagrante.

Sous l'influence de mouvements comme Arts & Crafts (1874-1910) en Angleterre, les Roycrafters (1895-1938) aux États-Unis et les Wiener Werkstaette (1903-1932) en Autriche, les fabricants de sac accordent une plus grande attention au travail artisanal du cuir, qui est alors traité et décoré de manière à mettre particulièrement en valeur la beauté de la matière elle-même.

De 1906 à 1932, les Wiener Werkstaette fabriquent des portefeuilles et des sacs en cuir sombre aux motifs repoussés dorés. Les dessins sont d'abord surtout linéaires ; après 1915 toutefois, la maroquinerie adopte des motifs de fleurs et de plantes plus stylisés. On associe aussi différentes sortes ou couleurs de cuir, comme pour le sac à main de cuir orange décoré par insertion d'étroites rayures de couleur.

L'Art déco, mouvement artistique international né vers 1910 et qui se prolongera jusqu'à la fin des années vingt et trente, apporte des formes cubiques et géométriques, de nouvelles matières et des couleurs primaires vives. Les sacs à main créés à cette époque sont rouges, bleus, noirs et argentés en chrome ou aluminium.

Dans les années vingt, c'est la mode du batik sur les sacs en tissu ou en cuir, comme le sac en velours de la créatrice Agathe Wegerif et le sac en cuir de l'artiste décoratif Cris Agterberg.

Eind negentiende en de eerste decennia van de twintigste eeuw kenden de toegepaste kunsten een bloeiperiode. Verschillende stijlen volgden elkaar op, en hun invloed op tassen uit die tijd is duidelijk zichtbaar. Onder invloed van kunststromingen als de Arts & Crafts (1874-1910) in Engeland, de Roycrafters (1895-1938) in de Verenigde Staten en de Wiener Werkstätte (1903-1932) in Oostenrijk ontstond er bij tassenmakers veel aandacht voor de ambachtelijke bewerking van leer. Men bewerkte en versierde het leer zo dat de schoonheid van het materiaal zelf er extra goed in uitkwam.

De Wiener Werkstätte vervaardigde vanaf 1906 tot in 1932 mappen, portefeuilles en tassen van veelal donkerkleurig leer met in goud geperste patronen. De ontwerpen hadden vaak lijnmotieven, maar na 1915 kreeg het leerwerk ook meer gestileerde bloem- en plantenmotieven. Ook combineerde men wel verschillende leersoorten of verschillende kleuren leer, zoals bij de oranje leren handtas die versierd is met smalle ingewerkte kleurrijke banden.

Art Deco, een internationale stroming in de toegepaste kunst die al rond 1910 opkwam en populair was in de jaren twintig en dertig, zorgde voor kubistische en geometrische vormen, nieuwe materialen en heldere primaire kleuren. Tassen werden in die periode uitgevoerd in chroom, aluminium en in de kleuren rood, blauw, zwart en zilver.

In de jaren twintig was batik op tassen van leer en textiel in zwang. Voorbeelden hiervan zijn de fluwelen tas van ontwerpster Agathe Wegerif en de leren tas van sierkunstenaar Cris Agterberg.

français

nederlands

El florecimiento de las artes decorativas tuvo lugar a finales del siglo XIX y en las primeras décadas del siglo XX. En las bolsas personales de aquella época se aprecian con claridad los diversos estilos que se sucedieron y su influencia.

Influidos por movimientos como el de las Arts & Crafts (1874-1910) en Inglaterra, los Roycrafters (1895-1938) en Estados Unidos y el Wiener Werkstaette (1903-1932) en Austria, los fabricantes de bolsos centraron su atención en el cuero labrado a mano. Este material se trabajaba y se decoraba para hacer destacar especialmente su belleza intrínseca.

De 1906 a 1932, el Wiener Werkstaette confeccionó portadocumentos, carteras y bolsos, casi todos en cuero negro con motivos estampados en oro. A menudo se realizaban motivos lineales, pero después de 1915 las creaciones en cuero presentaban dibujos de flores y plantas más estilizados. También se combinaban distintas clases o colores de cuero como es el caso del bolso de cuero naranja decorado con finas cintas de color.

El *art déco*, un movimiento internacional de artes aplicadas que surgió alrededor de 1910 y que gozó de gran popularidad en los años veinte y treinta, empleaba formas cubistas y geométricas, materiales nuevos y colores primarios vivos. En esta época, se creaban bolsos de mano de cromo y aluminio, y en color rojo, azul, negro y plateado.

En la década de 1920, estaba de moda la técnica del *batik* en los bolsos de cuero y tela. Ejemplos de ello es el bolso de terciopelo de la diseñadora Agathe Wegerif y el bolso de cuero del artista decorativo Cris Agterberg.

Alla fine del XIX secolo e nei primi decenni del XX secolo, le arti applicate conobbero un periodo di grande fioritura. Diversi stili si succedettero, esercitando una chiara influenza sulle borse e borsette dell'epoca.

Sotto l'influenza di movimenti artistici come l'Arts & Crafts (1874-1910) in Inghilterra, i Roycrafters (1895-1938) negli Stati Uniti e la Wiener Werkstaette (1903-1932) in Austria, i produttori di borse prestarono grande attenzione alla pelle lavorata a mano. La pelle veniva lavorata e decorata in modo da mettere in particolare risalto la sua bellezza naturale.

Tra il 1906 e il 1932, la Wiener Werkstaette produsse porta-documenti, portafogli e borse, solitamente in pelle scura con decorazioni in foglia dorata. Spesso i motivi decorativi erano lineari, ma dopo il 1915 si adottarono motivi floreali e di piante più stilizzati. Inoltre si combinavano tra loro diversi tipi e colori di pellami, come nella borsetta di pelle arancione con strisce verticali formate da sottili inserti di pelle di altri colori.

L'Art Déco, un movimento internazionale di arti applicate che emerse intorno al 1910 e restò popolare fino agli anni Venti e Trenta, adottò forme cubiste e geometriche, nuovi materiali e colori decisi e luminosi. In questo periodo, si crearono borse in cromo e in alluminio, in colori come il rosso, il blu, il nero e l'argento.

Negli anni Venti, divennero di moda borse di pelle decorate con la tecnica del batik e borse di tessuto. Ne sono esempio la borsetta di velluto della stilista Agathe Wegerif e la borsetta di pelle dell'artista decorativo Cris Agterberg.

Español

Italiano

Gegen Ende des 19. und zu Anfang des 20. Jahrhunderts erlebten die angewandten Künste eine besondere Blüte. Ein Stil folgte auf den anderen. Die ständig wechselnden modischen Ansprüche spiegeln sich auch im Taschendesign dieser Zeit deutlich wieder.

Unter dem Einfluss der Bewegungen im Kunsthandwerk - wie der Arts & Crafts (1874-1910) in England, der Roycrafters (1895-1938) in den Vereinigten Staaten und der Wiener Werkstätte (1903-1932) in Österreich – gewann die Herstellung von Ledertaschen an Bedeutung. Leder wurde so bearbeitet und verziert, dass seine materialeigene Qualität voll zur Geltung kam.

Von 1906 bis 1932 stellte die Wiener Werkstätte Dokumententaschen, Brieftaschen und Handtaschen, die meist in dunklem Leder mit Goldpressung produziert wurden. Das Design war oft ein Linienmotiv, aber nach 1915 kamen vermehrt stilisierte Blumen- und Pflanzenmotive dazu. Es wurden ebenfalls verschiedene Lederfarben und -typen kombiniert, so wie bei der orangefarbenen Ledertasche mit den schmalen, eingearbeiteten Streifen.

Das Art Déco, eine internationale Strömung in der angewandten Kunst, begann um 1910 und wurde in den 20er und 30er Jahren allgemein populär. Es dominierten geometrische und kubistische Formen, neue Materialien und vor allem leuchtende Farben. In dieser Zeit entstanden Taschen aus Chrom, aus Aluminium und Taschen in hellem Rot, Blau und Silber, aber auch in Schwarz.

In den 20er Jahren waren Taschen aus Leder oder Stoff mit Batikdrucken groß in Mode. Ein Beispiel hierfür ist die Samttasche der Designerin Agathe Wegerif sowie die Ledertasche des Künstlers Cris Agterberg.

応用美術は 19 世紀後期から 20 世紀最初の 10 年間にかけて開花します。さまざまな様式が次から次へと入れ替わり、バッグがその都度、流行した応用美術に影響を受けとことははっきりと表れています。

バッグ製造者の関心は大部分が手細工のレザーへ注がれました。レザーに手を加え装飾を施すようになり、素材自体の美しさが特に脚光を浴びるようになります。1906 年から 1932 年までの書類鞄、札入れ、バッグ類は濃色レザーに金箔押しの模様が入ったものがほとんどでした。デザインは線状のモチーフを施したものがよく出回っていましたが、1915 年以降、レザー加工には花や植物のモチーフを取り入れたものが様式化されていきます。さまざまな種類または色のレザーは組み合わせて使用されるようにもなり、オレンジ色のレザーに異なる色の細長いレザーを差し込んだものなどがその例です。

国際的な応用美術、アールデコは 1910 年頃に浮上し、20 年代、30 年代に入ってもその人気を保ち続け、キュービズムと幾何模様、新素材と明るい原色などでデザインや装飾が統一されていました。この期間、ハンドバッグはクロム、アルミニウムで作られ、色は赤、青、黒、シルバーなどが使用されました。

20 年代になって、ろうけつ染めを施したレザー、布製バッグが流行します。代表的なものには、デザイナーのアガーテ・ヴェゲリフによるベルベット製バッグや装飾アーティスト、クリス・アグテルベルグのレザーバッグなどがあります。

deutsch

日本語

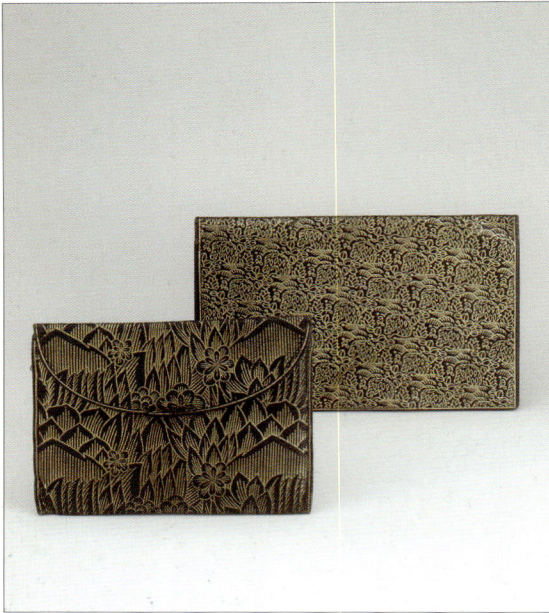

▲ Leaf-patterned lettercase no. 162 (l) and 'Strawberry' clutch bag (r), gold tooled leather, Wiener Werkstätte, Josef Hoffmann. Designs by Dagobert Peche Austria, 1922 and 1918.
▼ Leather handbag, Wiener Werkstätte, Maria Likarz Austria, 1929.

▲ Embossed and coloured leather handbag with matching comb-holder European, 1920s.
▼ Embossed and coloured leather handbag Italy, 1923-1925.

▲ Leather handbag with brass frame and clasp
The Netherlands, 1920s.
▼ Silk handbag with brass frame France, 1920s.

▲ Batik velvet handbag with plastic frame and chain, Agathe Wegerif
The Netherlands, ca. 1919.
▼ Embroidered fabric reticule The Netherlands, ca. 1910.

▲ Two embossed and batik leather pochettes, Cris Agterberg
The Netherlands, ca. 1926.

▲ Fabric pochette with chrome frame France, ca. 1930.
▼ Leather handbag with chrome decoration, lock and handle
England, 1930s.

▲ Pochette with chrome frame and enameled decoration
France, ca. 1930.
▼ Aluminium handbag with plastic trim France, ca. 1930.

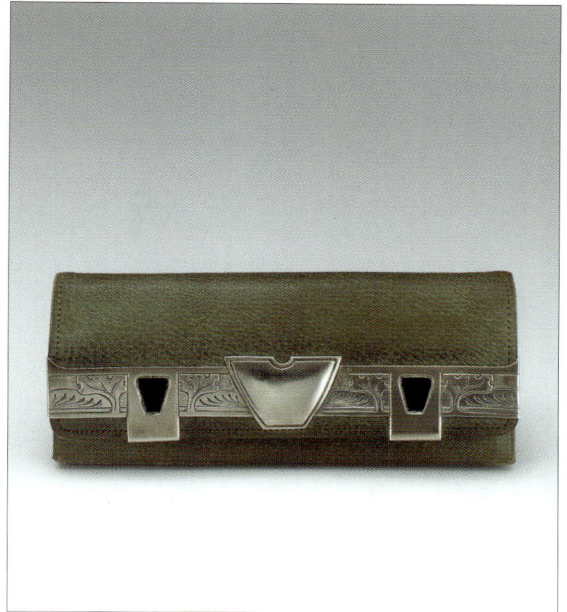

▲ Silver enameled vanity case with mirror, rouge, powder and
lipstick England, ca. 1930.
▼ Small brass pink bag with enameled decoration France, 1920s.

▲ Leather pochette with silver mounting France, 1910s.

Vanity cases and minaudières

Vanity-cases et minaudières

Vanity cases en minaudières

Neceseres y minaudières

Trousse e minaudière

Schminktäschchen und Minaudières

ヴァニティーケースとミノディエール

After the First World War, the use of cosmetics increased sharply under the influence of women's emancipation and the enormous popularity of film stars. Because of this, a need arose for special bags for cosmetics. In around 1905, handbags were sold with a purse, scent bottle, mirror and compartment with powder and puffs. In the twenties, the vanity case became popular: a small bag with compartments for powder, rouge, lipstick, perfume and/or cigarettes. The shape of the vanity case was attributed to the Japanese *inro*, a small box with compartments for medicinal herbs and perfumed water. Exclusive vanity cases were made by jewellers such as Cartier and Van Cleef & Arpels in silver or gold, enamel, mother of pearl, jade and lapis lazuli. Cheap vanity cases were made from coloured plastic decorated with glass stones. It is characteristic for the lipstick to often be hidden in the tassel.

At the beginning of the thirties, a customer of the Paris jeweller Van Cleef & Arpels used her cigarette case as a handbag. This inspired the jeweller to design the minaudière: a small, usually rectangular, metal box with compartments for powder, rouge, lipstick and cigarettes, and with a mirror, comb and/or a lighter. Minaudières were often made of silver or gold and decorated with enamel or precious stones. With this luxurious (evening) bag, Van Cleef & Arpels set a trend followed by many well-known jewellers and brands, while cosmetics companies came out with more affordable versions. Jewellers, bag manufacturers and cosmetics companies also sold special powder boxes, lipstick holders and similar items in the most curious shapes: hidden in a bracelet, for example, or in the form of a gramophone record, telephone dial or piano.

English

Après la Première Guerre mondiale, l'usage des cosmétiques se généralise avec l'émancipation féminine et l'immense popularité des stars de cinéma. Un besoin naît alors de sacs spécial maquillage. Vers 1905, tous les sacs à main sont vendus avec un porte-monnaie, un flacon à parfum, un miroir et un compartiment pour la poudre et sa houppe. Dans les années vingt, c'est le vanity-case qui s'impose, un petit sac avec différents compartiments pour la poudre, le rouge à joues, le rouge à lèvres, le parfum et/ou les cigarettes. Il doit sa forme à l'*inro* japonais, une petite boîte comportant divers compartiments pour les herbes médicinales et eaux parfumées. Des vanity-cases très chics sont proposés par des bijoutiers comme Cartier ou Van Cleef & Arpels, en argent, or, émail, nacre, jade et lapis-lazuli. Les moins chers sont en plastique coloré et décoré de cailloux de verre imitant des pierres précieuses. Tous ont pour caractéristique commune de souvent dissimuler le rouge à lèvres dans le gland.

Au début des années trente, le bijoutier parisien Van Cleef & Arpels constate que l'une de ses clientes utilise son étui à cigarettes comme un sac à main et s'en inspire pour créer la minaudière, une petite boîte métallique généralement rectangulaire, avec plusieurs compartiments pour la poudre, le rouge à joues, le rouge à lèvres et les cigarettes, et fournie avec un miroir, un peigne et/ou un briquet. Les minaudières étaient souvent en or ou argent décorées d'émaux ou de pierres précieuses. Avec ce sac de luxe (du soir), Van Cleef & Arpels lance une mode qui sera suivie par de nombreux bijoutiers et marques célèbres, sans compter les fabricants de cosmétiques qui en sortiront des versions plus abordables.

Bijoutiers, fabricants de sacs et de cosmétiques vendent alors aussi des boîtes spéciales pour la poudre, des étuis à rouge à lèvres et d'autres articles de ce type dans les formes les plus étranges : cachés dans un bracelet, ou en forme de disque pour gramophone, de cadran de téléphone ou de piano.

Na de Eerste Wereldoorlog nam onder invloed van de vrouwenemancipatie en de enorme populariteit van filmsterren het cosmeticagebruik sterk toe. Hierdoor ontstond de behoefte aan speciale tassen voor cosmetica. Rond 1905 werden al handtassen verkocht met een beurs, een reukflesje, een spiegel en een vakje met poeder en dons. In de jaren twintig werd de vanity case populair: een kleine tas met vakjes voor poeder, rouge, lippenstift, parfum en/of sigaretten. De vorm van de vanity case wordt wel toegeschreven aan de Japanse inro, een kleine tas met vakjes voor geneeskrachtige kruiden en reukwater. Exclusieve vanity cases werden door juweliers als Cartier en Van Cleef & Arpels vervaardigd in zilver of goud, email, parelmoer, jade en lapis lazuli. Goedkope vanity cases werden gemaakt van gekleurde kunststof versierd met glasstenen. Kenmerkend is dat de lippenstift vaak in de kwast verscholen zit.

In het begin van de jaren dertig gebruikte een klant van de Parijse juwelier Van Cleef & Arpels haar sigaretten-doosje als handtas. Dit inspireerde de juwelier tot het ontwerpen van de minaudière: een kleine veelal recht-hoekig metalen tas met vakjes voor poeder, rouge, lipstick en sigaretten, en met een spiegel, een kam en/of een aansteker. Minaudières waren vaak van zilver of goud en versierd met email of edelstenen. Met deze luxueuze (avond)tas zette Van Cleef & Arpels een trend die door vele bekende juweliers en merken werd gevolgd; cosmeticahuizen kwamen met goedkope versies.

Ook verkochten juweliers, tassenfabrikanten en cosme-ticahuizen speciale poederdozen, lipstickhouders en dergelijke in de meest bizarre vormen: verborgen in een armband, bijvoorbeeld, of in de vorm van een grammofoonplaat, telefoonschijf of piano.

français   nederlands

Después de la Primera Guerra Mundial, el uso de los cosméticos aumentó de forma drástica debido a la emancipación de la mujer y a la enorme popularidad que adquirieron las estrellas cinematográficas. Por ello, surgió la necesidad de disponer de bolsas especiales para los productos cosméticos. En torno a 1905, todos los bolsos que se comercializaban contaban con un monedero, un frasco de perfume, un espejo y un compartimento con polvos y una esponjita para aplicarlos. En los años veinte se popularizó el uso del neceser. Se trataba de una bolsa pequeña con compartimentos para los polvos, el colorete, el pintalabios y/o los cigarrillos. Su forma se inspiró en el *inro* japonés, una pequeña caja con compartimentos para guardar hierbas medicinales y agua perfumada. Joyeros como Cartier y Van Cleef & Arpels crearon neceseres en plata u oro, esmalte, madreperla, jade y lapislázuli. Los neceseres más económicos se realizaban con plástico de colores y se decoraban con piedras de cristal. A menudo, el pintalabios aparece escondido en la borla.

Entrados los años treinta, una clienta del joyero parisino Van Cleef & Arpels utilizó su pitillera como bolso de mano. Esto fue motivo de inspiración para el joyero, que diseñó la *minaudière*, una caja metálica pequeña, de forma rectangular, con compartimentos para la polvera, el colorete, el pintalabios y los cigarrillos, así como un espejo, un peine y/o un mechero. A menudo, las *minaudières* se realizaban en plata u oro y se decoraban con esmaltes o piedras preciosas. Con este lujoso bolso (de noche), Van Cleef & Arpels fijó una tendencia que siguieron numerosos joyeros y marcas de renombre, mientras que las empresas de cosmética ofrecían versiones algo más asequibles.

Los joyeros, los fabricantes de bolsos y las empresas de cosmética también vendían polveras especiales, fundas para pintalabios y otros artículos similares de las más variadas formas: escondidos en un brazalete, por ejemplo, o en forma de disco de gramófono, de disco telefónico o de piano.

Dopo la prima guerra mondiale, l'utilizzo dei prodotti cosmetici aumentò notevolmente, a causa dell'emancipazione della donna e sotto l'influsso dell'enorme popolarità delle attrici del cinema. Ciò, a sua volta, creò la necessità di contenitori particolari per i cosmetici. Intorno al 1905, le borsette erano vendute insieme a un borsellino, a una boccetta per il profumo e a uno specchietto e avevano uno scomparto per cipria e piumino. Negli anni Venti, divenne popolare la *trousse* o *vanity case*: un astuccio con scomparti per la cipria, il *rouge* per le guance, il rossetto, il profumo e/o le sigarette. La forma della *trousse* risalirebbe all'*inro* giapponese, un astuccio provvisto di scomparti per le erbe medicinali e l'acqua profumata. Gioiellieri come Cartier e Van Cleef & Arpels producevano *trousse* esclusive in argento e oro, smalto, madreperla, giada e lapislazzuli, ma ve ne erano anche modelli più economici, fatti di plastica colorata e decorati con pietre di vetro. Un dettaglio caratteristico è che spesso il rossetto era nascosto nella nappa.

All'inizio degli anni Trenta, una cliente del gioielliere parigino Van Cleef & Arpels cominciò a utilizzare il proprio portasigarette come borsetta. Ciò ispirò il gioielliere a ideare la *minaudière*, un astuccio di metallo, di solito rettangolare, con scomparti per la cipria, il *rouge*, il rossetto e le sigarette e provvisto di specchietto, pettine e/o un accendino. Spesso le *minaudière* erano d'argento o d'oro, decorate con smalti o pietre preziose. Con questa lussuosa borsetta (da sera), Van Cleef & Arpels fece tendenza e il suo esempio venne seguito da molti gioiellieri e stilisti di fama, mentre i produttori di cosmetici ne misero in vendita versioni più economiche. I gioiellieri, i produttori di borsette e le ditte di cosmetici vendevano anche speciali scatolette per cipria, portarossetto ed oggetti simili, spesso creati nelle forme più stravaganti: ad esempio nascosti in un braccialetto, oppure a forma di disco per grammofono, disco di telefono o pianoforte.

Español

Italiano

Nachdem ersten Weltkrieg nahm im Zuge der Emanzipation der Frau und der enormen Popularität der Filmstars der Verbrauch an Kosmetik schlagartig zu. Ein neuer Markt für spezielle Schminktaschen entstand. Um 1905 wurden Handtaschen mit dazu passender Geldbörse, Parfüm-fläschchen, Spiegel und einem Fach für Puderdose und Puderquaste verkauft. In den 20ern bereits wurde ein besonderes Schminktäschchen, das sogenannte Vanity-Case modern. Es handelte sich um eine kleine Tasche mit Platz für Puder, Rouge, Lippenstift, Parfüm und evtl. Zigaretten. Die Form des ersten Vanity-Case wurde der Japanischen *Inro* abgeguckt, einer schmalen Schachtel mit Fächern für medizinische Heilkräuter und parfümiertes Wasser. Exklusive Vanity-Cases wurden von Gold-schmieden wie Cartier oder Van Cleef & Arpels aus Silber, Gold, Email, Perlmutt, Jade oder Lapislazuli angefertigt. Billigere Vanity-Cases waren aus farbigem Plastik und mit Glassteinen dekoriert. Typisch ist hier, dass der Lippenstift oft in der Quaste versteckt ist.

Zu Beginn der 30er Jahre besuchte den Pariser Juwelier Van Cleef & Arpels eine Kundin, die ihr Zigarettenetui als Handtasche benutzte. Dies inspirierte den Juwelier zum Design des Minaudière: Das ist ein kleines, schmales, für gewöhnlich rechteckiges Metalletui mit Innenfächern für Rouge, Lippenstift, Puder und Zigaretten. Es hatte auch einen Spiegel, einen Kamm und manchmal ein Feuerzeug. Minaudières wurden oft aus Silber und Gold angefertigt und mit Email und Edelsteinen besetzt. Mit dieser luxuriösen Abendtasche schuf Van Cleef & Arpels einen neuen Trend, der sich rasch verbreitete und den viele Juweliere und Kosmetikfirmen in oftmals erschwing-licheren Ausführungen übernahmen.

Juweliere, Taschenhersteller und die Kosmetikindustrie boten auch spezielle Puderdosen an, Lippenstiftbehälter und ähnliche Utensilien in den bizarrsten Varianten: Versteckt in einem Armreif zum Beispiel, in Form einer Grammophonplatte, einer Wählscheibe des Telefons oder tatsächlich in Form eines Pianos.

第一次世界大戦後、女性解放の動きと映画女優の爆発的な人気が影響して化粧品の使用が急増します。このため、化粧品を入れる専用バッグの必要性が生じました。1905 年頃、ハンドバッグはパース、芳香瓶、鏡、パウダーとパフの収納仕切り付きで売られていました。20 年代にはヴァニティーケースが人気になります。小ぶりのバッグで中にパウダー、頬紅、口紅、香水と煙草を収納する仕切りがあるものです。ヴァニティーケースの形は日本の印籠—薬草や香りをつけた水などを入れる仕切り付き小箱—から来たものです。カルティエやヴァン クリーフ＆アーペルなどの宝石商によって作られた専売のヴァニティーケースが登場し、金・銀、エナメル、真珠層、ヒスイやラピスラズリなどを作製に使用したものでした。色つきのプラスチックにガラス宝石をあしらった安価なヴァニティーケースもありました。口紅はしばしば飾り房によって隠されていたことは特徴的です。

30 年代のはじめ、パリの宝石商、ヴァン クリーフ＆アーペルの顧客の一人が煙草ケースをハンドバッグ代わりにしていました。ここからひらめきを得たヴァン クリーフ＆アーペルはミノディエールをデザインします。パウダー、頬紅、口紅・煙草、鏡、コーム・ライター用に収納仕切りを付けた小さな金属箱で、通常は長方形です。ミノディエールはしばしば銀や金で作られエナメルや宝石で装飾されました。この贅沢な（イブニング用）バッグでヴァン クリーフ＆アーペルは流行を生み出し、多くの有名宝石商や有名ブランドが後を追う一方で、化粧品会社はより手ごろな価格のものを販売するようになりました。

また、宝石商やバッグ製造者、化粧品会社は特製のパウダーボックス、口紅ホルダー、関連商品などをめずらしい形に作って売り出していました。たとえば、ブレスレットに隠れるものや蓄音機のレコード、電話のダイアル、またはピアノの形をしたものなどがありました。

deutsch

日本語

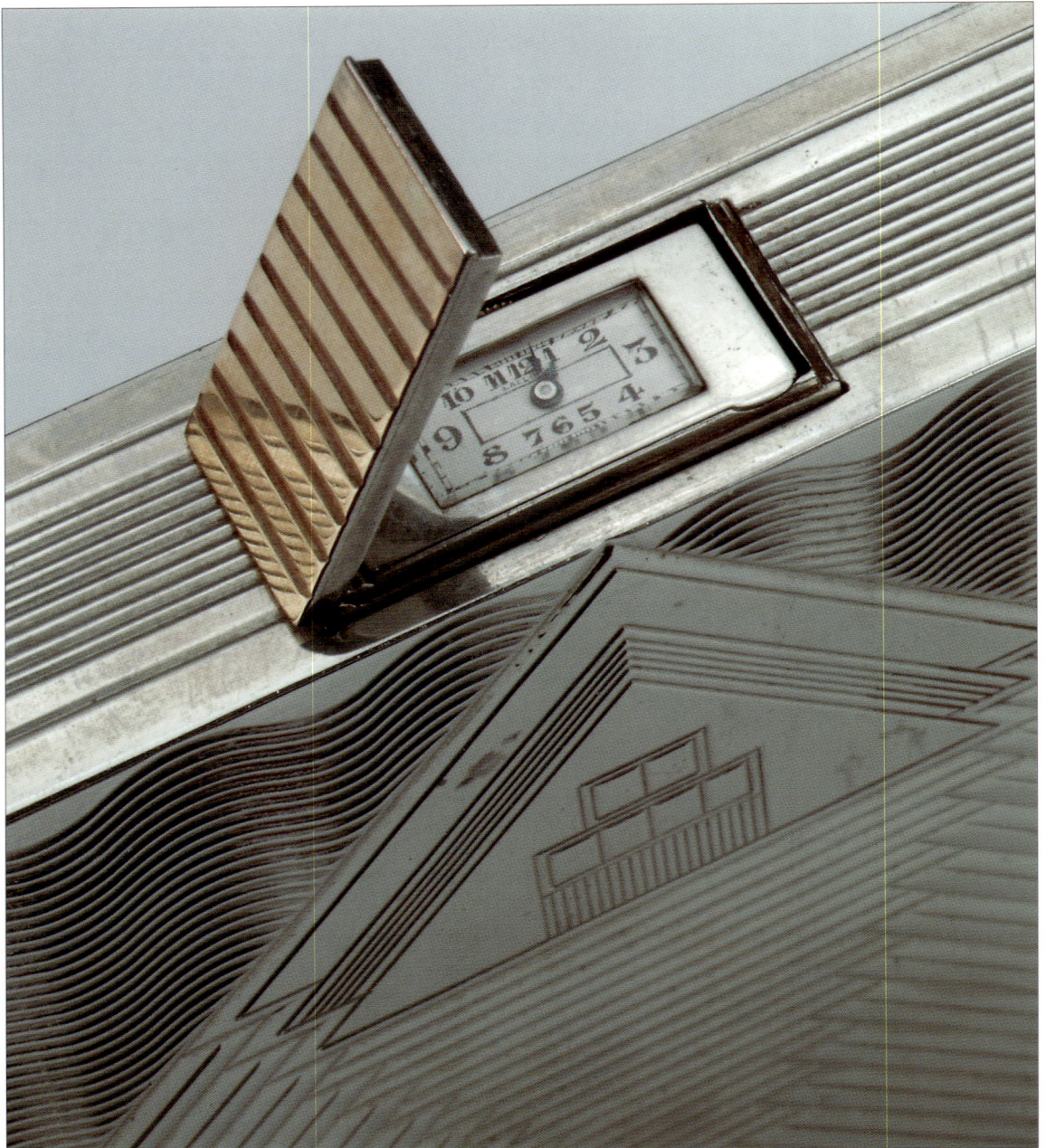

◀ Chrome bracelet with compact and comb Austria, 1920s.

◄▲ Minaudière with gold and sapphires, watch in lock, Lacloche Frères France, 1930s.

▼ Gold-coloured metal vanity case with engraved portrayal of crane France, 1920s.

▲ Enamelled minaudière with jewelled clasp which can also be used as brooch, Asprey England, 1939.

▼ Plastic vanity case decorated with red glass stones France, 1920s.

► Plastic vanity case with lipstick in silk tassel France, 1920s.

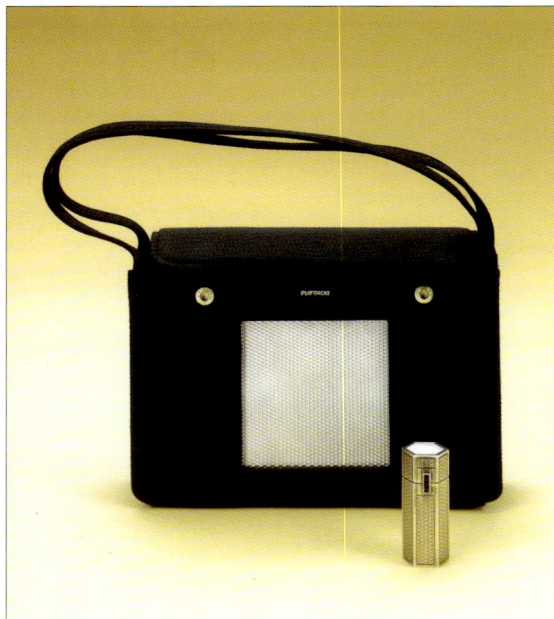

▲ Silk vanity bag with fittings, Evans U.S.A., 1940s.
▼ Silk evening bag with compact and lipstick in silver with sapphires, Puiforcat France, 1930s.
◄ Vanity case France, 1920s.

▲ Vanity bag with gilt filigree design printed on enamel background, Stratton U.S.A., 1950s.

▲ Plastic vanity case with lipstick in silk tassel France, 1920s.
▼ Galalith vanity case with three fittings in silk tassels, sold at
Harrods 1924.

▲ Plastic vanity case with lipstick in silk tassel France, 1925.
▼ Plastic vanity case with silk tassel hiding lipstick France, 1920s.

Evening bags

Sacs du soir

Avondtassen

El bolso de noche

Borsette da sera

Abendhandtaschen

イブニングバッグ

At the beginning of the twentieth century, women had a bag for every occasion including a city or visiting bag for the afternoons and an opera or evening bag for the evening. Daytime bags were often made of leather, but for evening bags, materials included shiny silk and brocade extravagantly decorated with embroidery, beads, foliage or colourful sparkling stones.

Real diamonds are seen less often on bags, although the evening bags from jewellers such as Cartier are an exception. In order to make evening bags glitter, artificial glass diamonds were mostly used, such as strass. Strass is named after the Strasbourg jeweller G.F. Strass, who invented the artificial diamond in around 1730. In the 1920s and 1930s, strass became widely popular, partly through the costume jewellery by the fashion designer Coco Chanel. In addition to being used on ornaments and bags, strass is also set into hats, hatpins, shoes and calling card cases. Coloured strass is used to imitate precious stones for ornaments and bag frames.

Marcasite (a frequently used but incorrect name for the mineral pyrite) was also used quite frequently to imitate diamonds in ornaments and bag frames. It was extremely popular as a decoration on frames and clasps for evening bags in black suede or silk. Just like diamonds, it was cut and set in mountings.

Sablé beads were also used to decorate evening bags. One of the companies that made them was the Paris firm Mayer, which exported these bags all over the world. During the twentieth century, countries such as India have started to play a major role in making evening bags with embroidery and beads.

English

Au début du vingtième siècle, les femmes ont des sacs pour toutes les occasions, dont notamment un sac de ville ou de visite pour l'après-midi et un sac d'opéra ou du soir pour la nuit. Les sacs de jour sont souvent en cuir, ceux du soir dans des matières allant de la soie chatoyante au brocart et décorées avec extravagance de broderies, perles, feuillages ou pierres colorées brillant de mille feux.

Les vrais diamants sont rares sur les sacs, à l'exception des modèles de bijoutiers comme Cartier. Pour faire briller les sacs du soir, on préfère le plus souvent des diamants artificiels de verre, comme le strass qui doit son nom au bijoutier strasbourgeois G.F. Strass (son invention remonte à 1730). Dans les années 1920 et 1930, le strass connaît un grand succès, notamment grâce aux bijoux fantaisies de la grande couturière Coco Chanel. Outre les bijoux et les sacs, les chapeaux, épingles à chapeaux, chaussures et étuis à cartes de visite en sont assortis. Le strass coloré sert à imiter les pierres précieuses pour les bijoux et les fermoirs.

La marcassite (terme souvent utilisé à tort pour désigner la pyrite) est elle aussi fréquemment employée pour imiter les diamants sur les bijoux et fermoirs de sacs. Elle est particulièrement appréciée pour orner les fermoirs et les boucles des sacs du soir en daim noir ou en soie. Comme les diamants, elle est taillée et sertie dans des montures.

On utilise aussi le sablé de perles pour décorer les sacs du soir, comme c'est le cas pour la firme parisienne Mayer qui exporte ses sacs dans le monde entier. Au vingtième siècle, des pays comme l'Inde se sont imposés dans la fabrication de sacs du soir ornés de broderies et de perles.

In het begin van de twintigste eeuw hadden vrouwen voor elke gelegenheid een tas: voor 's middags een stads- of visitetas en voor 's avonds een opera- of avondtasje. Tassen voor overdag waren vaak van leer, maar voor avondtassen gebruikte men materialen als glanzende zijde en brokaat, opvallend versierd met borduursels, kralen, lovertjes of kleurrijke, flonkerende stenen.

Echte diamanten ziet men minder vaak op tassen, hoewel de avondtassen van juweliersmerken als Cartier hierop een uitzondering vormen. Om avondtassen te laten glinsteren werden meestal namaakdiamanten van glas gebruikt, zoals stras. Stras is vernoemd naar de Straatsburgse juwelier G.F. Strass, die de namaakdiamant rond 1730 uitvond. In de jaren twintig en dertig van de twintigste eeuw werd stras populair, mede door de namaaksieraden van modeontwerper Coco Chanel. Behalve op sieraden en tassen werd stras ook op hoeden, hoedenspelden, schoenen en visitekaarthouders verwerkt. Gekleurd stras werd ter imitatie van edelstenen voor sieraden en tasbeugels gebruikt.

Ook markasiet (een algemeen gebruikte, maar onjuiste benaming voor het mineraal pyriet) werd veel toegepast ter imitatie van diamanten op sieraden en tasbeugels. Het was uitermate populair als decoratie op beugels en sluitingen van avondtassen van zwarte suède of zijde. Het werd net als diamant geslepen en in vattingen gezet.

Ook werden sablékralen gebruikt om avondtassen te versieren. Ze werden onder andere gemaakt door de Parijse firma Mayer, die deze tasjes over de hele wereld exporteerde. In de loop van de twintigste eeuw zijn landen als India een grote rol gaan spelen bij de vervaardiging van avondtassen met borduursels en kralen.

français

nederlands

A principios del siglo XX, las mujeres disponían de un bolso para cada ocasión, lo cual incluía un bolso de ciudad o un bolso de visita para la tarde y un bolso de noche o para la ópera, que usaban en las salidas nocturnas. Los bolsos de día solían realizarse en cuero, mientras que para los bolsos de noche se empleaban materiales como la seda brillante y los brocados, que se decoraban de forma extravagante con bordados, abalorios, láminas metálicas o relucientes piedras de colores.

Los diamantes auténticos son menos frecuentes en los bolsos, si bien los bolsos de noche de joyeros como Cartier constituyen una excepción. Para que los bolsos de noche relucieran se empleaban sobre todo diamantes de cristal artificial como el *strass*, el cual toma su nombre del joyero de Estrasburgo G. F. Strass, que inventó el diamante artificial alrededor de 1730. En las décadas de 1920 y 1930 el *strass* alcanzó gran popularidad, en parte gracias a la pedrería que añadía a los vestidos la diseñadora de moda Coco Chanel. Además de aplicarse en bisutería y bolsos, el strass también se utiliza para ornamentar sombreros, pasadores, calzado y estuches para las tarjetas de visita. El strass de colores se emplea para imitar piedras preciosas en bisutería y boquillas para bolsos.

La marcasita (un nombre utilizado con frecuencia pero incorrectamente para referirse al mineral pirita) también se empleaba a menudo para imitar diamantes en bisutería y boquillas para bolsos.

 Gozaba de gran aceptación como elemento decorativo de boquillas y asas de bolsos de noche realizados en seda o ante negro. Igual que los diamantes, el strass se facetaba y se engarzaba.

Las cuentas *sablé* también se empleaban para decorar bolsos de noche. Una de las empresas que los comercializaba era la firma parisina Mayer, que exportaba estos bolsos a todo el mundo. Durante el siglo XX, países como la India comenzaron a desempeñar un papel destacado en la confección de bolsos de noche con bordados y abalorios.

All'inizio del XX secolo, le donne possedevano una borsetta per ogni occasione, tra cui una borsetta da città o da passeggio per il pomeriggio e una borsetta da teatro o da sera. Le borse da giorno erano spesso di pelle, mentre per quelle da sera i materiali utilizzati comprendevano lucida seta o broccato con abbondanti decorazioni in ricami, perline, foglie metalliche o scintillanti pietre colorate.

Con l'eccezione di alcuni modelli da sera prodotti da gioiellieri quali Cartier, era raro che si usassero brillanti veri come decorazione. Di solito, per far brillare le borsette da sera si utilizzavano brillanti artificiali di vetro, come lo strass. Lo strass prende il nome dal gioielliere di Strasburgo G. F. Strass, che inventò questa pietra artificiale intorno al 1730. Negli anni Venti e Trenta, lo strass divenne popolarissimo, anche grazie alla bigiotteria disegnata dalla stilista Coco Chanel. Oltre a essere impiegato per la bigiotteria e le borsette, lo strass viene usato anche per decorare cappelli, spilloni per cappelli, scarpe e portabiglietti. Nella sua versione colorata, lo strass veniva utilizzato anche per imitare pietre preziose su vari ornamenti e sulle cerniere delle borsette.

Anche la marcasite (nome spesso impiegato, sebbene erroneamente, anche per indicare la pirite) veniva usata di frequente per imitare i brillanti suoggetti de bigiotteria e cerniere per borsette. Sfaccettata e inserita in castoni, proprio come i veri brillanti, era una decorazione diffusissima, in particolare, per le cerniere e i fermagli di chiusura delle borsette da sera di seta o di pelle scamosciata nera.

Anche le perline *sablé* venivano usate per decorare le borsette da sera. Una delle ditte che le produceva era la parigina Mayer, che esportava le sue borsette in tutto il mondo. Nel corso del XX secolo, paesi come l'India hanno iniziato ad avere un ruolo importante nella produzione di borsette da sera abbellite da ricami e perline.

Español

Italiano

Zu Beginn des 20. Jahrhunderts hatten viele Frauen Handtaschen für jede Gelegenheit, darunter eine Handtasche für Besuche und Einkäufe am Nachmittag und eine Opern- oder Abendtasche für abends. Die Taschen für den Gebrauch tagsüber waren zumeist aus Leder. Die Abendtaschen waren aus glänzender Seide mit zierlicher Stickerei, häufig wurden sie auch mit Perlen und Brokat, Glasperlen, Spiegelchen oder farbenprächtig funkelnden Steinen verziert.

Echte Diamanten zieren diese Taschen weniger, wenn auch berühmte Juweliere wie Cartier für Ausnahmen sorgten. Damit die Abendtaschen glitzerten und glänzten, verwendete man gewöhnlich künstliche Glasdiamanten sowie Strass-Steine. Die Bezeichnung Strass geht auf den bekannten Straßburger Juwelier G.F. Strass zurück, der diese künstlichen Glitzersteine um 1730 entworfen hatte. In den 20er und 30er Jahren des 20. Jahrhundert war Strass sehr „in" - teilweise angeregt durch den Modeschmuck der französischen Modedesignerin Coco Chanel. Man trug Strass nicht nur als Schmuck, sondern auch auf Taschen, Hüten, Hutnadeln, Schuhen und Visitenkartenhaltern. Farbiger Strass wird als Imitation von Edelsteinen häufig für Schmuck und Bügel verwendet.

Auch Markesiten (eine häufig gebrauchte, jedoch falsche Bezeichnung für das Mineral Pyrit) wurden gerne zur Dekoration und speziell zur Imitation von Diamanten benutzt. Sehr modern waren Abendtaschen mit Markesiten als Schmuck an Taschenbügeln, Verschlüssen und Schnallen kombiniert mit schwarzem Wildleder oder Seide. Die Strasssteine wurden wie Diamanten geschliffen und gefasst.

Feine, sandartige Sablé-Perlen wurden ebenfalls für das Dekor von Abendtaschen verwendet. Eine der Firmen, die diese Taschen herstellte, war die Pariser Firma Mayer, die Taschen in die ganze Welt vertrieb. Im Laufe des 20. Jahrhunderts stieg Indien zu einem der führenden Hersteller von Abendtaschen mit Stickereien und feinen Glasperlen auf.

20 世紀のはじめ、女性は目的別にバッグを揃え、日中はシティーバッグまたは訪問バッグ、夕方はオペラバッグまたはイブニングバッグと使い分けていました。日中のバッグはしばしばレザー製でしたが、イブニングバッグは光沢のある絹や錦織の素材を使用し、刺繍、ビーズ、葉飾りや色とりどりに輝く宝石などをふんだんにあしらい、豪華に仕上げられたものでした。

本物のダイアモンドをバッグにあしらった例はそれほど頻繁に見かけませんが、カルティエなどの宝石商によるイブニングバッグは別です。イブニングバッグに輝きを持たせるため、ストラス（strass:鉛ガラス）など人工のガラスダイアが最も頻繁に使用されました。ストラスは 1730 年頃人工ダイアを発明したシュトラスブルグの宝石商、ストラス（G.F. Strass）の名前を取って名づけたものです。1920 年代、1039 年代にはストラスの人気が広まり、その影にはファッションデザイナー、ココ・シャネルによるコスチューム・ジュエリーの影響もありました。装飾品やバッグへの応用に加えて、帽子、ハットピン、靴、名刺ケースなどにも使用されるようになります。色つきのストラスは装飾品やバッグの金属口金に宝石のイミテーションとして使用されました。

白鉄鋼―高頻度で使用されましたが、黄鉄鉱を指すには不正確な呼び名―も装飾品やバッグの口金にわりと頻繁に使用されました。白鉄鋼は黒のスエードまたは絹製イブニングバッグの金属口金や留金の装飾として非常に人気がありました。ダイアモンド同様にカットが施され、台の上に固定されました。

サブレビーズもイブニングバッグの装飾に使用されました。サブレビーズのイブニングバッグ製造会社のうちの一社に当たるのがパリのメイヤー社で、同社は世界中にバッグを輸出していました。20 世紀中、インドのような国が刺繍やビーズをあしらったイブニングバッグの製造面で重要な役割を担い始めるようになります。

deutsch

日本語

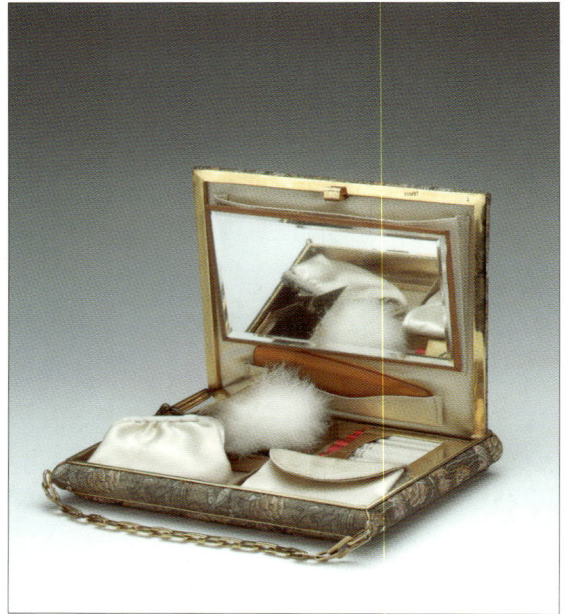

▲ Satin pochette, silver border with marcasite, onyx and red stones
Germany, ca. 1930.
▼ Evening clutch bag embroidered with sablé beads, silver frame,
Mayer France, ca. 1928.

▲ Brocade and brass evening bag France, 1950s.
▼ Plastic vanity case with strass decoration France, 1920s.
▶ Brocade evening bag with silver and enamel frame, Mayer
France, 1920s.

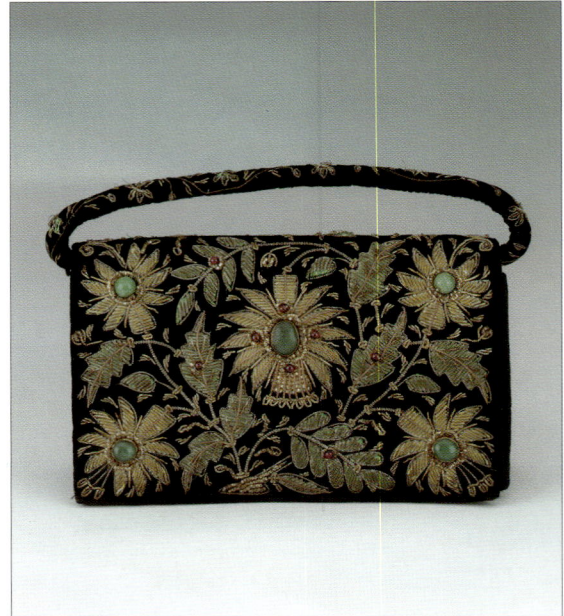

▲ Brocade evening clutch bag, imitation coral clasp, Maison de Bonneterie The Netherlands, 1930s.
▼ Brocade clutch evening bag, brass frame with mosaic France, 1930s.

▲ Envelop evening bag embroidered with silk and gold-coloured thread France, 1940s.
▼ Velvet and silk evening bag embroidered with silk, metal thread, beads and stones India, 1970s.

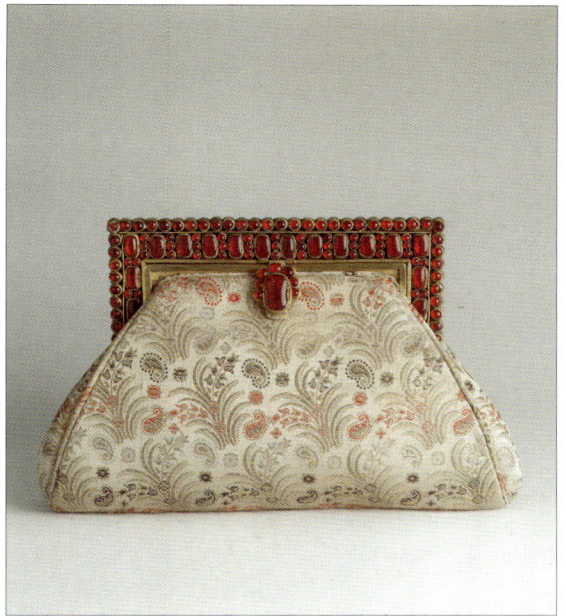

▲ Evening bag decorated with gold-coloured leather and silk
France, 1920s.
▼ Silk evening bag embroidered with gold thread, brass frame
encrusted with glass stones France, early 1930s.

▲ Brocade evening clutch bag, brass frame with imitation garnets
France, 1930s.
▼ Embroidered silk evening bag, brass frame encrusted with
turquoise stones, Mayer France, 1920s.

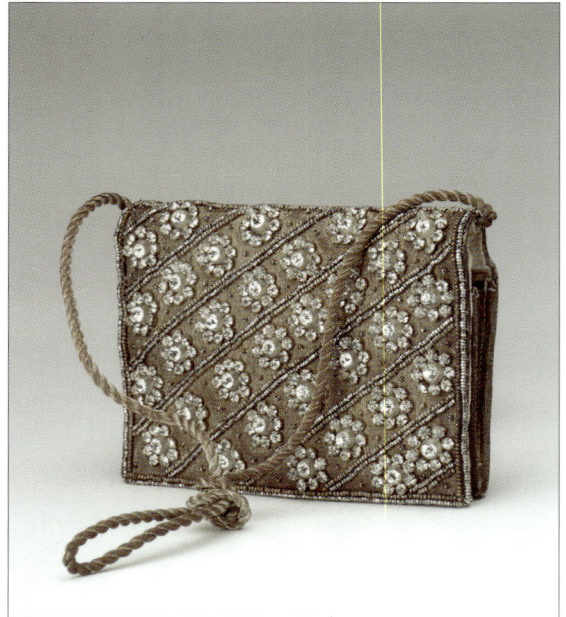

▲ Silk evening envelop bag embroidered with silk and silver thread,
Louise Fontaine Belgium, 1930s.
▼ Brocade pochette, clasp with coral and diamonds, Cartier
France, 1925.

▲ Silk evening bag with brass frame and imitation coral decoration
France, 1920s.
▼Evening bag decorated with strass France, 1920s.

▲ Brocade evening clutch bag, Mayer France, 1925.
▼ Brocade evening clutch bag embroidered with silver and gold thread, Silk Emporium Agra India, 1970s.

▲ Silk pochette embroidered with silk and cut-steel beads, Duvelleroy France, 1930s.
▼ Silk evening bag embroidered with silk and beads encrusted with glass stones India, 1970s.

▲ Silk evening bag, gilt frame and clasp decorated with stones
France, 1920s.
▼ Brocade evening bag with gold-coloured leather
England, 1950-1980.

▲ Embroidered silk evening bag, brass frame encrusted with glass
stones European, 1930s.
▼ Satin evening bag with clasp of plastic and strass ca. 1920.
▶ Two suede evening bags, silver frame with marcasite. With
carnelian (l) and onyx and enamel (r) Germany, 1929 and 1931.

▲ Silk evening bag decorated with strass, silver frame with onyx and strass France, ca. 1930.
▼ Silk envelop bag with decoration of strass and imitation pearls France, 1920s.
◄ Silk evening envelop bag encrusted with strass France, 1920.

▲ Silk evening bag with strass decoration, perspex frame, Maison de Bonneterie The Netherlands, 1930s.
▼ Evening bag extensively decorated with strass and green-coloured glass stones The Netherlands, 1950s.

▲ Satin evening bag with strass decoration 1950s.
▼ Velvet evening bag with embroidery India, 1970s.
◄ Silk evening bag handpainted with granular paint, Waldy bag
England, 1950s.

▲ Plastified straw evening bag, clasp decorated with strass and
turquoise, Roberto Rice Italy, 1970s.
▼ Shoulder evening bag decorated with mirrors 1960-1980.

New materials

Nouvelles matières

Nieuwe materialen

Nuevos materiales

Nuovi materiali

Neue Materialien

新素材

In the first thirty years of the nineteenth century, reticules and bags were made in forms and from materials distinct from those used before. Due to the new technologies brought about by the Industrial Revolution (which is usually considered to have begun in around 1760 in England), materials and products could be produced much better and faster. A good example is the papier-mâché bag in the form of a vase, with a cut steel frame and decorations.

Papier-mâché is finely powdered paper that, mixed with chalk or clay, is pressed into all kinds of shapes and then dried and varnished. Papier-mâché techniques originated in Asia and arrived in Europe in the seventeenth century via France. Not until the Industrial Revolution was papier-mâché used on a large scale: snuffboxes, trays, pen and ink sets, candlesticks, card tables, chairs and bags were made in great numbers. Steel had already been known in Europe since the Middle Ages, but due to improvements in the production process, cut steel became popular in the nineteenth century. It was used for ornaments, decorative combs, buckles, buttons, chatelaines and watch chains. Bags were decorated with sequins, foliage, beads, frames and clasps made of cut steel. On bags made of dark velvet or leather, steel was a good imitation of diamonds. Another trend between 1813 and 1850 was the use of fine filigrain ironwork, the so-called *fer de Berlin* (or Berlin iron), for bags and ornaments. Because of their matte black lustre, these accessories were also sought after as mourning ornaments.

English

Au cours des trente premières années du dix-neuvième siècle, les réticules et les sacs adoptent des formes et des matières différentes de celles utilisées auparavant. Avec les nouvelles technologies introduites par la Révolution industrielle (dont le début est généralement daté vers 1760 en Angleterre), la fabrication de matières et de produits gagne en qualité et en rapidité. Le sac de papier mâché en forme de vase, avec un fermoir et des décorations en fil d'acier coupé, en est un parfait exemple.

Le papier mâché est du papier finement réduit en poudre et mélangé à la craie ou de l'argile, puis moulé en formes diverses, séché et verni. Cette technique est née en Asie et arrivée en Europe au dix-septième siècle par la France. Il faudra cependant attendre la Révolution industrielle pour voir son usage se généraliser à grande échelle et assister à la production en grandes quantités de tabatières, plateaux, encriers et porte-plumes, bougeoirs, tables de jeu, chaises et sacs.

L'acier était connu en Europe depuis le Moyen Âge, mais les progrès des processus de production le rendront populaire au dix-neuvième siècle. Il sert alors à divers bijoux, peignes d'ornement, boucles, boutons, châtelaines et chaînes de montre. Les sacs sont ornés de sequins, feuillage, perles, fermoirs et boucles en acier coupé, une bonne imitation des diamants pour les sacs en velours ou cuir sombre.

Parmi les autres tendances entre 1813 et 1850 s'inscrit l'utilisation de ferronnerie filigrane, dite *fer de Berlin*, pour les sacs et bijoux. Du fait de leur éclat noir mat, ces bijoux étaient aussi recherchés pour les ornements de deuil.

In de eerste dertig jaar van de negentiende eeuw werden reticules en tassen gemaakt in andere vormen en uit andere materialen dan voorheen. Door de nieuwe technieken van de Industriële Revolutie (die men in Engeland meestal rond 1760 laat beginnen) konden materialen en producten veel beter en sneller geproduceerd worden. Een goed voorbeeld hiervan is de papier-maché-tas in de vorm van een vaas met een beugel en decoraties van geslepen staal.

Papier-maché is fijngestampt papier dat, vermengd met krijt of klei, in allerlei vormen geperst en vervolgens gedroogd en gevernist wordt. De papier-maché-techniek is oorspronkelijk afkomstig uit Azië en kwam in de zeventiende eeuw via Frankrijk naar Europa. Pas tijdens Industriële Revolutie werd papier-maché op grote schaal toegepast: snuifdozen, presenteerbladen, inktstellen, kandelaars, speeltafels, stoelen en tassen werden toen in grote oplagen vervaardigd.

Staal kende men in Europa al sinds de Middeleeuwen, maar door verbeteringen in het productieproces werd geslepen staal in de negentiende eeuw populair. Het werd gebruikt voor sieraden, sierkammen, gespen, knopen, chatelaines en horlogekettingen. Tassen werden versierd met pailletten, lovertjes, kralen, beugels en sluitingen van geslepen staal. Op tassen van donker fluweel of leer was het een goede imitatie van diamanten. Een ander modesnufje tussen 1813 en 1850 was het gebruik van fijn filigraanijzerwerk: het zogenaamde *fer de Berlin* (ijzer uit Berlijn) voor tassen en sieraden. Deze sieraden waren vanwege hun zwarte doffe uitstraling ook geliefd als rouwsieraden.

français

nederlands

En las tres primeras décadas del siglo XIX, las retículas y los bolsos se realizaban con formas y materiales diferentes a los empleados hasta entonces. Gracias a las nuevas tecnologías que trajo consigo la revolución industrial (la cual se considera que tiene sus orígenes en Inglaterra alrededor de 1760), podían producirse materiales y productos de mejor calidad y con más rapidez. Un buen ejemplo de ello es el bolso de cartón piedra en forma de jarrón, con una boquilla de acero cortado y motivos decorativos.

El cartón piedra es un papel finamente espolvoreado que, si se mezcla con yeso o arcilla, puede modelarse en múltiples formas y, posteriormente, secarse y barnizarse. Las técnicas para trabajarlo tienen sus orígenes en Asia y entraron en Europa en el siglo XVII a través de Francia. Nunca antes de la revolución industrial se había utilizado el cartón piedra a tan gran escala. Con él se produjeron grandes cantidades de tabaqueras, bandejas, conjuntos de pluma y tinta, candelabros, mesas de juego, sillas y bolsos.

El acero ya se conocía en Europa desde la Edad Media, pero como resultado de las mejoras en el proceso de producción, el acero cortado adquirió popularidad en el siglo XIX. Se utilizaba en joyas, peines decorativos, hebillas, botones, chatelaines y cadenas de reloj. Los bolsos se decoraban con lentejuelas, láminas metálicas, cuentas, boquillas y broches realizados con acero cortado. En los bolsos que se realizaban en cuero o terciopelo oscuro, el acero resultaba una acertada imitación de los diamantes.

Otra tendencia entre los años 1813 y 1850 fue el uso de filigranas de hierro, el denominado fer de Berlin (hierro de Berlín), en los bolsos y joyas. Debido al lustre de color negro mate que les caracterizaba, estas joyas también eran codiciados ornamentos de luto.

Nei primi trent'anni del XIX secolo, si cominciò a produrre *reticule* e borsette di forma e di materiali diversi dal passato. A causa delle nuove tecnologie ideate dalla Rivoluzione Industriale (il cui inizio di solito si data in Inghilterra intorno al 1760), era diventato possibile lavorare materiali e prodotti molto più rapidamente e con maggiore precisione. Un buon esempio di questa evoluzione è la borsetta in *papier-mâché* a forma di vaso, con cerniera e decorazioni in acciaio tagliato.

Il *papier-mâché* è carta ridotta in polvere finissima che, mescolata a gesso o argilla, viene modellata nella forma prescelta, fatta essiccare e quindi verniciata. Le sue tecniche di lavorazione sono nate in Asia, per diffondersi in Europa nel XVII secolo attraverso la Francia. Occorre però attendere la Rivoluzione Industriale perché questo materiale venga impiegato su larga scala: è in questo periodo che vengono fabbricati in serie tabacchiere, vassoi, completi per scrittura con portapenne e calamaio, candelieri, tavolini da gioco, sedie e borsette.

L'acciaio era conosciuto in Europa sin dal Medioevo, ma divenne popolare grazie ai miglioramenti del suo processo di produzione ideati nel XIX secolo. Questo materiale veniva usato per ornamenti, pettini decorativi, fibbie, bottoni, châtelaine e catenine per orologi. Come decorazione per borsette, veniva utilizzato sotto forma di lustrini, piccole foglie, perline, cerniere e chiusure. Sullo sfondo di materiali come il velluto o pelle scuri, l'acciaio era una buona imitazione di diamante.

Un'altra tendenza tra il 1813 e il 1850 era l'impiego di ferro lavorato a filigrana, il cosiddetto *fer de Berlin* (ferro di Berlino), usato per borsette e gioielli. Questo materiale aveva un aspetto scuro e opaco che lo rendeva ricercato anche per gli accessori da usare nei periodi di lutto.

Español

Italiano

In den ersten dreißig Jahren des 19. Jahrhundert wurden Taschen in neuen Formen und Materialien produziert. Dank neuer Technologien, die im Zuge der Industriellen Revolution (deren Beginn normalerweise auf die Jahre um 1760 in England datiert wird) aufkamen, konnten Produkte und Materialien schneller und billiger hergestellt werden als bislang. Ein gutes Beispiel ist die reich dekorierte Pappmaché-Tasche in Form einer Vase, mit einem Bügel aus poliertem Stahl.

Pappmaché ist zu Staub zermahlenes Papier, das mit Kreide oder Ton vermischt und dann in alle mögliche Formen gepresst wird. Nach dem Trocknen wird das fertige Stück lackiert. Pappmaché-Techniken stammen ursprünglich aus Asien und erreichten Europa im 17. Jahrhundert über Frankreich. Seit der industriellen Revolution wurde Pappmaché in vielen Bereichen verwendet: Man fertigte Schnupftabakdosen, Tabletts, Tuschesets, Kerzenhalter, Kartentische, Stühle und Taschen in großer Zahl.

Stahl ist in Europa schon seit dem Mittelalter bekannt. Durch die technologischen Neuerungen der Verarbeitung wurde polierter Stahl jedoch im 19. Jahrhundert vermehrt eingesetzt. Man stellte Schmuck, dekorative Kämme, Schnallen und Spangen, Knöpfe, Chatelaines und Uhrketten her. Taschen wurden mit Pailletten verziert, oder mit Metallfolienapplikationen, Glasperlen, Bügeln, oder Schnallen aus poliertem Stahl. Auf schwarzen Taschen aus Samt oder Leder galt das Metall als schöne Diamantimitation.

Ein anderer Trend zwischen 1813 und 1850 ist die Verwendung von filigranem Eisenmaschennetz, das aus dem sogenannten Fer de Berlin (Berliner Eisen) bestand und für Taschen und Schmuck verwendet wurde. Aufgrund des dunklen schimmernden Glanzes wurde dieser Schmuck auch häufig als Trauerschmuck verwendet.

19 世紀のはじめの 30 年間、レティキュールやバッグ類はそれ以前に使用されていたものと全く違った形や素材で作られるようになります。産業革命（通常、1760 年頃に英国で始まったと考えられている社会現象）がもたらした新技術によって、素材も製品もより高品質になり、より早く仕上げることが可能になりました。そのよい例に、花瓶の形をした張子でできたバッグでカットスチールの口金と装飾を施したものがあります。

張子は細かい粉末状にした紙に石灰粉や粘土を混ぜ合わせ、いろいろな形に押し型して成型後、乾燥させニス塗りを行って完成させます。張子技術はもともとアジアで生まれたもので、17 世紀にフランスを介して欧州にやってきました。産業革命が起こるまで大規模に張子が使用されることはありませんでした。産業革命後、嗅ぎ煙草入れ、トレー、ペン・インクセット、キャンドル、トランプ台、椅子、戸棚、バッグなどが大量に生産されました。

鋼鉄は中世からヨーロッパに広まっていましたが、生産過程が向上したことから 19 世紀にカットスチールの人気が高まりました。カットスチールは装飾品、髪飾り用コーム、バックル、ボタン、シャトレーン、時計のチェーンに利用されました。バッグはスパンコール、葉飾り、ビーズ、カットスチールでできた口金や留金などで装飾されるようになります。濃色のベルベットやレザーのバッグと一緒に使うと、鋼鉄は銀そっくりに見えした。

19 世紀初期のもうひとつの傾向はバッグや装飾に繊細な鉄線細工を施すことで、いわゆるフェール・ド・ベルリン（またはベルリン鉄）と呼ばれるものでした。この素材は鉄の装飾品や小道具の製造を行ったベルリンの鋳造工場の名称にちなんで付けられたものです。その曇りのある黒い輝きから、これらのアクセサリーは喪中の装飾品として引く手あまたでもありました。

▲ Papier-mâché handbag covered with silk and cut steel sequins,
cut steel frame France, 1820s.

▲ Papier-mâché handbag with cut steel frame France, 1820s.

▲ Fer de Berlin handbag with decoration and lock of cut steel
Germany, ca. 1820.
▼ Papier-mâché handbag with cut steel frame France, ca. 1820.

▲ Fer de Berlin coin purse Germany, ca. 1820.
▼ Velvet handbag decorated with cut steel France, ca. 1820

▲ Velvet handbag decorated with cut steel beads, cut steel frame
France, 1910s.
▼ Leather handbag with cut steel decoration France, 1900s.

▲ Velvet handbag decorated with cut steel beads, cut steel frame
France, ca. 1918.
▶ Crocheted coin purse decorated with cut steel beads, cut steel lid
France, 19th c.

Tortoiseshell, ivory and imitations

Écaille, ivoire et imitations

Schildpad, ivoor en imitaties

Carey, marfil e imitaciones

Tartaruga, avorio e loro imitazioni

Schildpatt, Elfenbein und Imitationen

べっ甲、象牙、イミテーション

From the nineteenth century on, tortoiseshell was used for decorating or making fashion accessories such as bags, combs, spectacle cases, etuis and coin purses. It was difficult to work with, so objects made of tortoiseshell were true luxury articles. What is more, tortoiseshell accessories were often also inlaid with gold, silver or mother of pearl. To imitate tortoiseshell, horn was used. Ivory was also used in the nineteenth and the first quarter of the twentieth century for bags and purses. Detailed images were often carved from ivory, which showed up well against the bag's dark leather background. A special set of leather bags from the Museum of Bags and Purses collection has cover sheets of carved ivory which are set off with a silver border.
The best example is without a doubt a snakeskin bag depicting Eve plucking an apple in paradise.
As a substitute for ivory buttons and handcrafted accessories in the nineteenth century, the much cheaper vegetable ivory was used, made from ivory nuts from the ivory palm.
After the arrival of the first plastics, such as celluloid (1868), casein (1897) and cellulose acetate (1926), tortoiseshell and ivory were often imitated. For bags in the twenties, this specifically meant semicircular frames that were flat in structure or decorated to excess with historical, romantic, oriental and Egyptian motifs. In the thirties, handbags and clutches appeared made completely from plastic. The plastics were no longer used as a cheap imitation but because of their modern rigid structure.

English

Depuis le dix-neuvième siècle, l'écaille de tortue est utilisée pour la décoration ou la fabrication d'accessoires de mode tels que sacs, peignes, étuis à lunettes, étuis et petits porte-monnaie. Du fait de la difficulté à la travailler, les objets en écaille étaient des articles de grand luxe, d'autant qu'ils étaient souvent incrustés d'or, d'argent ou de nacre. L'imitation de l'écaille se faisait avec de la corne.

L'ivoire aussi a été utilisé au dix-neuvième siècle et pendant le premier quart du vingtième pour des sacs et porte-monnaie. Des représentations très détaillées étaient souvent sculptées en ivoire, qui tranchait sur un fond de cuir sombre. Le Musée des sacs possède dans sa collection une série spéciale de sacs en cuir avec des feuilles de couverture en ivoire sculpté et garnies d'une bordure en argent. Le meilleur exemple est sans aucun doute le sac en peau de serpent représentant Ève au Paradis en train de cueillir une pomme.

Au dix-neuvième siècle, on utilisait, en guise de substitut pour les boutons et accessoires artisanaux en ivoire, l'ivoire végétal tiré des noix du palmier à ivoire et nettement moins cher.

Avec l'arrivée des premiers plastiques comme le celluloïd (1868), la caséine (1897) et l'acétate de cellulose (1926), les imitations d'écaille et d'ivoire se multiplient. On les retrouve en particulier, pour les sacs des années vingt, dans les fermoirs semi-circulaires de structure plate ou décorée à l'excès de motifs historiques, romantiques, orientaux et égyptiens. Dans les années trente, des sacs à main et pochettes entièrement en plastique apparaissent : les plastiques ne sont plus désormais utilisés comme une imitation moins onéreuse mais pour leur texture rigide moderne.

Vanaf de negentiende eeuw werd schildpad gebruikt voor het versieren of maken van modeaccessoires als tassen, haarkammen, brillenkokers, etuis en beursjes. De verwerking ervan was duur, waardoor voorwerpen met schildpad tot de echte luxeartikelen behoorden. Bovendien werden accessoires van schildpad vaak ook nog ingelegd met goud, zilver of parelmoer. Ter imitatie van schildpad werd hoorn gebruikt.

Ook ivoor werd in de negentiende eeuw en het eerste kwart van de twintigste eeuw gebruikt voor tassen en beursjes. Vaak werden in het ivoor gedetailleerde voorstellingen gesneden, die goed uitkwamen tegen de donkere achtergrond van het leer van de tas. Een bijzondere serie leren tassen uit de collectie van het Tassenmuseum is voorzien van dekplaten van bewerkt ivoor, afgewerkt met een zilveren rand. Het mooiste exemplaar is zonder twijfel een slangenleren tas met daarop in ivoor een afbeelding van Eva die een appel plukt in het paradijs.

Als substituut voor ivoren knopen en handwerk-accessoires gebruikte men in de negentiende eeuw wel het veel goedkopere ivoriet, gemaakt van de kiem van de ivoorpalm.

Na de komst van de eerste kunststoffen, zoals celluloid (1868), caseïne (1897) en celluloseacetaat (1926), werden schildpad en ivoor vaak nagebootst. Bij tassen in de jaren twintig ging het vooral om halfronde beugels, die vlak van structuur waren of overdadig versierd werden met historische, romantische, oosterse en Egyptische motieven. In de jaren dertig verschenen handtassen en onderarmtassen die helemaal van kunststof waren gemaakt. De kunststoffen werden niet meer gebruikt als goedkope imitatie, maar vanwege hun moderne, strakke structuur.

français   nederlands

A partir del siglo XIX, el carey se utilizó para decorar o elaborar accesorios de moda tales como bolsos, peines, fundas de binóculos, estuches y portamonedas. Resultaba un material difícil de trabajar, por lo que los objetos realizados con carey eran verdaderos artículos de lujo. Y, más aún, en los accesorios de este tipo a menudo se realizaban incrustaciones de oro, plata o madreperla. Para imitar el carey se utilizaba el cuerno. También se empleó el marfil en el siglo XIX y el primer cuarto del siglo XX en la confección de bolsos y monederos. Este material solía utilizarse para labrar imágenes detalladas, que resaltaban bien con el fondo de cuero oscuro del bolso. Hay un conjunto especial de bolsos de cuero procedente de la colección del Museum of Bags and Purses que presenta cubiertas de marfil tallado que se hacen resaltar con un borde de plata. El mejor ejemplo sin ninguna duda es un bolso de piel de serpiente con la imagen de Eva cogiendo una manzana en el Paraíso.

Como sustituto de los accesorios tallados a mano y los botones de marfil, en el siglo XIX también se empleaba el marfil vegetal, que resultaba mucho más económico y se obtenía de las semillas de la tagua.

Con la aparición de los primeros plásticos, como el celuloide (1868), la caseína (1897) y el acetato de celulosa (1926), el carey y el marfil fueron objeto de numerosas imitaciones. En la década de 1920, esto se traducía en bolsos de boquillas semicirculares con una estructura plana o decorados en exceso con motivos históricos, románticos, orientales y egipcios. Los *clutches* y los bolsos de mano que aparecieron en la década siguiente estaban elaborados íntegramente en plástico. Este material ya no se utilizaba tanto como imitación barata sino por su moderna estructura rígida.

A partire dal XIX secolo, la tartaruga veniva usata per decorare o fabbricare accessori di moda come borsette, pettini, portaocchiali, étuis e borse per monete. Poiché questo materiale era di difficile lavorazione, gli accessori in tartaruga erano articoli di gran lusso. Inoltre, venivano spesso decorati con intarsi d'oro, d'argento o di madreperla. Per imitare la tartaruga si utilizzava il corno. Nel XIX secolo e nel primo quarto del XX secolo, anche l'avorio veniva utilizzato per borsette e borsellini. Spesso veniva intagliato in immagini dettagliate che risaltavano bene sullo sfondo di pelle scura della borsetta. Una serie speciale di borsette in pelle della collezione del Museo della Borsetta è ricoperta da lamine di avorio intagliato, messo in risalto da una cerniera d'argento. L'esempio migliore è senza dubbio una borsetta di pelle di serpente che raffigura Eva nell'atto di cogliere una mela nel Giardino dell'Eden.

Nel XIX secolo, si producevano imitazioni dei bottoni e degli accessori d'avorio lavorati a mano utilizzando il più economico avorio vegetale o tagua, ricavato dalla noce di una pianta della famiglia delle palme.

Dopo l'arrivo delle prime plastiche sintetiche come la celluloide (1868), la caseina (1897) e l'acetato di cellulosa (1926), questi materiali vennero utilizzati spesso per imitare la tartaruga e l'avorio. Nelle borse degli anni Venti, ciò significava soprattutto cerniere piatte e semicircolari, che potevano essere abbondantemente decorate con motivi di ispirazione storica, romantica, orientale ed egiziana. Negli anni Trenta, comparvero le prime borse a mano e pochette fatte completamente di plastica. In questi modelli, le plastiche sintetiche non venivano più usate per imitare materiali più costosi, ma erano apprezzate per la loro moderna struttura rigida.

Español

Italiano

Ab dem 19. Jahrhundert wurde Schildpatt häufig für die Dekoration von modischen Accessoires, wie z. B. von Kämmen, Taschen, Brillenetuis und kleinen Geldbörsen verwendet. Das Material war schwer zu bearbeiten. Also hatten Objekte aus Schildpatt einen stolzen Preis. Die Accessoires aus Schildpatt waren oft mit kostbaren Einlegearbeiten aus Silber und Gold oder Perlmutt verziert. Zur Imitation von Schildpatt benutzte man Horn.

Elfenbein wurde im 19. und zu Beginn des 20. Jahrhundert häufig für die Herstellung von Taschen und Beuteln verarbeitet. Oft wurden in das Elfenbein minuziöse Darstellungen geschnitzt, die sich von dem Hintergrund des dunklen Leders sehr wirkungsvoll abhoben. Ein besonderes Set dieser Ledertaschen aus dem Taschenmuseum besitzt auf der Vorderseite ein kunstvoll geschnitztes Elfenbeinrelief und ist elegant mit silbernem Rand abgesetzt. Ohne Zweifel das beste Beispiel ist die Schlangenledertasche mit einer Darstellung von Eva, wie sie gerade den Apfel im Paradies pflückt.

Ein Ersatz für Elfenbeinknöpfe und andere handgearbeitete Accessoires waren im 19. Jahrhundert die weitaus billigeren Knöpfe aus vegetabilem (pflanzlichem) Elfenbein: Das waren die Elfenbeinnüsse von der sogenannten Elfenbeinpalme.

Nach der Entwicklung der ersten Kunststoffe wie Zelluloid (1868), Kasein (1897) und Zellulose-Acetat (1926), wurden Schildpatt und Elfenbein häufig imitiert. Am Beispiel der Taschen waren das in den 20er Jahren fast immer halbkreisförmige Bügel, manchmal flach und schmucklos und manchmal übermäßig mit historischen, romantischen, fernöstlichen oder ägyptischen Motiven dekoriert. In den 30ern tauchten Handtaschen und Unterarmtaschen auf, die vollständig aus Plastik hergestellt worden waren. Die neuen Kunststoffe wurden nicht mehr nur als billige Imitation, sondern vor allem aufgrund ihrer modernen glatten Oberflächen geschätzt.

19 世紀以降、べっ甲がバッグ、コーム、眼鏡ケース、エテュイ（小ケース）、コインパースなどファッション・アクセサリーの装飾または製作に利用されるようになります。加工するのが難しかったため、べっ甲は真の贅沢品でした。それだけでなく、べっ甲のアクセサリーは金、銀、真珠層と象がんされていることがよくありました。べっ甲のイミテーションとして、角が利用されました。

象牙もまた 19 世紀、20 世紀のはじめの 25 年間はバッグやパースに使われていました。詳細な彫像は象牙から彫られることが多く、バッグの濃い色のレザーを背景にするととてもよく映えます。

19 世紀の象牙製ボタンや手細工アクセサリーの代用品として、格段に安い植物性象牙が使用されるようになります。これはゾウゲヤシのアイボリーナッツからできたものです。

セルロイド（1868 年）、カゼイン（1897 年）、セルロースアセテート（1926 年）など、最初のプラスチックが登場した後、べっ甲や象牙はイミテーションが多くなります。20 年代のバッグ類において特にこれは、平らな構造をした半円の口金または歴史的、ロマンチック、オリエンタルエジプト調の過度な装飾を意味しました。30 年代には完全にプラスチックでできたハンドバッグやクラッチバッグが登場します。プラスチックはもはや安価なイミテーションとして利用されるだけではなく、その近代的で硬い構造が注目されるようになったのです。

deutsch

日本語

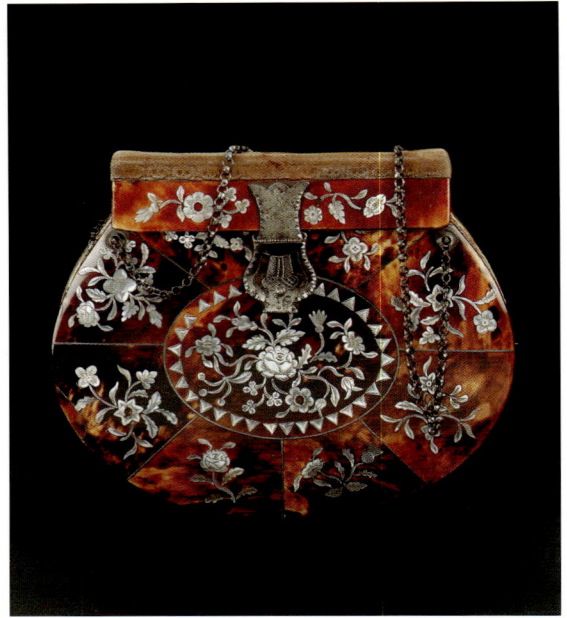

▲ Leather handbag with cover-sheet of tortoise-shell inlaid with
mother-of pearl Germany, 1810-1820.
▼ Silk reticule decorated with tortoise-shell, mother-of-pearl and
gilt leaves France, 1820-1850.

▲ Leather handbag with cover-sheet of tortoise-shell inlaid with
mother-of pearl Germany, ca. 1820.

▲ Plastic (imitation tortoise-shell) handbag France, 1930s.
▼ Fabric handbag decorated with cut steel beads and fringe,
plastic frame France, 1920s.

▲ Imitation tortoise-shell handbag, Koret U.S.A., 1950s.
▼ Beaded handbag with plastic (imitation tortoise-shell) frame
Czechoslovakia, 1920s.

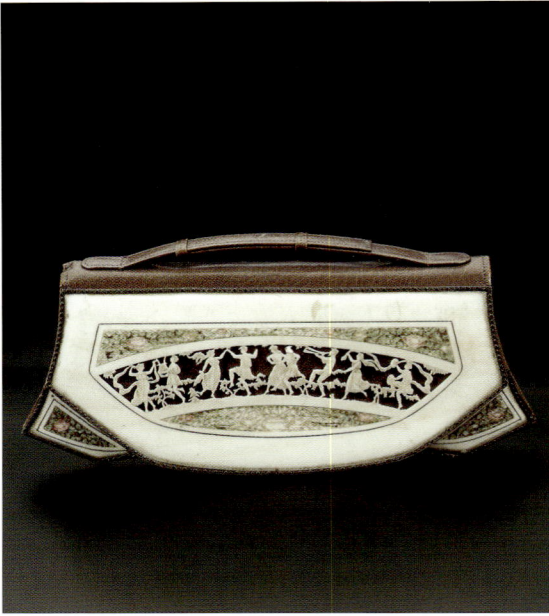

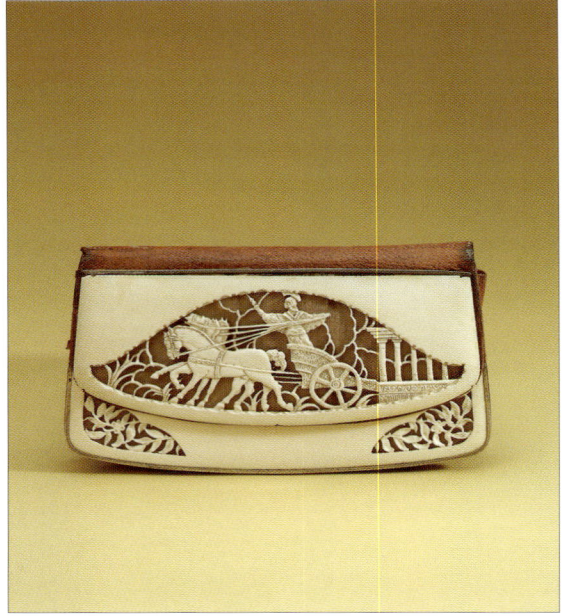

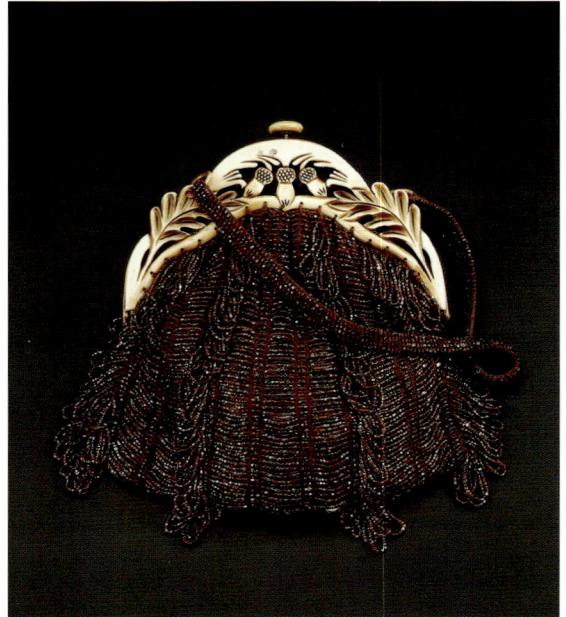

▲ Leather handbag with ivory cover-sheet, Greek dancers, silver border Germany, 1920s.
▼ Brocade handbag with plastic (imitation ivory) frame European, 1920s.

▲ Leather pochette with ivory cover-sheet, Pallas Athena, silver border Germany, ca. 1925.
▼ Beaded handbag with plastic (imitation ivory) frame France, 1920s.

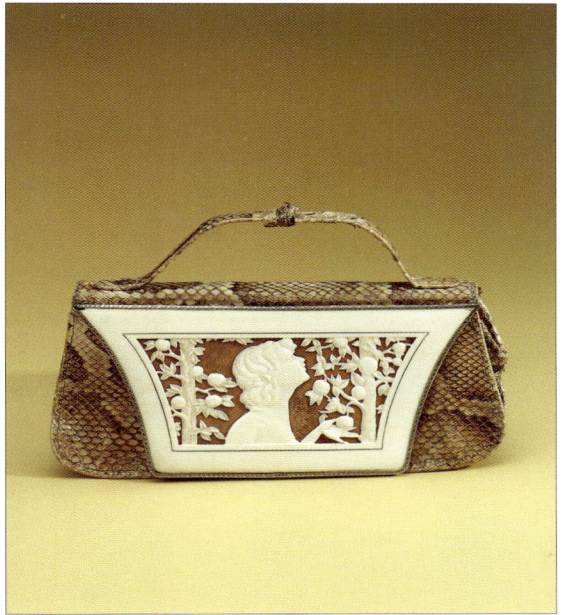

▲ Leather handbag with ivory cover-sheet and silver border
Germany, ca. 1920.
▼ Fabric handbag with ivory decoration of Greek god Pan
France, 1920-1925.

▲ Snakeskin handbag with ivory cover-sheet, Eve and the apple,
silver border Germany, 1920s.
▼ Silk handbag with plastic (imitation ivory) frame France, 1920s.

▲ Silk reticule with decoration of celluloid and ivory (l) and ivory handbag with silver border and chain (r) Germany, early 20th c.
▼ Fabric handbag decorated with net of imitation shells, coloured plastic frame (l) and leather handbag with plastic frame (r) France, 1920s.

▲ Fabric tobacco-pouch in shape of monk with face, feet and hands in vegetable ivory Austria, 19th c.
▶ Fabric handbag with special grip and plastic (imitation ivory) frame France, 1920s.

Special kinds of leather

Cuirs spéciaux

Bijzondere leersoorten

Tipos de cuero especiales

Pellami speciali

Besondere Ledersorten

特殊皮革（レザー）

Leather is one of the oldest materials used by human beings. After plastic, in the twentieth century leather was still the most frequently used material for handbags. It was valued not just for its durability but also because of its sleek or sometimes striking texture.

In theory, all skins can be converted into leather, but mainly those from cattle, goats, donkeys, sheep and pigs are used. The leather from exotic animals such as snakes, crocodiles, ostriches, lizards and armadillos are valued for their unique textures. Fish leather has also been used for bags; for example, skate and shark leather have been used in the past, and currently Nile perch are also made into leather.

In accordance with the prevailing fashion, leather handbags are furnished with decorations, clasps and frames, from silver fittings to clasps and decorations in chrome and plastic.

English

Le cuir est l'un des matériaux travaillés depuis le plus longtemps par l'homme. Après le plastique, il reste le plus utilisé pour les sacs à main au vingtième siècle et est apprécié pour sa longévité et sa texture lisse parfois superbe.

En théorie, toutes les peaux peuvent être transformées en cuir, mais on utilise essentiellement celles de bovins, chèvres, ânes, moutons et porcs, ou d'animaux exotiques comme les serpents, crocodiles, autruches, lézards et tatous, appréciées pour leurs textures uniques. On trouve également dans le passé des sacs en cuir de poisson, notamment de raie ou de requin ; aujourd'hui, les perches du Nil sont transformées en cuir.

La mode actuelle équipe les sacs à main en cuir de décorations, boucles et fermoirs de divers matériaux, de l'argent au chrome ou au plastique.

Leer is een van de oudste door de mens gebruikte materialen. Naast kunststof was leer in de twintigste eeuw nog altijd het meest toegepaste materiaal voor de vervaardiging van tassen. Het werd niet alleen gewaardeerd om zijn duurzaamheid, maar ook om zijn gladde of soms juist opvallende structuur.

In principe kunnen alle huiden tot leer worden verwerkt, maar vooral die van runderen, geiten, ezels, schapen en varkens worden veel gebruikt. Het leer van exotische dieren als slangen, krokodillen, struisvogels, hagedissen en gordeldieren werd gewaardeerd om hun bijzondere structuur. Ook vissenleer werd wel gebruikt voor tassen. Dat gebeurde bijvoorbeeld met roggen- en haaienleer; tegenwoordig wordt ook de nijlbaars tot leer verwerkt. Overeenkomstig de heersende mode werden leren tassen van decoraties, sluitingen en beugels voorzien, uiteenlopend van zilverbeslag tot sluitingen en decoraties van chroom en kunststof.

français

nederlands

El cuero es uno de los materiales más antiguos utilizados por el ser humano. Tras el plástico, en el siglo XX el cuero seguía siendo el material más utilizado en la producción de bolsos. Su valor reside no sólo en su durabilidad sino también por su textura lisa o a veces consistente.

En teoría pueden usarse todo tipo de pieles, pero las más utilizadas son las de bovinos, cabras, equinos, ovinos y cerdos. El cuero de animales exóticos como serpientes, cocodrilos, avestruces, lagartos y armadillos se aprecia por su textura única. En la elaboración de bolsos también se ha empleado la piel de peces. Así, en otros tiempos se utilizó el cuero de raya y de tiburón, y en la actualidad también se usa la piel de las percas del Nilo.

Según la moda del momento, los bolsos de cuero se ornamentan con motivos decorativos, cierres y boquillas, desde accesorios de plata hasta hebillas y ornamentos de cromo y plástico.

La pelle è uno dei primi materiali utilizzati nella storia dell'uomo. Dopo la plastica, anche nel XX secolo la pelle restò il materiale più diffuso per le borsette. Veniva apprezzata non solo per la sua resistenza, ma anche per il tatto piacevole o, a volte, per la curiosa provenienza.

In teoria, tutte le pelli possono essere conciate, ma si usano soprattutto quelle di bestiame, di capra, d'asino, di pecora e di maiale. Alcune pelli di animali esotici come serpenti, coccodrilli, struzzi, lucertole e armadilli sono apprezzate per il loro aspetto particolare. Per confezionare borsette si sono utilizzati anche pellami derivati da pesci: ad esempio, in passato si è usata la pelle di razza e di squalo, e attualmente viene conciata anche la pelle di persico del Nilo.

A seconda della moda prevalente, le borsette di pelle presentano decorazioni, chiusure e cerniere diverse, dalle finiture d'argento a chiusure e decorazioni in cromo e in plastica.

Español

Italiano

SPECIAL KINDS OF LEATHER

Leder ist eines der ältesten Materialen, das vom Menschen überhaupt verwendet wird. Nach den Kunststoffen war Leder im 20. Jahrhundert das meist benutzte Material für Handtaschen. Es wurde nicht nur aufgrund seiner Beständigkeit geschätzt, sondern auch wegen seiner glatten, geschmeidigen Oberfläche oder gerade wegen seiner fantastischen Struktur.

Theoretisch kann man jede Tierhaut in Leder verwandeln. Hauptsächlich wird jedoch Kuh-, Ziegen-, Esels-, Schafs- oder Schweineleder verwendet. Lederarten exotischer Tiere, wie z.B. von Schlangen, Krokodilen, Straußen, Eidechsen und Gürteltieren wurden auf Grund ihrer exotischen Maserung hoch gehandelt. Auch gab es Taschen aus Fischleder, zum Beispiel aus Haifisch- oder Rochenleder. Heutzutage wird z.B. Nil-Barsch zu Leder verarbeitet.

Je nach der vorherrschenden Mode werden die Taschen mit Verzierungen, Schnallen und Bügeln versehen. Es gibt Silbereinlagen, Schnallen und Verzierungen aus Plastik oder Chrom.

レザーは人類が利用してきた最も古い素材のひとつです。プラスチック登場後の 20 世紀になってもまだ、レザーはハンドバッグの素材として最も頻繁に使用される素材でした。その丈夫さが重宝されただけでなく、滑らかで、時には印象的な感触が高く評価されました。

理論上では全ての皮がレザーに加工可能ということになりますが、主に使用されるのは畜牛、ヤギ、ロバ、ヒツジ、ブタの皮です。ヘビ、ワニ、ダチョウ、トカゲ、アルマジロなどエキゾチックな動物の皮は、その特有の感触で貴重とされています。魚の皮からできたレザーもバッグに使用されてきました。たとえば、ガンキエイやサメの皮は過去にも使用された経歴があり、現在ではナイル川に生息するスズキもレザーとして使われています。

一般的な流行に伴って、レザーのハンドバッグには装飾、留金、口金などが施され、その種類は銀の金具からクロムやプラスチックの留金や装飾に至るまでさまざまです。

deutsch　　　　日本語

▲ Handbag in antelope leather, Comtesse Belgium, 1950s.
◀ Leather handbag with leopard skin Botswana, 1962.
◀◀ Armadillo shoulder bag 1920-1940.

▲ Handbag in elephant leather Italy, ca. 1965.
▶ Foalskin shoulderbag with chrome lock 1970s.

▲ Leather handbag covered with peacock feathers, plastic and metal frame 1970s.
▼ Two leather pochettes covered with peacock feathers 1970s.

▲ Leather handbag covered with peacock feathers, metal and leather handle 1970s.

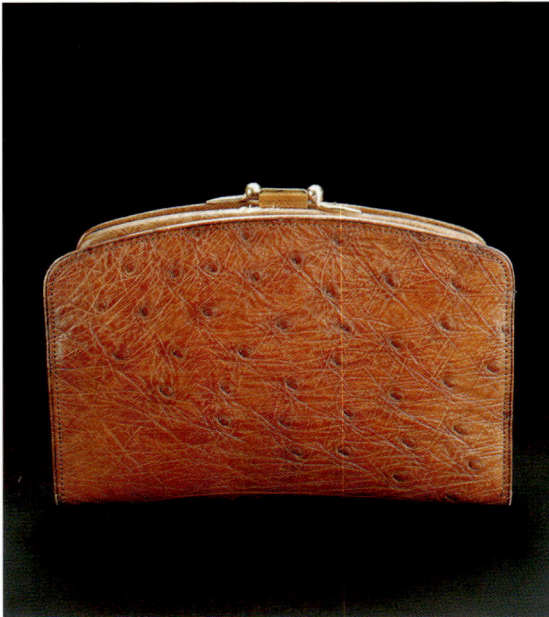

▲ Ostrich leather handbag, Asprey England, 1990s.
▼ Ostrich leather pochette England, 1920s.

▲ Ostrich leather shoulderbag, Asprey England, 1990s.

▲ Ostrich leather handbag Germany, 1950s.

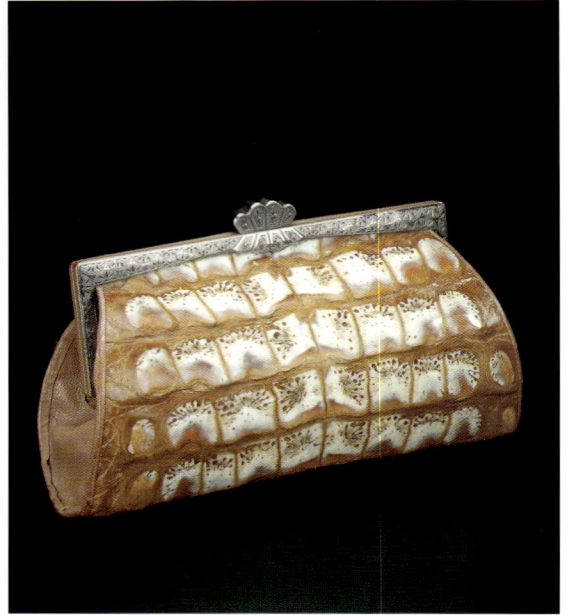

▲ Alligator handbag with silver decoration Indonesia, 1933.
▼ Alligator pochette with chrome frame and closure Belgium, 1930s.

▲ Alligator pochette with silver frame and lock Austria, 1920s.
▼ Alligator beauty-case, once owned by French actress Martine Carol France, 1950s.

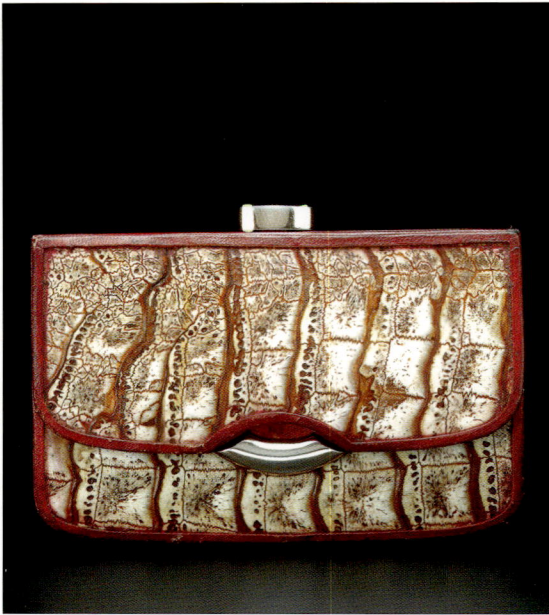

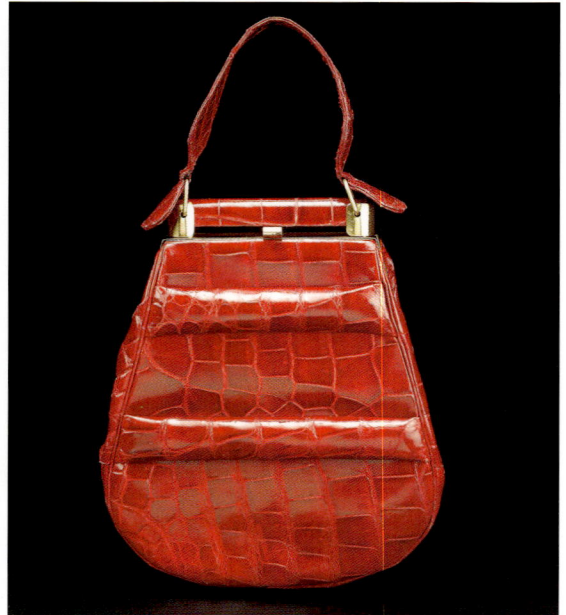

▲ Alligator pochette with two chrome closures European, 1930s.
▼ Imitation alligator handbag European, 1970s.

▲ Alligator handbag, Asprey England, 1990s.
▼ Alligator handbag with brass frame England, 1940s.

▲ Alligator handbag with brass frame and alligator handle
Argentina, 1960s.

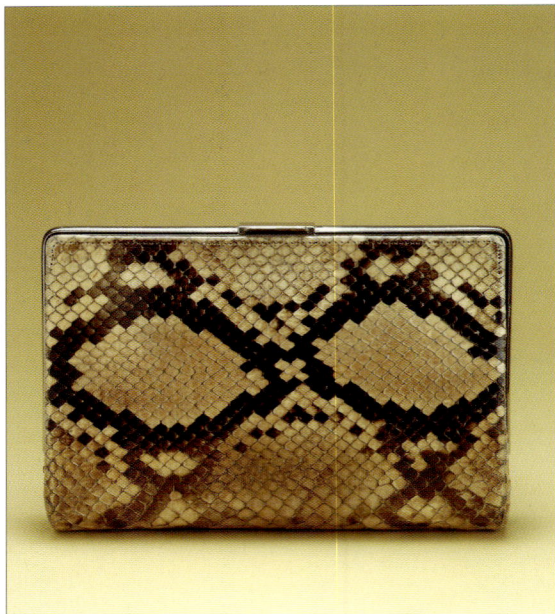

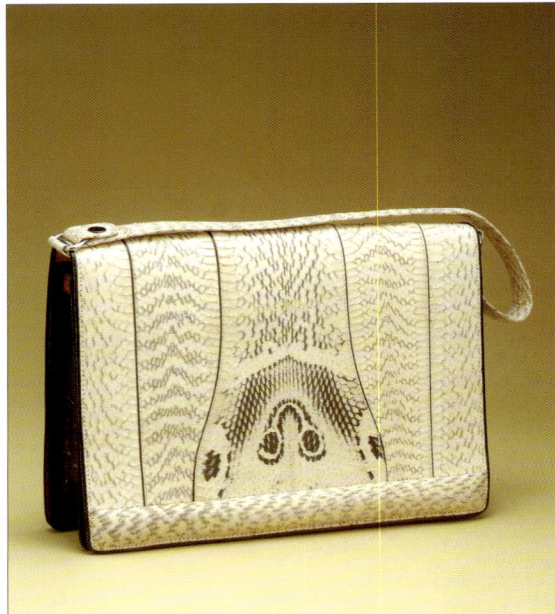

▲ Reticulated snakeskin pochette with chrome frame European, 1930s.
▼ Snakeskin handbag with brass closure The Netherlands, 1950s.

▲ Spectacled cobra handbag Indonesia, 1950s.
▼ Snakeskin handbag with matching shoes Indonesia, 1950s.

▲ Two coloured snakeskin handbags European, 1950-1980.

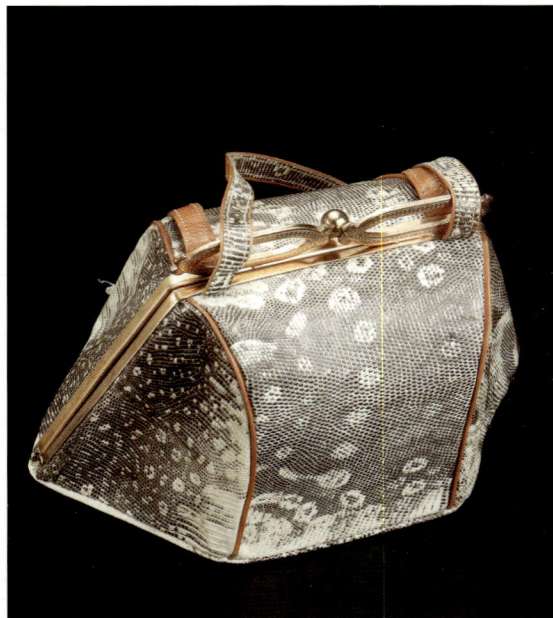

▲ Leather handbag with salamander France, 1920s.
▼ Two lizard handbags, both with chrome frame European, 1930s.

▲ Lizard handbag 1930s.
▼ Lizard handbag 1930s.
▶ Lizard handbag Indonesia, 1950s.

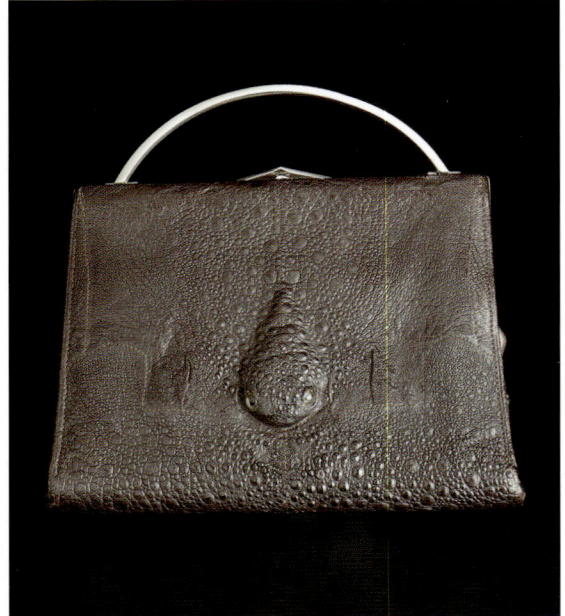

▲ Toad leather pochette Indonesia, 1930s.
▼ Toad leather pochette European, 1930s.

▲ Toad leather handbag England, 1930s.
▼ Toad leather handbag with chrome frame European, 1930s.

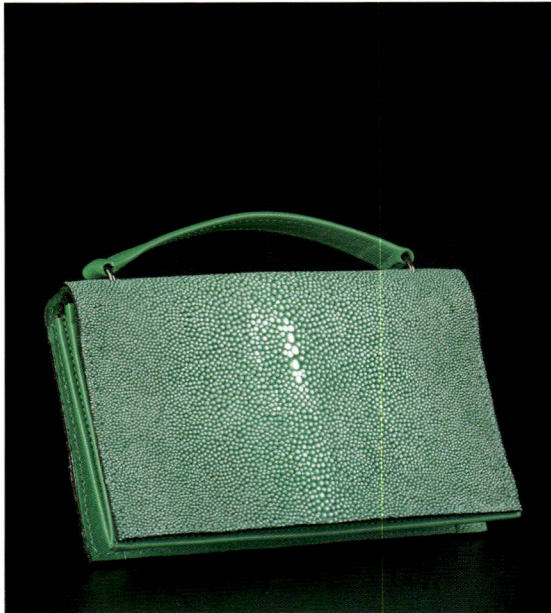

▲ Ray skin pochette with silver border Germany, 1920s.
▼ Stingray handbag, 'Jackie O' by Judith Leiber (designed in 1963)
U.S.A., 1995.

▲ Ray skin evening bag, Hester van Eeghen The Netherlands,
ca. 1998.
▶ Leather and ray skin handbag with brass frame England, 1920s.

Plant-derived materials

Matières végétales

Plantaardige materialen

Materiales de origen vegetal

Materiali vegetali

Materialien auf Pflanzenbasis

植物派生素材

Plant-derived products such as straw, wicker, raffia and wood have been used throughout the ages to make or decorate implements. In the eighteenth and nineteenth centuries, many bags and letter cases or wallets were decorated with straw. Apart from straw, wicker, aloe and cactus fibres, wood and nuts have also been used. The straw was first split and pressed flat and then applied to the wood, leather, cardboard or cloth background that was to be decorated. When used to decorate wallets or letter cases and bags, straw was, depending on the background, embroidered or pasted on. As is well-known, straw is naturally golden in colour; various colour nuances were obtained by heating the straw with a flatiron. The result could be further embellished by sprinkling and pasting on granules of gold or other metals, or by staining it in various colours.

In the twentieth century, plant-derived materials such as straw, raffia, wicker, wood and bamboo were mainly used to make woven bags and baskets. Although they are associated with being simple shopping bags, these baskets and bags were certainly prime fashion accessories in the spring and summer. In the fifties, bags made of imitation bamboo and straw were popular.

◀ Nile perch handbag, Maria Hees The Netherlands, 1993

English

Les produits d'origine végétale comme la paille, l'osier, le raphia et le bois ont toujours été utilisés pour fabriquer ou décorer de petits ustensiles. Aux dix-huitième et dix-neuvième siècles, nombre de sacs et de portefeuilles étaient ornés de paille, sans compter les fibres d'osier, d'aloès et de cactus, ainsi que le bois et les noix. La paille était d'abord fendue, puis pressée à plat et appliquée sur une base de bois, de cuir, de carton ou de tissu à décorer. Pour les portefeuilles et sacs, la paille était brodée ou collée selon le fond. Outre sa couleur naturelle dorée, on obtenait différentes nuances colorées en la chauffant au fer à repasser; le résultat pouvait être amélioré en appliquant dessus des granules d'or ou d'autres métaux ou par teinture.

Au vingtième siècle, les matériaux d'origine végétale comme la paille, le raphia, l'osier, le bois et le bambou ont surtout été utilisés pour des sacs et paniers tressés. Bien qu'assimilés à de simples paniers à provisions, ils constituent aussi des accessoires de mode essentiels au printemps et en été. Les sacs en imitation de bambou et paille ont connu un grand succès dans les années cinquante.

Plantaardige producten als stro, riet, raffia en hout zijn door de eeuwen heen gebruikt om gebruiksvoorwerpen te maken of te decoreren. In de achttiende en negentiende eeuw werden veel tassen en portefeuilles met stro gedecoreerd. Behalve stro werden ook riet, aloë- en cactusvezels, hout en noten gebruikt.

Het stro werd eerst gesplitst en platgeperst en daarna aangebracht op de te decoreren ondergrond van hout, leer, karton of textiel. Stro ter decoratie van portefeuilles en tassen werd afhankelijk van de ondergrond geborduurd of geplakt. Van nature is stro, zoals men weet, goudkleurig; verschillende kleurnuances verkreeg men door het stro met de strijkbout te verhitten. Het resultaat kon nog verder verfraaid worden door het te bestrooien en te beplakken met korreltjes goud of ander metaal, of door het in verschillende kleuren te beitsen.

In de twintigste eeuw werden van plantaardige materialen als stro, raffia, riet, hout en bamboe voornamelijk gevlochten tassen en manden gemaakt. Hoewel ze met eenvoudige boodschappentassen geassocieerd worden, waren deze manden en tassen wel degelijk modieuze accessoires van het voorjaars- en zomerseizoen. In de jaren vijftig waren tassen van imitatie-bamboe en –stro gewild.

français

nederlands

Los productos derivados de plantas como la paja, el mimbre, la rafia y la madera se han utilizado en todas las épocas para elaborar o decorar utensilios. En los siglos XVIII y XIX, muchos bolsos y portadocumentos o carteras se decoraban con paja. Además de la paja, el mimbre y las fibras de áloe y cactos, también se han empleado madera y cáscaras de frutos secos. En primer lugar, la paja se separaba y se prensaba, y posteriormente se aplicaba al fondo de madera, cuero, cartón o tela que debía decorarse. En su uso como decoración de carteras o portadocumentos y bolsos, los adornos se bordaban o se pegaban sobre la paja, siempre dependiendo de las características del fondo. Como es sabido, el color natural de la paja es dorado, pero podían obtenerse variados matices cromáticos calentando la paja con la ayuda de una plancha. A su vez, el resultado podía embellecerse esparciendo por encima y pegando gránulos de oro u otros materiales o tiñéndola de varios colores.

En el siglo XX, los materiales de origen vegetal como la paja, la rafia, el mimbre, la madera y el bambú se empleaban sobre todo para realizar cestos y bolsas trenzados. A pesar de que generalmente se consideran simples recipientes para transportar la compra, estos cestos y bolsas eran accesorios de moda de primera línea en primavera y en verano. En la década de 1950 se popularizaron los bolsos confeccionados en paja y bambú de imitación.

Materiali di origine vegetale come la paglia, il vimini, la rafia e il legno sono stati utilizzati in ogni epoca per fabbricare o decorare svariati oggetti. Nel XVIII e nel XIX secolo, molte borsette, portadocumenti e portafogli erano decorati con la paglia. Oltre alla paglia, si sono usati vimini, fibre di aloe e di cactus, legno e gusci di noci. La paglia veniva tagliata nel senso della lunghezza, appiattita e applicata allo sfondo di legno, pelle, cartone o tessuto da decorare. Quando l'oggetto da decorare era un portafogli o una borsetta, la paglia vi veniva ricamata o incollata, a seconda del materiale di cui era fatto il supporto. Come è noto, il colore naturale della paglia è dorato; scaldandola con un ferro da stiro, si potevano ottenere diverse sfumature di colore. Il risultato poteva essere abbellito ancora incollandovi una spruzzata di granelli d'oro o di altri metalli, oppure tingendo il materiale in diversi colori. Nel XX secolo, i materiali vegetali come la paglia, la rafia, il vimini, il legno e il bambù venivano usati soprattutto per produrre borse intrecciate e cestini. Anche se in generale vengono considerati semplici contenitori per la spesa, in primavera e in estate queste borse e cesti diventavano accessori di moda di primo piano. Negli anni Cinquanta, godettero di una certa popolarità le borsette fatte di bambù e paglia artificiali.

Español

Italiano

Pflanzliche Materialien, wie Stroh, Weidenruten, Bast und Holz wurden seit Urzeiten für die Herstellung oder Verzierung von Objekten verwendet. Im 18. und 19. Jahrhundert wurden Taschen, Brieftaschen und Geldbörsen häufig mit Stroh dekoriert. Neben Stroh benutzte man auch Weide, Aloe- und Kaktusfasern, Holz und Nussschalen. Das Stroh wurde zunächst geteilt und flach gepresst und dann auf Holz, Leder, Karton oder Stoff appliziert. Für das Dekor von Brieftaschen und Taschen wurde es aufgeklebt oder aufgestickt. Von Natur aus ist Stroh bekanntlich goldfarben. Man konnte aber verschiedene Farbtöne erzielen, indem man das Stroh mit dem Bügeleisen vorsichtig erwärmte. Danach wurden häufig auch noch goldene oder metallene Körner aufgetragen. Manchmal wurde Stroh auch zum Färben gebeizt.

Im 20. Jahrhundert werden Naturmaterialien wie Stroh, Bast, Weide, Holz oder Bambus hauptsächlich für die Herstellung von Körben oder geflochtenen Taschen benutzt. Auch wenn man bei diesen Körben und Taschen zuerst an Einkauf denkt, waren diese in der Frühlings- und Sommersaison groß in Mode. In den 50er Jahren waren Stroh- und Bambusimitationen besonders gefragt.

植物派生製品の麦わら、籐、ラフィアヤシ繊維、木材などは道具作製、装飾にいつの時代も利用されてきたものです。18 世紀、19 世紀、多くのバッグやレターケース、札入れは麦わらで装飾されていました。麦わらのほかに、籐、アロエ、サボテン繊維、木材、ナッツなども使用されていたようです。麦わらはまず裂いて平らにプレスし、その後装飾を施す木材、レザー、厚紙または布地にあしらいます。札入れまたはレターケース、バッグなどを装飾する際には、装飾する素材にもよりますが、麦わらを刺繍または糊付けしました。周知の通り、麦わらはもともと黄金色です。さまざまな色のニュアンスを作り出すにはこてで麦わらに熱を加えます。さらに金や他の金属粒をちりばめたり糊付けしたりする、またはさまざまな色に染めるなどして仕上がりに豪華さを出していきます。

20 世紀には麦わら、ラフィアヤシ繊維、籐、木材、竹などを主に編みこみ細工のバッグやバスケットに利用しました。通常、簡素な買い物バッグに利用されていたのですが、これらのバスケットやバッグは春夏には主要ファッション・アクセサリーだったことも確かです。50 年代にはイミテーションの竹や麦わらで作られたバッグが人気を集めました。

deutsch

日本語

▲ Reticule of silk and straw 19th c.
▼ Coin purse made of walnut and silk Germany, 1868.

▲ Straw basket with decoration of plaited straw roses France, 19th c.
▼ Lettercase covered with coloured straw and with gilt decorations
France, 18th c.

▲ Straw handbag Indonesia, 1970s.
▼ Pochette in coloured raffia (l) and pochette in coloured straw (r)
The Netherlands, 1930s, Hong Kong, 1980s.

▲ Shopping bag made of leather, wood and straw France, 1920-1940.
▼ Handbag in coloured raffia 1950s.

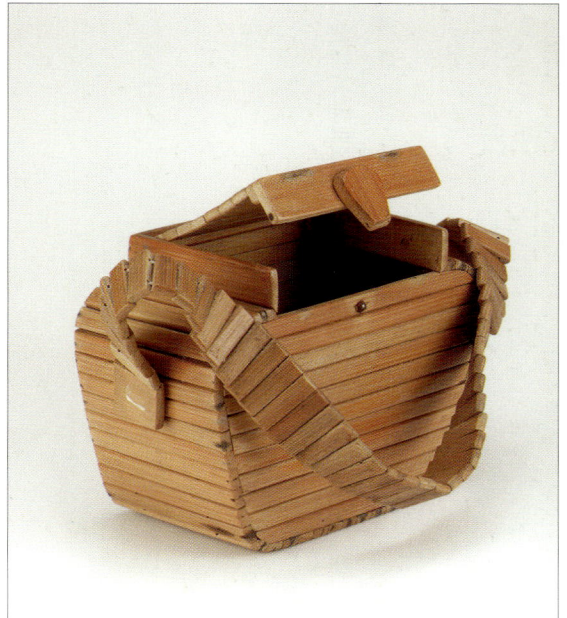

▲ Handbag made of leather and reed Belgium, 19th c.
▼ Bamboo and straw handbag with shell decoration, Straw World, Hialeah, U.S.A., 1950s.
◄ Basket with appliqué decoration and fabric lining, Annie Laurie Originals U.S.A., 1950s.

▲ Bamboo and wood handbag Indonesia, 1970s.
▼ Bamboo handbag Indonesia, 1970s.
► Bamboo basket bag Italy, 1974.
►► Folding bamboo handbag Japan, 1970s.

Beadwork

Perles

Kralen

Cuentas y abalorios

Perline

Perlenarbeiten

ビーズ

In the past two hundred years, beaded bags and pouches have been very popular in certain periods. Although it certainly was not easy, knitting with beads became popular at the beginning of the nineteenth century. An experienced knitter needed two full working weeks to complete a beaded bag: more than 50,000 beads had to be strung in the right order according to the pattern - without making a mistake - before the bag could be knitted. Patterns were sold in many versions or could be obtained from almanacs and women's magazines. Flowers, temples, gravestones, weeping willows, harps, hunting scenes and smoking Chinese people frequently adorned nineteenth century beaded bags and pouches. Because of the arduous and time-consuming technique, owning one of these beaded bags was considered a true luxury.

In the early decades of the twentieth century, beaded bags were fitted with drawstrings as handles or finished off with decorative frames made of metal, tortoiseshell or plastic. Popular motifs included flowers, picturesque landscapes with traditional houses, castles and ruins, children, historical tableaux and oriental carpets. Other bags had Cubist or Art Deco motifs.

In the twenties, handbags were also made from cut steel beads or aluminium beads. The cut steel beads were at first only available in gold, silver and bronze colours, but later in France they were also made in other colours.

After 1930, beaded bags lost some of their prominence. But a particular type of beaded bag was still fashionable for some time: the envelope style. Large, heavy, box-shaped bags in gleaming bronze, black, blue and white beads were all the rage in the United States in the forties.

English

Depuis deux cent ans, les sacs et bourses perlés ont connu plusieurs périodes de grand succès. Malgré la difficulté que la technique représente, le tricotage de perles était très populaire au début du dix-neuvième siècle. Un tricoteur expérimenté mettait alors deux bonnes semaines pour un sac perlé : plus de 50 000 perles devaient être enfilées dans le bon ordre selon le motif voulu (sans droit à l'erreur) avant de pouvoir tricoter le sac. Des motifs de toutes sortes étaient vendus ou offerts dans les almanachs et journaux : fleurs, temples, tombes, saules pleureurs, harpes, scènes de chasse et des Chinois en train de fumer étaient les plus fréquents. En raison de la complexité et de la longueur de la tâche, posséder un sac perlé était alors considéré comme un véritable luxe.

Dans les premières décennies du vingtième siècle, les sacs perlés étaient dotés de cordons en guise de poignées ou fermés par des fermoirs décoratifs en métal, écaille ou plastique. Les motifs les plus en vogue comprenaient les fleurs, les paysages pittoresques aux maisons traditionnelles, les châteaux et les ruines, les enfants, les tableaux historiques et les tapis d'Orient. Certains sacs affichent aussi des motifs cubistes ou art déco.

Dans les années vingt sont apparus des sacs à main en perles d'acier coupé ou d'aluminium. Le premier type n'a d'abord été disponible que dans les teintes doré, argenté et bronze, puis d'autres couleurs sont venues s'y ajouter en France.

Après 1930, les sacs perlés ont perdu leur place de choix, à l'exception d'un style particulier resté en vogue quelque temps : l'enveloppe. Ces grands sacs lourds en forme de boîte et ornés de perles bronze , noires, bleues et blanches luisantes ont fait fureur aux Etats-Unis dans les années quarante.

De afgelopen tweehonderd jaar waren kralentassen en -buidels in bepaalde periodes zeer gewild. Hoewel het bepaald niet gemakkelijk was, werd begin negentiende eeuw het breien met kralen populair. Een geoefend breister had twee volledige werkweken nodig om een kralentas te maken: meer dan 50.000 kralen moesten volgens patroon in de juiste volgorde geregen worden – zonder fouten te maken –, voordat de tas gebreid kon worden. Patronen waren in vele uitvoeringen te koop of over te nemen uit almanakken en tijdschriften. Bloemen, tempels, grafzerken, treurwilgen, harpen, jachttaferelen en rokende Chinezen sierden de negentiende-eeuwse kralentassen en -buidels. Door de bewerkelijke en tijdrovende techniek behoorden deze kralentassen tot de luxueuze producten.

In de eerste decennia van de twintigste eeuw werden kralentassen uitgevoerd met trekkoorden als hengsel of afgewerkt met decoratieve beugels van metaal, schildpad of kunststof. Populaire motieven waren bloemen, pittoreske landschappen met traditionele huizen, kastelen en ruïnes, kinderen, historische taferelen en oosterse tapijten. Andere tassen hadden kubistische of Art Deco-motieven.

In de jaren twintig werden tassen ook van geslepen stalen kralen of van aluminiumkralen gemaakt. De kralen van geslepen staal waren in eerste instantie alleen in goud-, zilver- en bronskleur te krijgen, maar werden later in Frankrijk ook in andere kleuren gemaakt.

Na 1930 speelde de kralentas een bescheidener rol. Wel was een bijzonder type kralentas nog enige tijd in de mode: de envelopstijl. Grote, zware doosvormige tassen in glinsterende bronzen, zwarte, blauwe en witte kralen waren in de jaren veertig een rage in de Verenigde Staten.

français   nederlands

En los últimos doscientos años, los bolsos y morrales con abalorios han gozado de gran aceptación en determinados momentos. A pesar de que resultaba realmente complicado, tejer con abalorios cobró gran popularidad a principios del siglo XIX. Una persona especializada precisaba de dos semanas enteras de trabajo para terminar un bolso de este tipo, pues tenía que colocar más de 50.000 cuentas o abalorios en el orden correcto –sin cometer un solo error– según dictara el patrón, antes de poder tejer el bolso. Había patrones de todo tipo a la venta y también podían extraerse de almanaques y revistas femeninas. Los motivos más frecuentes en la ornamentación de bolsos con cuentas o morrales del siglo XIX eran: flores, templos, lápidas, sauces llorones, arpas, escenas de caza e imágenes de personas de origen chino fumando. Puesto que era una técnica ardua y laboriosa, poseer uno de estos bolsos se consideraba un verdadero lujo.

En las primeras décadas del siglo XX, los bolsos con abalorios se proveían de cordones a modo de asas o se remataban con boquillas decorativas realizadas en metal, carey o plástico. Entre los motivos más populares encontramos flores, paisajes pintorescos con casas tradicionales, castillos y ruinas, niños, tableros históricos y alfombras orientales. Otros bolsos presentan motivos cubistas o *art déco*.

En la década de 1920, los bolsos de mano también se realizaban con cuentas de acero cortado o de aluminio. Al principio, las cuentas de acero cortado sólo se comercializaban en los colores oro, plata o bronce pero, posteriormente, en Francia también se encontraban en otros colores.

Si bien después de 1930, los bolsos con cuentas o abalorios perdieron parte de su importancia, hubo un tipo muy especial de bolso que siguió en boga: el bolso de estilo sobre. Estos bolsos largos, pesados y en forma de caja con relucientes cuentas de color bronce, negro, azul y blanco fueron el último grito en Estados Unidos durante los años cuarenta.

Negli ultimi due secoli, le borsette e i borsellini di perline hanno vissuto alcuni periodi di grande popolarità. All'inizio del XIX secolo, si diffuse molto la difficile arte di lavorare a maglia con le perline. La lavorazione di una borsetta di perline richiedeva a un'esperta due intere settimane di lavoro: infatti occorreva intrecciare più di 50.000 perline nell'ordine preciso indicato dallo schema, senza commettere errori. Si trovavano in vendita diversi tipi di schemi, che venivano pubblicati anche da almanacchi e riviste femminili. Motivi decorativi ricorrenti nelle borse e nei borsellini di perline di questo periodo erano fiori, templi, lapidi funerarie, salici piangenti, arpe, scene di caccia e fumatori di pipa cinesi. Poiché la tecnica di lavorazione era difficile e richiedeva molto tempo, possedere una di queste borsette di perline era considerato un vero lusso.

Nei primi decenni del XX secolo, le borsette di perline erano rifinite con spaghi a scorrimento che fungevano da manico, oppure con cerniere decorative in metallo, in tartaruga o in plastica. Tra i motivi più diffusi c'erano fiori, paesaggi pittoreschi con case tradizionali, castelli e rovine, bambini, scene storiche e tappeti orientali. Vi erano anche borsette di perline decorate con motivi in stile cubista o déco.

Negli anni Venti, si confezionavano anche borsette in perline d'acciaio tagliato o di alluminio. Inizialmente, le perline di acciaio tagliato erano disponibili solo nei colori oro, argento e bronzo, ma in seguito in Francia si iniziò a produrne anche di altri colori.

Dopo il 1930, le borsette di perline persero in parte la loro popolarità. Tuttavia, un tipo particolare di borsette di perline restò in voga ancora per diverso tempo: quelle a busta. Negli Stati Uniti degli anni Trenta, erano in gran voga borse grandi e pesanti a forma d'astuccio fatte di lucenti perline color bronzo, nero, blu e bianco.

Español

Italiano

In den letzten 200 Jahren waren perlenbesetzte Taschen und Beutel zeitweise heiß begehrt. Auch wenn es zu Beginn des 19. Jahrhunderts ein nicht einfaches Unterfangen war mit Perlen zu stricken, waren Perlentaschen ausgesprochen beliebt. Ein geübter Stricker brauchte zwei volle Arbeitswochen, um eine Perlentasche zu vollenden: Mehr als 50.000 Glasperlen mussten – fehlerfrei - in der korrekten Reihenfolge nach Vorlage aufgefädelt werden, bevor die Tasche schließlich gestrickt werden konnte. Die Vorlagen konnte man in großer Vielfalt erwerben oder aus Jahrbüchern und Frauenzeitschriften kopieren. Blumen, Tempel, Grabsteine, Trauerweiden, Harfen, Jagdszenen und rauchende Chinesen schmückten häufig die Perlentäschchen im 19. Jahrhundert. Aufgrund der zeitaufwendigen und mühsamen Herstellung galten diese Taschen als Luxusartikel.

In den ersten Jahrzehnten des 20. Jahrhunderts fertigte man die Perlentaschen mit Ziehschnüren als Henkel oder man nähte sie an einen Taschenbügel aus Metall, Plastik oder Schildpatt. Beliebt waren Blumen und Landschaftsmotive, traditionelle Gebäude, Schlösser oder Ruinen, Kinderdarstellungen, historische Kunstwerke oder orientalische Teppiche. Wieder andere Beutel und Taschen hatten kubistische Motive oder Art-Déco-Verzierungen.

In den 20er Jahren kamen auch Perltäschchen aus Stahl- oder Aluminiumperlen auf den Markt. Die Perlen aus poliertem Stahl gab es anfangs nur in den Farbtönen Gold, Silber und Bronze. Später aber stellte man sie in Frankreich auch in anderen Farben her.

Nach 1930 traten die Perlentaschen mehr und mehr in den Hintergrund. Nur ein ganz bestimmter Taschentyp mit Perlenstickereien blieb noch einige Zeit in Mode: Die Tasche im Briefumschlagstil. Große, schwere, schachtelförmige Taschen mit schimmernden, bronzefarbenen, schwarzen, blauen und weißen Perlen waren in den Vereinigten Staaten der 40er Jahre der letzte Schrei.

過去 200 年間で一時的にビーズ製のバッグやポーチの人気が上昇した期間が幾度かあります。明らかに容易な作業ではありませんでしたが、19 世紀のはじめビーズを用いた編み物が人気となりました。編み物のベテランがビーズバッグを 1 個仕上げるに労働週でまる 2 週間を要しました。5 万個以上のビーズを図柄にあわせて―ビーズ一個一個間違えずに―正確に連ねてからやっとバッグの編みこみ作業に取りかかるのです。豊富な種類の図柄が売り出されていたほか、婦人雑誌の年鑑から図柄を入手することもできました。花、寺院、墓石、枝垂れ柳、狩猟風景、煙草をふかした中国人などが 19 世紀のビーズバッグやポーチの装飾として頻繁に選ばれていました。骨の折れる、そして時間を要する技術でしたので、この種のバッグをひとつ持っているということは真の贅沢と考えられていました。

20 世紀早期の何十年間かはビーズバッグに引き紐を取り付け、それを持ち手として兼用したか、あるいは仕上げに装飾的な金属、べっ甲、プラスチック製の装飾口金を施していました。

20 年代ではハンドバッグはカットスチールやアルミニウムのビーズを使って作られることもありました。カットスチールのビーズははじめゴールド、シルバー、ブロンズの 3 色しかありませんでしたが、後にフランスで他の色も作られるようになります。

1930 年以降、ビーズバッグは人気が低迷してしまいます。しかし、ある種類のビーズバッグだけはその後もしばらく流行し続けました。封筒型のものです。大型で重い箱型のバッグにブロンズ、黒、青、白のビーズきらきらと輝くバッグは 40 年代のアメリカ合衆国で爆発的人気を記録しました。

deutsch

日本語

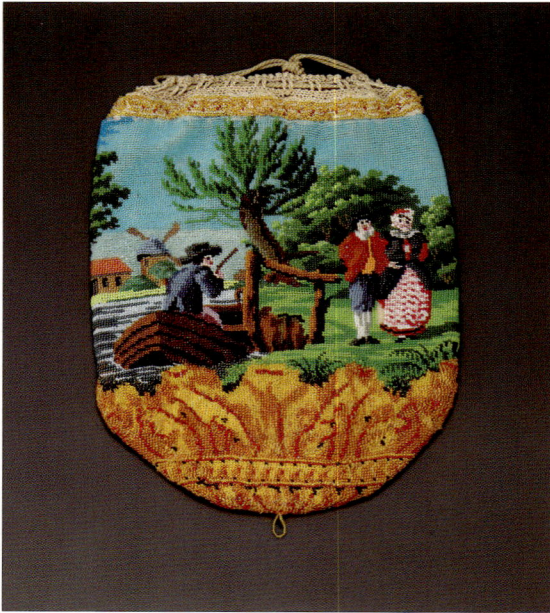

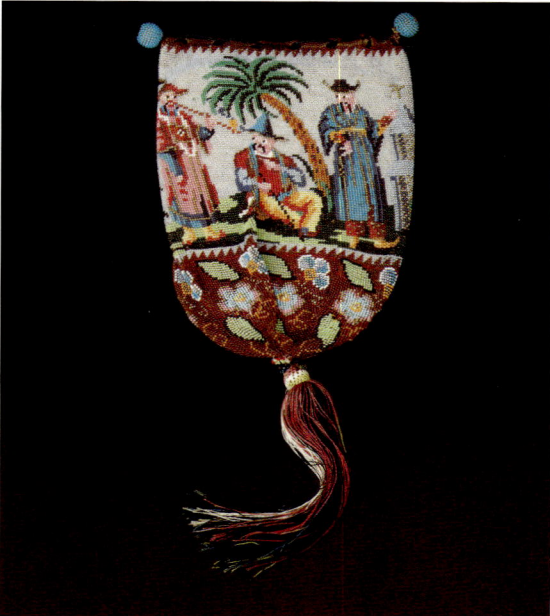

▲ Glass beaded reticule European, 19th c.
▼ Glass beaded tobacco-pouch, probably later used as reticule
European, 19th c.

▲ Glass beaded bag with Indian motifs U.S.A., late 19th c.
▼ Unfinished beaded bag, knitted on five needles
The Netherlands, 19th c.

▲ Glass beaded reticule with text: 'Glück auf' and 'Zum Andenken 1826' Germany, 1826.
▼ Two glass beaded tobacco pouches, probably later used as reticules France, 1820-1850.

▲ Silk reticule partly covered with glass beads, beaded handle and fringes U.S.A., late 19th c.
▼ Cotton reticule embroidered with beads European, ca. 1820.
▶ Glass beaded handbag with 'King of hearts' and imitation tortoise-shell frame and chain European, 1920s.

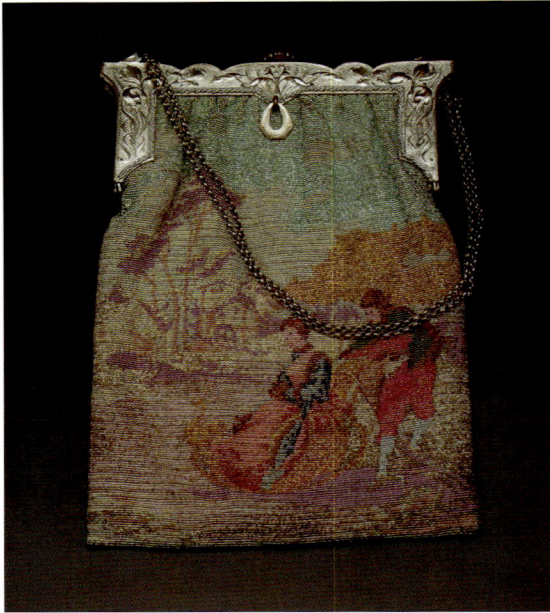

▲ Cut steel beaded handbag with steel frame France, 1920s.
▼ Glass beaded handbag with Venetian motif and brass frame with stone mosaic Italy, 1920s.

▲ Beaded handbag with ornate gilded frame encrusted with glass stones European, 1910s-1920s.
▼ Evening bag with aluminium beads and gold-coloured frame with mother-of-pearl France, 1920s.

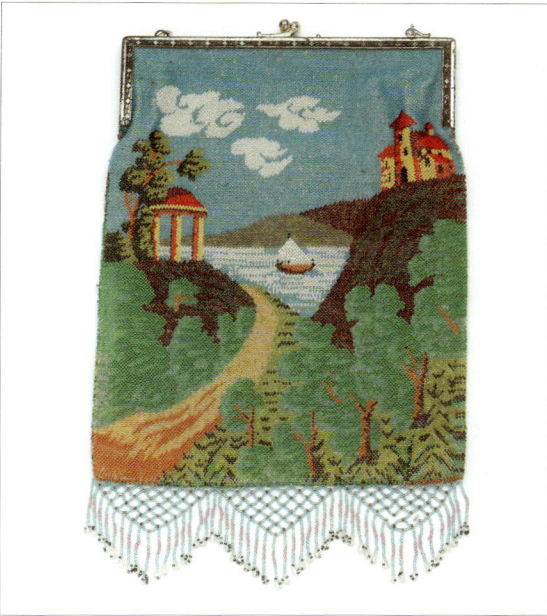

▲ Beaded handbag with silver frame and chain Germany, 1920s.
▼ Beaded handbag with plastic frame and beaded handle
European, 1920s.

▲ Beaded handbag with enameled gold-coloured frame and chain
Germany, 1920s.
▼ Beaded handbag with silver frame and chain
The Netherlands, 1830s.

▲ Beaded handbag with elaborately-shaped plastic frame and link chain France, 1920s.

▼ Black silk pochette with beads European, 1920s.

◄ Beaded handbag with poppy plant, plastic frame with strass and beaded handle Czechoslavakia, 1920s.

▲ Evening bag in blue beads with plastic frame and link chain European, 1920s.

▼ Beaded handbag with plastic frame and beaded handle France, 1920s.

▲ Evening bag with cut steel beads, Egyptian pattern
France, ca. 1923.
▼ Steel beaded handbag with gold-coloured frame and chain,
Metro Bag Works France, 1927.

▲ Glass beaded reticule European, 1920s.
▼ Cut steel beaded handbag France, 1920s.
▶ Glass beaded handbag in carpet motif pattern with gold coloured
frame and chain Germany, 1920s.

▲ Alumimium beaded handbag England, 1927.
▼ Clutch bag with black silk, partly covered with red and black beads, Gerzon The Netherlands, 1930s.

▲ Evening bag in blue- and pearl-coloured beads with silver frame and chain Belgium, 1930s.
▼ Clutch evening bag with black and white glass beads European, 1930s.

▲ Alumimium beaded handbag England, ca. 1927.

▲ Glass beaded bag with bead-covered frame France, 1950s.
▼ Two evening bags with beads and silver-, gold- and pearl-coloured sequins European, 1930s.

▲ Glass beaded handbag with bead-covered frame, Winifred Peniston, Bermuda France, 1950s-1960s.
▼ Glass beaded bag, partly with petit point and metal frame France, 1930s.

▲ Beaded handbag with gold-coloured frame and beaded handle
Belgium, 1950s.

▲ Glass beaded box-shaped handbag with beaded handle
U.S.A., 1940s.
▼ Evening bag with zipper and matching wallet in pearl-coloured
beads Germany, 1930s.
◄ Beaded evening bag with beaded handle Belgium, 1940s-1950s.

▲ Evening bag with white and pearl-coloured beads and gold-
coloured frame France, 1960s.
▼ Silk clutch bag with glass beads and sequins Hong Kong, 1970s.

Petit-point, lace and cloth

Petit point, dentelle et toile

Petit-point, kant en textiel

Petit-point, encajes y tela

Piccolo punto, pizzo e stoffa

Petit-Point, Spitze und Stoff

プチポワン刺繍、レース、布

Until the nineteenth century, fine needlework was performed not only by women as a home industry, but also by professional embroiderers. Partly due to technological developments, the variety of needlework techniques increased sharply. Although less very fine needlework was done at that time, there were many techniques for making reticules, such as Berlin woolwork, blackwork, lace, weaving, embroidery, crocheting and knitting.

One of the techniques still used today in the manufacture of handbags is petit point: embroidery in half cross-stitch on canvas. Petit point became popular in the nineteenth century due to the use of coloured grid patterns, in which each grid cell stood for a stitch. These patterns were also used for other needlework techniques. The technique was so simple that both professional embroiderers and women at home used them. Paris and Vienna were the most important centres for professional petit-point bags. Depictions of animals, flowers and people are often seen on petit-point bags.

Another needlework technique that has been around for a long time is lace making. Little bridal bags or communion bags were often made of white lace. Irish needlework technique is also used for this kind of bag. There are also white lace bags that have most likely been used as evening bags. Due to the delicate nature of the material, lace bags are not often found.

Printing on cloth is a technique that was employed quite frequently in the twentieth century, also in the production of bags.

English

Jusqu'au cours du dix-neuvième siècle, les travaux d'aiguille délicats n'étaient pas uniquement l'apanage des femmes au foyer car des brodeurs professionnels exerçaient aussi. Grâce, entre autres, aux progrès techniques, les méthodes se sont grandement diversifiées : les travaux d'aiguille très raffinés se sont réduits à cette époque, alors que les techniques de fabrication des réticules y sont nombreuses, comme la broderie de laine, le blackwork (broderie contrastée), la dentelle, le tissage, la broderie, le crochet ou le tricot.

L'une de ces techniques sert aujourd'hui encore à la confection de sacs à main, à savoir le petit point ou broderie sur canevas. Le petit point perce au dix-neuvième siècle avec l'emploi de canevas aux motifs colorés dont chaque trou de la grille représente un point. Ces canevas étaient aussi utilisés pour d'autres travaux d'aiguille, avec une technique si simple qu'elle était employée autant dans les maisons que par les brodeurs professionnels. Paris et Vienne étaient alors les principaux centres de sacs au petit point, dont la plupart portent des représentations d'animaux, fleurs et de figures humaines.

Autre technique d'aiguille très ancienne, la dentelle (notamment blanche) a été amplement utilisée pour les petites bourses de mariage ou de communion (également confectionnées en dentelle irlandaise). On trouve aussi des sacs de soirée en dentelle blanche, même si leur fragilité fait qu'ils sont rares et difficiles à trouver.

L'impression sur tissu est une technique également employée au vingtième siècle et se retrouve dans la production de sacs.

Het fijne handwerk werd tot in de negentiende eeuw door vrouwen in huisvlijt uitgevoerd, maar ook door professionele borduurders. Mede door technologische ontwikkelingen nam de variatie in handwerktechnieken snel toe. Hoewel het zeer fijne handwerk in die tijd steeds minder gedaan werd, waren er vele technieken voor het maken van reticules, zoals Berlijns wolwerk, blackwork, kant, weven, borduren, haken en breien.

Een van de technieken die tegenwoordig bij de fabricage van tassen nog steeds worden gebruikt, is petit-point: met halve kruissteken op stramien borduren. *Petit-point* werd in de negentiende eeuw populair door het gebruik van gekleurde ruitjespatronen, waarbij ieder ruitje stond voor een steek. Deze patronen werden ook voor andere handwerktechnieken benut. De techniek was zo eenvoudig, dat zowel professionele borduurders als vrouwen thuis er gebruik van maakten. Parijs en Wenen waren de belangrijkste centra voor professionele petit-point-tassen. Men ziet op petit-point-tassen vaak voor-stellingen van dieren, bloemen en mensen.

Een andere handwerktechniek die al lang bestaat, is het maken van kant. Vaak werden bruidstasjes of communietasjes van wit kant gemaakt. Ook de Ierse haakwerktechniek werd bij dit soort tasjes toegepast. Daarnaast kennen we tasjes van wit kant die hoogst-waarschijnlijk als avondtasjes gediend hebben. Gezien de kwetsbaarheid van het materiaal komen kanten tasjes niet veel voor.

Het bedrukken van stof is een techniek die in de twintigste eeuw veel werd toegepast, ook bij de productie van tassen.

Hasta el siglo XIX, las labores de costura eran realizadas no sólo por mujeres en el ámbito de la industria casera sino también por profesionales del bordado. En parte como resultado de los avances técnicos, la variedad de técnicas de costura aumentó de forma espectacular. A pesar de que en aquella época se realizaba una menor cantidad de labores de costura delicadas, existían muchas técnicas para confeccionar retículas, como la técnica berlinesa, los bordados negros, las puntillas, el tejido, el bordado, el ganchillo y el punto de media.

Una de las técnicas que se siguen empleando hoy en día en la producción de bolsos de mano es el *petit-point*, el bordado sobre lona. Esta técnica se difundió en el siglo XIX debido al uso de patrones de rejilla coloreados, en los que cada cuadrado de la rejilla representaba un punto. Estos patrones también se utilizaban para aplicar otras técnicas de costura. Era una técnica tan sencilla que podían usarla tanto los profesionales de la costura como las mujeres en sus casas. París y Viena eran los centros más importantes de producción profesional de bolsos realizados en *petit-point*. En ellos abundan los motivos de animales y plantas, y también se representaban personas.

Otra técnica de costura que ha perdurado durante largo tiempo son los encajes. Era frecuente confeccionar pequeños bolsos nupciales o de comunión con puntillas blancas. Para este tipo de bolsos también solía utilizarse la técnica de costura irlandesa. Existen asimismo algunos bolsos hechos con encajes blancos que probablemente se usaran como bolsos de noche. Debido a la delicada naturaleza del material, encontramos pocos ejemplos de estos bolsos.

La impresión sobre tela es una técnica que se difundió ampliamente en el siglo XX, también en la producción de bolsos.

Fino al XIX secolo, il ricamo a mano non era solo un'attività casalinga che impegnava le donne comuni, ma veniva eseguito anche da ricamatrici professioniste. In seguito, la varietà delle tecniche di ricamo aumentò notevolmente, anche grazie al progresso tecnologico. Anche se in quest'epoca il ricamo a mano veniva praticato molto meno, vi erano molte tecniche utilizzate per confezionare *reticule*: ricamo berlinese, *blackwork*, pizzo o merletto, tessitura, ricamo, uncinetto e maglia. Una delle tecniche che vengono ancora oggi utilizzate nella fabbricazione di borsette è il piccolo punto, un ricamo a fili contati eseguito su tela che divenne popolare nel XIX secolo, quando si diffusero schemi a colori tracciati su carta quadrettata, in cui a ogni quadretto corrispondeva un punto. Questo tipo di schemi veniva usato anche per altre tecniche di ricamo. Il piccolo punto era talmente semplice che veniva impiegato sia dalle ricamatrici professioniste, sia dalle donne di casa. Parigi e Vienna divennero i maggiori centri della manifattura professionale di borse a piccolo punto, spesso decorate con motivi che riproducevano animali, fiori e persone.

Un'altra tecnica antichissima è il pizzo o merletto. Spesso, le borsette da sposa o quelle portate dalle comunicande erano fatte di pizzo bianco. Per questo tipo di borse si utilizza anche il pizzo irlandese. Esistono anche borsette di pizzo bianco che probabilmente sono state utilizzate come borsette da sera. Tuttavia, è raro trovare borsette di pizzo, perché si tratta di un materiale molto delicato. La stampa su tessuto è una tecnica utilizzata molto spesso nel XX secolo, anche nella produzione di borsette.

Español   Italiano

Bis ins 19. Jahrhundert wurde die Handarbeit nicht nur von Hausfrauen in Hausarbeit, sondern auch von professionellen Nähern und Stickern ausgeführt. Dank der technischen Neuerungen entstanden immer mehr neue Handarbeitstechniken. Auch wenn allerfeinste Handarbeiten immer weniger ausgeführt wurden, gab es viele Techniken zur Herstellung der Retikül-Handtaschen, sowie zum Beispiel Berliner Wollstickerei, Schwarzstickerei, Spitzenstickerei, Weberei, Stickerei, Häkeln und Stricken.

Eine der Techniken, die bis heute für die Herstellung von Damenhandtaschen in Gebrauch sind, ist die Petit-Point-Stickerei, d.h. Stickerei in halben Kreuzstichen auf Stramin. Diese Handarbeitstechnik wurde im 19. Jahrhundert populär, als auf Karopapier gedruckte Stickvorlagen erschienen, bei denen jedes Karo einen Stich bedeutete. Diese Vorlagen wurden auch für andere Handarbeitstechniken benutzt.

Die Techniken waren so einfach, dass sie nicht nur von professionellen Arbeiterinnen, sondern auch oft von Hausfrauen ausgeführt wurden. Paris und Wien waren die wichtigsten Städte für die Herstellung von Täschchen aus Petit-Point-Stickerei. Besonders häufig wurden Pflanzen, Tiere oder Menschen dargestellt.

Eine weitere Handarbeitstechnik, die sich großer Beliebtheit bei der Taschenherstellung erfreute, war die Spitzentechnik. Kleine Brauttäschchen, oder Kommunionsbeutel wurden häufig aus feiner, weißer Spitze angefertigt. Oft wird auch die sogenannte Irish-Needlework-Technik zur Herstellung dieser Taschen benutzt. Es gab auch weiße Spitzentaschen, die höchstwahrscheinlich zur Abendgarderobe getragen wurden. Aufgrund des sehr empfindlichen Materials sind jedoch nicht allzu viele Spitzentaschen erhalten geblieben.

Der Stoffdruck ist eine Technik, die im 20. Jahrhundert häufig angewendet wurde, so auch bei der Herstellung von Taschen.

19 世紀のはじめまで見事な手芸作品には家内工業として女性が携わったばかりでなく、専門の手芸職人によっても行われていました。技術発展が加担してか、多種多様な手芸技術が急激に増えました。当時、素晴しさという面で少々劣るような手芸も行われていましたが、レティキュールを作るための多くの技術が存在し、ベルリン毛糸刺繍、黒糸刺繍、レース、編みこみ、刺繍、かぎ針編み、編み物などがそれに当たります。

前述の技術のうちひとつは、現在でもハンドバッグの製造に使われています。プチポワン刺繍です。キャンバス地に施す刺繍です。プチポワンは 19 世紀に人気が出た刺繍で、格子目が縫い目になるように付けられた色つきの格子柄が人気の発端となりました。これらの格子柄は他の手芸技術にも利用されました。この手法はとても簡単だったため、専門の刺繍職人と家庭の女性たちの両者が利用していました。パリとウィーンが専門職によるプチポワンバッグにとって重要な中心都市でした。動物や花の肖像などがしばしばプチポワンバッグにあしらわれていました。

もうひとつ手芸技術で息の長いものがレース製作です。小さな婚礼バッグや親交バッグがよく白いレースで作られました。アイルランドの手芸技術もまたこの種のバッグ作製に応用されました。白のレース製バッグの中には、ほぼ間違いなくイブニングバッグとして使われていたと思われるものもあります。素材が繊細であることから、レース製のバッグにお目にかかれる機会はそう頻繁にはありません。

布にプリントを施す技術は 20 世紀にわりと頻繁に応用され、バッグ製造の際にも応用されました。

deutsch   日本語

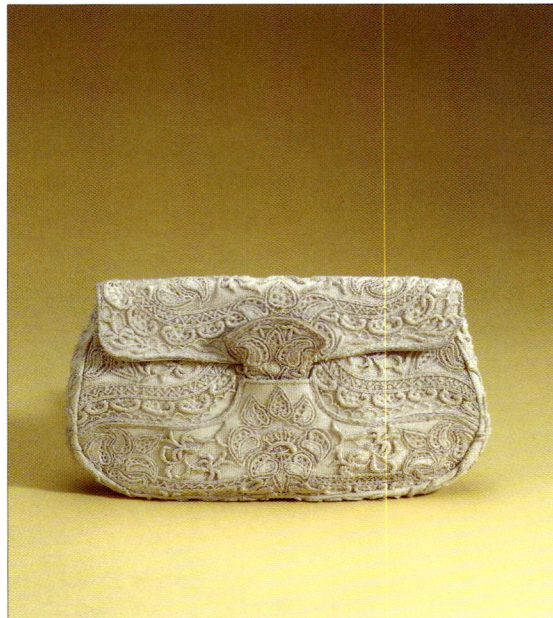

▲ Machine-made lace handbag, silver frame with strass, Mayer
France, 1920s.
▼ Bridal purse of Maltese lace and three bobbins European, 1910s.

▲ Irish crochet handbag with crocheted tassels European, 1910s.
▼ Brussels lace pochette, Mayer France, 1920-1940.
▶ Silk communion chatelaine bag with embroidery France,
late 19th c.

▲ Petit point handbag, silver frame with carnelians Austria, 1920s.
▼ Handbag with silk embroidery, brass frame with inlay
European, 1920s.

▲ Petit point handbag, brass frame with imitation pearls and enamel
France, 1920-1930.
▼ Petit point handbag, brass frame with coral in silver setting
Austria, 1920s.

▲ Petit point handbag, hammered silver frame by Sybil Dunlop with
glass stones England, ca. 1925.

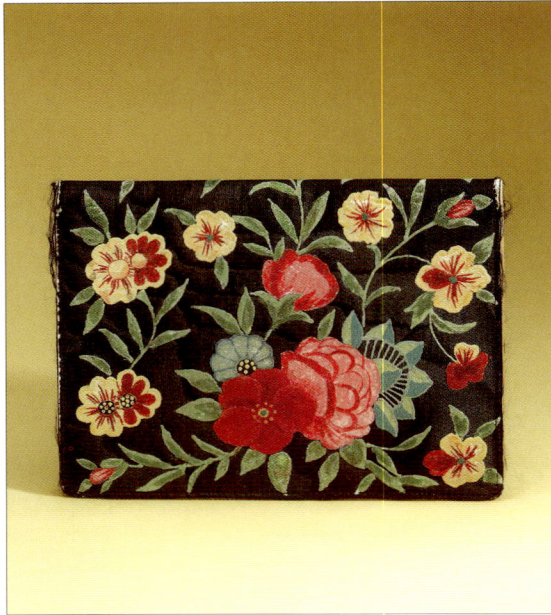

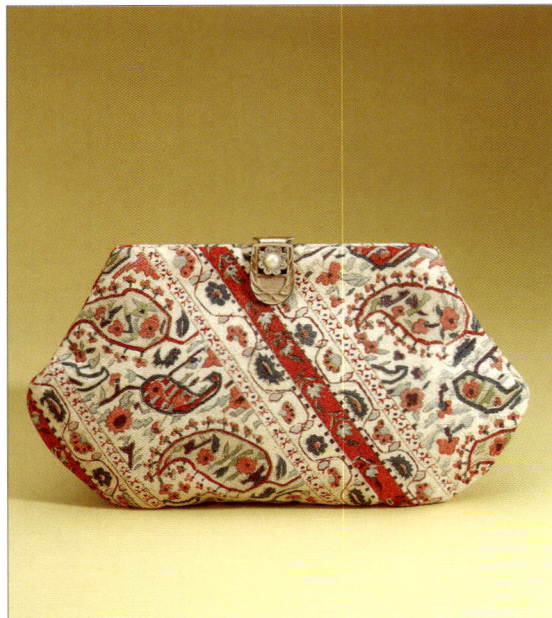

▲ Silk pochette embroidered with Chinese scene England, 1934.
▼ Fabric pochette, brass clasp with imitation pearl European, 1920s-1930s.

▲ Moiré silk handbag handpainted with granular paint France, 1930s.
▼ Fabric pochette with embroidery, chrome frame France, 1925-1935.

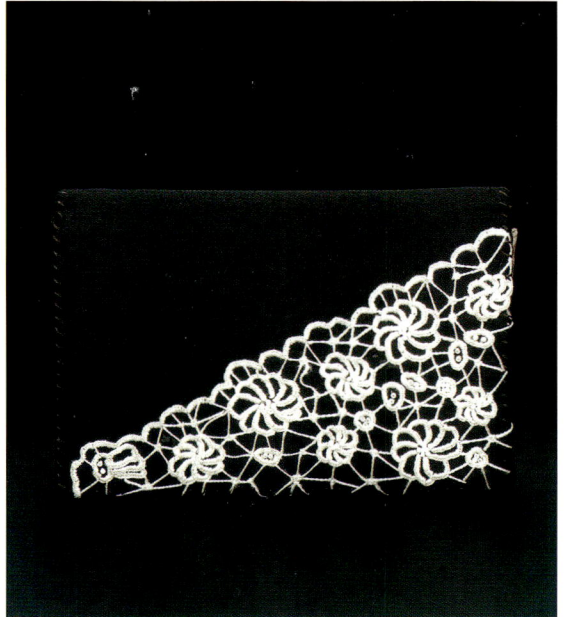

▲ Fabric pochette European, 1920s.
▼ Moiré silk pochette embroidered with silk and gilt thread
France, 1920s.

▲ Moiré silk handbag with embroidery France, 1920s.
▼ Leather pochette with crocheted silk and bead decoration
Germany, 1920s.

▲ Brass box bag with velvet decoration, Lou Taylor U.S.A., 1950s.
▼ Petit point handbag, Maison de Bonneterie Austria, 1950-1975.

▲ Printed velvet handbag with brass frame France, 1960s.
▶ Two velvet handbags with leather lining England, 1880s.

▲ Crocheted handbag with perspex handles France, 1940s.

▲ Silk handbag woven in the Japanese Saga-Nishiki technique
The Netherlands, 1968-1971.

Metal and ring mesh

Métal et mailles

Metaal en maliën

El metal y la malla de aros

Maglia metallica e ad anelli

Metall- und Netztaschen

金属とリングメッシュ

Starting at the end of the nineteenth century, bags and purses made of metal were highly popular, especially silver and ring mesh. Ring mesh consists of little metal rings or plates linked to each other to form a web, like in the chain mail coats of medieval knights. Ring mesh bags were expensive because the rings were attached to each other one by one. They were often made of silver, but silver-plated and other metal versions also appeared. Jewellers and accessory firms specialised in the construction of the ring mesh bags and purses. Germany and the United States were major producers. From 1909 onward, ring mesh bags became considerably cheaper due to the invention (by the American, A.C. Pratt) of a machine for manufacturing ring mesh. Another American company, Whiting & Davis, acquired the patent and became the best known company in the world in this field. They manufactured bags designed by well-known fashion designers such as Paul Poiret and Elsa Schiaparelli. Starting in 1918, Whiting & Davis sold bags made of so-called Dresden ring mesh, extraordinarily fine ring mesh named after the designer of this material, who lived in Germany. By enamelling the little plates or rings in various colours, in the twenties and thirties multi-coloured images were made that fitted in well with the prevailing Art Deco style. At present, the company still sells ring mesh bags, fashion accessories and clothing.

Another American company that was famous in the interwar years for its ring mesh bags was the Mandalian company. The founder Sahatiel G. Mandalian was of Turkish descent, which perhaps explains the subtle oriental influence in his bags.

English

À partir de la fin du dix-neuvième siècle, les sacs et bourses de métal deviennent très populaires, notamment ceux en maille d'argent et d'or. Le maillage consiste en de petits anneaux ou morceaux de métal reliés les uns aux autres pour former un entrelacs rappelant les cottes de mailles des chevaliers du Moyen Âge. Les sacs en maille coûtaient chers car les anneaux devaient être attachés un par un. Ils étaient souvent en argent, même s'il existe des versions en plaqué argent et autres métaux. Plusieurs bijoutiers et fabricants d'accessoires étaient spécialisés dans la fabrication de sacs et porte-monnaie en maille, avec les États-Unis et l'Allemagne en tête pour la production.

À partir de 1909, le prix des sacs en maille diminue grâce à l'invention (par l'Américain A.C. Pratt) d'une machine permettant la réalisation du maillage. Une autre société américaine, Whiting & Davis, acquiert le brevet et s'impose au niveau mondial dans ce domaine. Elle fabriquera des sacs conçus par de célèbres créateurs de mode comme Paul Poiret et Elsa Schiaparelli. À partir de 1918, Whiting & Davis vend des sacs en maille dite de Dresde, exceptionnellement fine et baptiséenommées d'après son créateur qui vivait en Allemagne. Par la suite, dans les années vingt et trente, l'émaillage en différentes couleurs des petites plaques ou anneaux permet d'obtenir des images multicolores en accord avec le style art déco du moment. Aujourd'hui, l'entreprise vend des sacs, des accessoires de mode et des vêtements en maille.

Une autre entreprise américaine était célèbre pour ses sacs en maille pendant l'entre-deux-guerres. La subtile influence orientale des sacs de Mandalian, dont le fondateur, Sahatiel G. Mandalian, était d'origine turque, s'explique peut-être par l'origine turque de son fondateur, Sahatiel G. Mandalian.

Vanaf het einde van de negentiende eeuw waren tassen en beurzen van metaal bijzonder populair, vooral zilver en maliën. Maliën zijn metalen ringetjes of plaatjes die met elkaar verbonden zijn tot een netwerk, zoals in de maliënkolders van middeleeuwse ridders. De maliëntassen waren kostbaar, doordat de ringetjes één voor één aan elkaar werden gezet. Vaak waren ze van zilver, maar ook verzilverde en andere metalen uitvoeringen kwamen voor. Juweliers en sieradenfirma's specialiseerden zich in de vervaardiging van de maliëntassen en -beursjes. Duitsland en Verenigde Staten waren belangrijke producenten.

Vanaf 1909 werden maliëntassen aanzienlijk goedkoper door de uitvinding (door de Amerikaan A.C. Pratt) van een machine voor de productie van maliën. De eveneens Amerikaanse firma Whiting & Davis verwierf de patenten en werd wereldwijd het bekendste bedrijf op dit gebied. Ze liet tassen ontwerpen door bekende modeontwerpers als Paul Poiret en Elsa Schiaparelli. Vanaf 1918 verkocht Whiting & Davis tassen van zogeheten Dresden-maliën: buitengewoon fijne maliën, genoemd naar de in Duitsland woonachtige ontwerper van dit materiaal. Door de kleine plaatjes of ringetjes in verschillende kleuren te emailleren, konden in de jaren twintig en dertig veelkleurige voorstellingen worden gemaakt die goed pasten in de populaire Art Deco-stijl. Tegenwoordig verkoopt het bedrijf nog steeds tassen, modeaccessoires en kleding van maliën.

Een ander Amerikaanse bedrijf dat in het interbellum beroemd was om zijn maliëntassen, was de firma Mandalian. De oprichter Sahatiel G. Mandalian was van Turkse afkomst, wat misschien de subtiele oosterse invloed in zijn tassen verklaart.

Ya a finales del siglo XIX, los bolsos y monederos realizados en metal gozaban de gran aceptación, sobre todo los de plata y malla de aros. La malla de aros está formada por pequeños aros metálicos unidos los unos a los otros para formar una especie de red, como ocurre en la cota de malla de los caballeros medievales. Los bolsos confeccionados con malla de aros resultaban caros porque los aros debían unirse entre sí uno a uno. A menudo se realizaban en plata, pero también aparecieron versiones chapadas en plata y otros metales. Hubo joyeros y empresas de accesorios que se especializaron en la construcción de bolsos y monederos de malla de aros. Entre los mayores productores se encuentran Alemania y Estados Unidos. A partir de 1909, los bolsos de malla de aros se volvieron bastante asequibles gracias al invento (por parte del estadounidense A. C. Pratt) de una máquina que producía la malla. Otra empresa americana, Whiting & Davis, adquirió la patente y se convirtió en la empresa más célebre en este campo a nivel mundial. Producía bolsos creados por célebres diseñadores de moda de la talla de Paul Poiret y Elsa Schiaparelli. En 1918, Whiting & Davis comenzó a vender bolsos confeccionados con malla de aros de Dresde, una malla extraordinariamente fina, bautizada así porque quien la diseñó vivía en esta ciudad alemana. Esmaltando las pequeñas planchas o aros de diversos colores, en los años veinte y treinta se realizaron imágenes multicolor que encajaban bien con la corriente del momento, el *art déco*. En la actualidad, esta empresa sigue vendiendo bolsos de malla de aros, accesorios de moda y ropa.

Otra empresa estadounidense famosa en los años de entreguerras por sus bolsos de malla de aros era Mandalian. Su fundador, Sahatiel G. Mandalian, era de ascendencia turca, lo cual puede explicar los sutiles resabios orientales que presentan sus bolsos.

A partire dalla fine del XIX secolo, divennero popolarissime le borse e i borsellini in metallo, soprattutto in maglia d'argento e in maglia ad anelli. La maglia ad anelli è formata da anelli o placchette di metallo fissati gli uni agli altri a formare una rete simile a quella delle cotte di maglia dei cavalieri medievali. Questo tipo di maglia era costosa, perché gli anelli dovevano venir fissati uno per uno. Spesso gli anelli erano d'argento, ma ne esistevano anche di placcati d'argento e di altri metalli. Le gioiellerie e i produttori di accessori si specializzarono nella fabbricazione di borse e borsellini in maglia ad anelli, di cui i maggiori produttori erano la Germania e gli Stati Uniti.

Dal 1909 in poi, le borsette in maglia ad anelli divennero molto più economiche, grazie all'invenzione di una macchina (ideata dall'americano A. C. Pratt) che fabbricava questo tipo di materiale. Una ditta americana, la Whiting & Davis, ne acquistò il brevetto e divenne la più famosa produttrice del mondo in questo campo, fabbricando borsette disegnate da famosi stilisti come Paul Poiret ed Elsa Schiaparelli. A partire dal 1918, la Whiting & Davis mise in vendita borsette fabbricate con la cosiddetta *Dresden mesh*, una maglia ad anelli finissima che prendeva il nome dalla città tedesca di Dresda, in cui viveva il suo inventore. Ricoprendo in smalto di diversi colori le piccole placche o gli anelli, negli anni Venti e Trenta si produssero borsette con decorazioni multicolori che ben si accordavano con il prevalente stile déco. La Whiting & Davis vende ancor oggi borsette, accessori moda e abiti in maglia ad anelli.

Un'altra società americana che divenne famosa per le sue borsette in maglia ad anelli nel periodo compreso tra le due guerre mondiali era la Mandalian. Il suo fondatore, Sahatiel G. Mandalian, era di origini turche, fatto che forse può spiegare la leggera influenza orientale riscontrabile nei suoi prodotti.

Español

Italiano

Seit dem ausklingenden 19. Jahrhundert waren Taschen und Beutel aus Metall, vor allem aus Silber und Metallnetzen, ausgesprochen beliebt. Gefertigt wurden sie aus Ringmaschen, d.h. kleinen Ringe oder platten Ösen, die zu einem Maschengewebe ineinander gehängt werden – etwas so wie die metallenen Maschenhemden der mittelalterlichen Ritter. Solche Metallnetztaschen waren sehr teuer, da alle Ringe einzeln, Ring für Ring, ineinander eingehängt werden mussten. Häufig wurden diese Taschen aus Silber, aus versilberten Materialien oder auch aus anderen Metallen angefertigt. Es gab Juweliere und Accessoirefirmen, die sich auf die Herstellung solcher Netzgitter für Taschen und Beutel spezialisiert hatten. Deutschland und die Vereinigten Staaten gehörten zu den führenden Herstellungsländern. Ab dem Jahre 1909 wurden die Metallnetztaschen deutlich billiger, da man in Amerika (A.C. Pratt) eine Maschine zur Produktion der Maschengewebe erfunden hatte. Eine andere amerikanische Firma, Whiting & Davis, erwarb das Patent und wurde zur angesehensten Firma weltweit in dieser Branche. Es gab Taschen, die von berühmten Modedesignern, wie Paul Poiret oder Elsa Schiaparelli, entworfen wurden. Ab 1918 entwickelte die Firma Whiting & Davis Taschen aus dem sogenannten Dresdner Metallnetz. Dies war ein außerordentlich feines Maschengewebe, benannt nach dem Designer dieses Materials, der in Deutschland wohnte. Indem man die winzigen Ringe des Gewebes in verschiedenen Farben emaillierte, konnten passend zur Art-Déko-Mode der 20er und 30er Jahre bunte Motive auf den Taschen angebracht werden. Heute verkauft die Firma noch immer Metallnetztaschen, sowie Accessoires und Bekleidung.

Eine weitere amerikanische Firma war in den Jahren zwischen den Kriegen mit ihrer Produktion von Metallnetztaschen berühmt geworden: Die Mandalian Company. Ihr Gründer Sahatiel G. Mandalian war türkischer Herkunft, was vielleicht die etwas orientalische Note seiner Taschen erklärt.

19 世紀の終わりから、金属製のバッグやパースに対する人気の高まりが始まり、とりわけ銀製とリングメッシュが流行ります。小さな金属のリングまたはプレートを組み合わせて網を構成するリングメッシュはまるで中世の騎士がまとうくさび帷子のようです。リングメッシュはリングをひとつひとつ組み合わせていくため高価なものでした。しばしば銀でできていましたが銀メッキ製や他の金属製のものも登場しました。宝石商やアクセサリー会社が専門にリングメッシュのバッグやパースの製作を手がけました。主要な生産国はドイツやアメリカ合衆国でした。

1909 年以降、リングメッシュのバッグはリングメッシュ製作機が発明されたことから価格が大幅に下がります。発明した会社とは別のホワイティング＆デイビス（Whiting & Davis）という会社が特許を取得し、一躍この分野では世界的に最も有名な会社になります。この会社ではポール・ポワレやエルザ・スキャパレリなどの有名デザイナーがデザインを手がけたバッグを製造していました。

小さなリングやプレートをエナメルでさまざまに着色されることで、20 年代、30 年代には多彩な風貌を演出し、広く普及していたアールデコ様式によくマッチしました。

戦争のあい間にリングメッシュのバッグ製造で有名だったもうひとつの会社にマンダリアン社があります。創設者のサハティエル G. マンダリアンはトルコ家系に生まれた人で、彼が製造したバッグにどことなくオリエンタルの影響が漂っているのはここからきているのでしょう。

deutsch   日本語

▲ Mesh handbag designed by Elsa Schiaparelli for Whiting & Davis
U.S.A., 1936-1937.
▼ Leather handbag with silver cover showing flower and leaves
Russia, 1908-1917.

▲ Compact bag with powderbox in lid, Evans U.S.A., 1940-1950.
▼ Silver finger case with notebook and pencil England, 1919.

▲ Silver ring mesh handbag with mirror, notebook and perfume bottle Germany, 1900-1910.
▼ Silver cigarette case decorated as envelop with enamel stamp, Georg Adam Scheid Austria, 1892.

▲▶ Silver ring mesh handbag with ivory ring to open and close Germany, 1910s.
▼ Leather handbag with silver cover showing spider in web Russia, 1908-1917.

▲ Dresden mesh handbag with enamel frame U.S.A., 1920s.
▼ Mesh handbag with silver frame, Mandalian U.S.A., 1920s.
◀ Silver mesh handbag with silver frame, Georg Adam Scheid
Austria, ca. 1900.

▲ Dresden mesh handbag, Whiting & Davis U.S.A., 1920s.
▶ Mesh handbag with vanity case, Whiting & Davis U.S.A., 1920s.

Plastic

Plastique

Kunststof

Plásticos

Plastica

Kunststoff

プラスチック

At first, plastics were used to imitate expensive tortoise-shell and ivory bag frames. They appeared in around 1919 and remained in fashion until about 1930. These semicircular plastic bag frames were flat or decorated with historical, romantic, oriental or Egyptian motifs. Initially they were only made from celluloid and casein, but from 1927 onwards they were also made from cellulose acetate.

At the beginning of the thirties, handbags and clutches appeared that were completely made of plastic. Plastic was no longer used in imitation of tortoiseshell and ivory but valued for its contemporary rigid lustre. These plastic bags stayed popular until the war. A beautiful example is the set of celluloid pochettes from 1937 in pastel shades of pink, blue and green.

In the thirties, many new plastics were invented which had many more possible applications. In the forties and fifties, they were so popular that bags were made from plastic beads, telephone wires and small tiles. In the United States in the fifties, plastic handbags dominated the fashion scene for more than a decade. These bags are box-shaped and made from hard plastic. Transparent as glass, made from Lucite (Perspex or Plexiglas) or in intense colours and decorated with strass, they were expensive bags at first. But they quickly became so popular that cheaper, lower quality versions were sold everywhere. With the arrival of softer plastics like vinyl, heavy, hard plastic handbags lost their popularity.

English

Le plastique a d'abord été utilisé pour imiter les fermoirs plus coûteux de sacs en écaille ou ivoire. Les matières plastiques sont apparues vers 1919 et sont restées à la mode jusque vers 1930. Les fermoirs semi-circulaires en plastique étaient mats ou décorés de motifs historiques, romantiques, orientaux ou égyptiens. D'abord uniquement en celluloïd et caséine, ils ont vu l'acétate de cellulose faire son entrée en 1927.

Au début des années trente, des sacs et pochettes entièrement en plastique apparaissent. Le plastique n'est plus désormais utilisé pour imiter l'écaille ou l'ivoire, mais pour son éclat moderne et sa rigidité. Ces sacs resteront à la mode jusqu'à la Guerre, comme c'est le cas de la série de pochettes en celluloïd de 1937 dans des tons pastel de rose, bleu et vert.

Dans les années trente, de nombreux autres plastiques sont inventés et offrent des possibilités multiples d'applications. Dans les années quarante et cinquante, ils sont si populaires que des sacs sont fabriqués en perles de plastique, câbles de téléphone et petits carreaux. En plastique rigide moulé en forme de boîte, les sacs à main domineront la scène de la mode américaine des années cinquante pendant plus d'une décennie. Aussi transparents que le verre, en lucite (perspex ou plexiglas) ou aux couleurs vives et décorés de strass, ils seront tout d'abord chers, pour rapidement devenir si populaires que des versions plus abordables et de qualité moindre proliféreront. Les lourds sacs à main en plastique rigide perdront les faveurs du public avec l'arrivée des plastiques plus mous comme le vinyle.

Kunststoffen werden in eerste instantie gebruikt ter imitatie van de dure tasbeugels van schildpad en ivoor. Ze verschenen rond 1919 en bleven tot circa 1930 in de mode. Deze halfronde kunststoftasbeugels waren vlak of versierd met historische, romantische, oosterse of Egyptische motieven. Aanvankelijk werden ze alleen van celluloid en caseïne gemaakt, maar vanaf 1927 ook van celluloseacetaat.

Begin jaren dertig verschenen hand- en onderarm-tassen die volledig vervaardigd waren van kunststof. Kunststof werd niet langer als imitatie van schildpad en ivoor gebruikt, maar men waardeerde het om zijn eigentijdse strakke uitstraling. Deze kunststoftassen bleven tot de oorlog populair. Een mooi voorbeeld hiervan is de serie onderarmtassen van celluloid in de pasteltinten roze, blauw en groen uit 1937.

In de jaren dertig werden vele nieuwe kunststoffen uitgevonden, die veel meer toepassingsmogelijkheden hadden. In de jaren veertig en vijftig waren ze zo populair, dat men tassen vervaardigde van kunststof kralen, telefoondraden en kleine tegels. In de Verenigde Staten domineerden kunststoftassen vanaf de jaren vijftig meer dan tien jaar lang het modebeeld. Deze tassen zijn doosvormig en gemaakt van harde kunststof. Doorzichtig als glas, van lucite (perspex of plexiglas), of in felle kleuren, versierd met stras, waren het in eerste instantie dure tassen. Al snel waren ze zo populair, dat goedkopere uitvoeringen van mindere kwaliteit overal te koop waren. Met de komst van zachtere kunststoffen als vinyl verloren de tassen van zwaar, hard plastic hun populariteit.

français

nederlands

Al principio, el plástico se utilizaba para imitar las costosas boquillas de carey y marfil de que se dotaban los bolsos. Las boquillas realizadas con este nuevo material aparecieron hacia 1919 y estuvieron de moda hasta aproximadamente 1930. Estas boquillas de bolso semicirculares de plástico eran planas o estaban decoradas con motivos históricos, románticos, orientales o egipcios. Al principio sólo se realizaban en celuloide y caseína, pero a partir de 1927 también se realizaron en acetato de celulosa.

A principio de la década de 1930, aparecieron bolsos de mano realizados íntegramente en plástico. Este material ya no se utilizaba para imitar el carey o el marfil, sino que se apreciaba por su lustre rígido y contemporáneo. Los bolsos de este tipo siguieron de moda hasta la Segunda Guerra Mundial. Constituye un bonito ejemplo el conjunto de *pochettes* de celuloide de 1937 en tonos rosas, azules y verdes pastel.

En la década de 1930 se inventaron numerosos plásticos con incontables posibilidades de aplicación. En las dos décadas siguientes, su uso se había difundido de tal manera que se elaboraron bolsos realizados con cuentas de plástico, cable de teléfono y pequeños azulejos. En la década de 1950, en Estados Unidos los bolsos de plástico dominaron el mundo de la moda durante más de una década. Estos bolsos tienen forma de caja y están realizados en plástico duro. Transparentes como el cristal, realizados con *lucite* (perspex o plexiglás) o de colores intensos y decorados con *strass*, al principio resultaban algo caros. Sin embargo, adquirieron tanta fama que rápidamente comenzaron a venderse por doquier versiones de menor calidad. Con la aparición de plásticos más blandos como el vinilo, los pesados bolsos de plástico duro perdieron popularidad.

All'inizio, la plastica veniva usata per sostituire materiali più preziosi, come la tartaruga e l'avorio, nella fabbricazione di cerniere per borsette. Queste imitazioni apparvero intorno al 1919 e restarono di moda fino al 1930 circa. Le cerniere da borsetta in plastica erano di forma semicircolare, piatte o decorate con motivi di ispirazione storica, romantica, orientale o egiziana. I primi materiali impiegati erano la celluloide e la caseina, ma a partire dal 1927 si utilizzò anche l'acetato di cellulosa.

All'inizio degli anni Trenta, comparvero borse a mano e pochette fatte interamente di plastica. Adesso, questo materiale non veniva più utilizzato come surrogato della tartaruga e dell'avorio, ma era apprezzato per la sua superficie lucida e la sua rigidità. Le borse di plastica restarono di moda fino allo scoppio della guerra. Un bell'esempio è fornito dalla serie di pochette di celluloide, datate dal 1937 in poi, in tinte pastello che vanno dal rosa, all'azzurro e al verde.

Negli anni Trenta si inventarono molte nuove plastiche sintetiche che presentavano diverse altre possibili applicazioni. Negli anni Quaranta e Cinquanta, tali materiali divennero tanto popolari che si fabbricavano borsette con perline di plastica, cavi telefonici e tessere di plastica. Negli anni Cinquanta, negli Stati Uniti, le borsette di plastica dominarono il mondo degli accessori di moda per più di un decennio. Queste borsette sono di struttura rigida, a forma di astuccio o scatola. Trasparenti come il vetro nelle versioni di Lucite (Perspex o Plexiglas), oppure tinte in colori vivaci e decorate con strass, inizialmente erano accessori costosi. Tuttavia, la richiesta di questi prodotti aumentò tanto rapidamente che si diffusero dovunque versioni più economiche, anche se di qualità inferiore. Con l'avvento di plastiche più morbide come il vinile, le rigide e pesanti borsette di plastica videro tramontare la loro popolarità.

Español

Italiano

Zunächst dienten Kunststoffe zur Imitation der teuren Taschenbügel aus Schildpatt und Elfenbein. Sie tauchten um 1919 auf und hielten sich bis in Anfang der 30er Jahre. Die halbkreisförmigen Plastikbügel der Taschen waren flach und mit historischen, romantischen, orient-alischen oder auch ägyptischen Motiven geschmückt. Anfangs wurden diese Bügel fast ausschließlich aus Zelluloid oder Kasein hergestellt, ab 1927 gab es sie dann auch aus Zelluloseacetat.

Zu Beginn der 30er Jahre tauchten schließlich Hand-taschen und Unterarmtaschen auf, die ausschließlich aus Plastik hergestellt wurden. Plastik wurde nicht mehr nur als Schildpatt- oder Elfenbeinimitation verwendet, sondern auch wegen seiner glänzenden, modernen Oberfläche geschätzt. Bis zum Krieg hielt sich diese Mode. Ein schönes Beispiel sind die kleinen Zelluloid-Unterarmtaschen aus dem Jahre 1937 in rosafarbenen, blauen und grünen Pastelltönen.

In den 30ern wurden viele neue Kunststoffe erfunden. Es boten sich immer mehr Verwendungsmöglichkeiten. In den 40ern und 50ern waren Kunststofftaschen so in Mode, dass man Taschen aus Plastikperlen herstellte, aus Telefonkabeln und kleinen Plastikplättchen. In den Vereinigten Staaten dominierten ab den 50er Jahren die Plastiktaschen die Modewelt über ein Jahrzehnt lang. Diese Taschen sind schachtelförmig und aus Hartplastik hergestellt. Sie sind transparent wie Glas (Perspex oder Plexiglas) oder leuchten in bunten Farben und sind oft reich mit Strass verziert. Anfangs waren das sehr teure Taschen. Aufgrund ihrer hohen Beliebtheit wurden jedoch bald überall billigere, weniger qualitative Modelle zum Verkauf angeboten. Mit der Entwicklung weicherer, flexiblerer Kunststoff-materialen wie z. B. Vinyl kamen die harten, schweren Plastiktaschen schnell außer Mode.

はじめ、プラスチックは高価なべっ甲や象牙のバッグ口金用イミテーションとして使われていました。プラスチックは 1919 年頃登場し、1930 年頃まで流行します。これらの半円形プラスチック製バッグ口金は平らに加工されるか、歴史的、ロマンチック、オリエンタル、またはエジプト調のモチーフで装飾されました。もともとセルロイドとカゼインからのみ作られていましたが、1926 年以降はセルロースアセテートからも作られるようになりました。

30 年代のはじめ、完全にプラスチックのみで作られたハンドバッグやクラッチバッグが登場します。プラスチックはもはやべっ甲や象牙のイミテーションとしてではなくその現代的な硬い艶に価値を見出されたのです。これらのプラスチックバッグは戦争が起こるまで人気を保っていました。この種の美しいバッグを代表するものに、1937 年のセルロイドポシェットのセットがあり、パステル調のピンク、ブルー、グリーンが使われています。

30 年代になって、応用の幅が広い新たなプラスチックが発明されます。40 年代、50 年代には、プラスチックは非常に人気が高まりプラスチックのビーズ、電話線、小さなタイルからできたバッグも作られました。50 年代のアメリカ合衆国ではプラスチックのハンドバッグが 10 年以上もファッションシーンを独占していました。これらのバッグは箱型で硬度の高いプラスチック製のものです。ガラス同様に透明なバッグは、ルーサイト（パースペクスまたはプレキシグラス）から製造されたもの、または強烈な色にストラスで装飾されたものなどあり、出始めは高額でした。しかしすぐに人気が高まったため、価格が下がり、品質面では劣るのものもあちらこちらで販売されるようになります。ビニールのようなより柔らかいプラスチックが登場してからは、重くて硬いプラスチックのハンドバッグの人気は衰えました。

deutsch

日本語

◄ Two handbags made from plastic beads, Maison de Bonneterie (r)
and Elizabeth Arden (l) U.S.A., 1950s.

◄◄ Four plastic Rodolac pochettes U.S.A., ca. 1937.

▲ Clear plastic handbag with applied fabric flowers U.S.A., 1950s.

▲ Plastic handbag with strass decoration U.S.A., 1950s.
▼ Clear plastic handbag U.S.A., 1950s.

▲ Plastic handbag with clear top carved with floral spray,
Charles S. Kahn U.S.A., 1950s.
▼ Silver-coloured metal and plastic handbag U.S.A., 1950s.

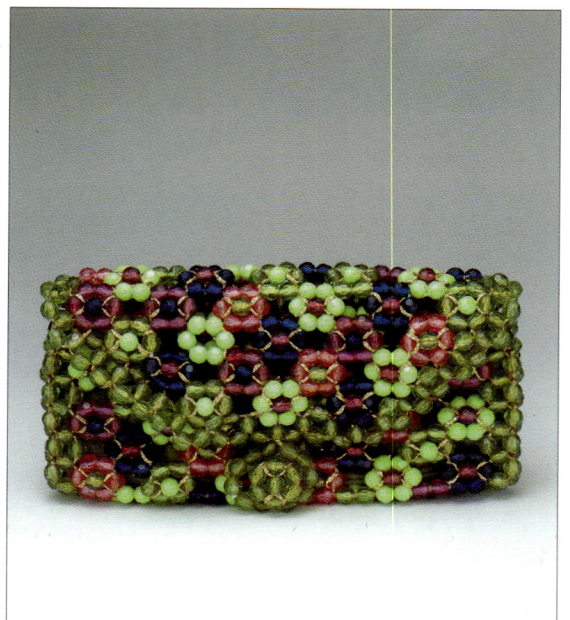

▲ Pochette made of lightweight square plastic tiles, Gadabout
England, 1947.
▼ Pochette made of lightweight square plastic tiles U.S.A., ca. 1942.

▲ Pochette made of lightweight square plastic tiles, Gadabout
England, 1947.
▼ Pochette made from plastic beads, made for Saks Fifth Avenue
Italy, 1950s.
▶ Plastic pochette U.S.A., 1950s.

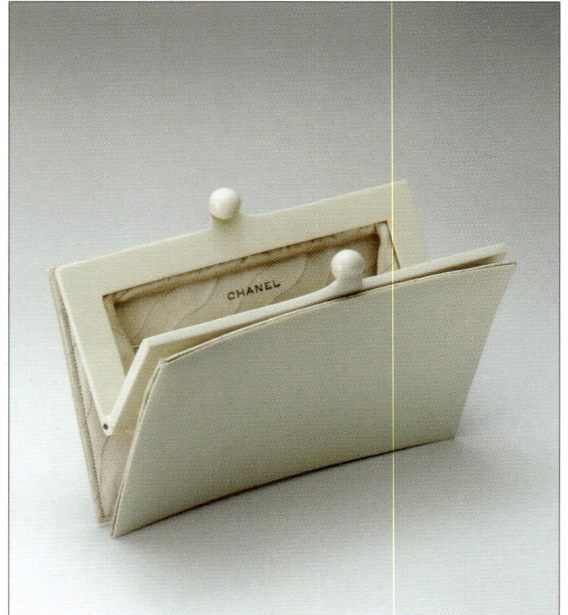

▲ Plastic cigarette-case France, 1920s.
▼ Two fabric handbags encased in plastic U.S.A., 1950s.

▲ Plastic handbag with decorations of Burma temple and swan (reverse) European, 1930s.
▼ Plastic pochette, Chanel France, 1950s.

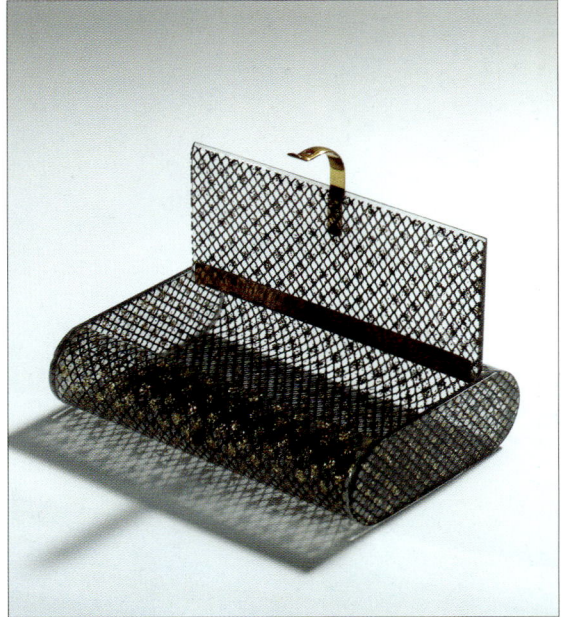

▲ Plastic 'telephone cord' handbag U.S.A., 1950-1955.
▼ Plastic handbag with confetti base U.S.A., 1950s.

▲ Imitation leather handbag with brass frame, Bally (l) and plastic vanity bag (r) Switzerland, ca. 1985 and U.S.A., 1950s.
▼ Clear plastic clutch bag U.S.A., 1950s.

Unusual models

Modèles inédits

Ongewone modellen

Ejemplares raros

Modelli inconsueti

Ungewöhnliche Modelle

希少なバッグ

In the thirties, fashion designer Elsa Schiaparelli created a stir with her Surrealist fashion accessories and bags. At that time, many bags were entirely made from out-of-the-ordinary models, such as the clutch bag in the form of the luxurious French cruise ship the Normandie. During its maiden voyage from France to the United States in 1935, all the first class passengers received one.

As a reaction to the sober war years, in the fifties handbags were made that were striking and novel in their use of material and shape, a development that led to some surprising bag shapes. And in certain periods, bags with unusual decorations or unconventional pictures were popular. The designers Enid Collins, Judith Leiber and Lulu Guinness created striking bags that are now sought after by collectors the world over. One example of such an unusual object is a bag with a little light. The first idea for such a bag comes from 1922. That year, the Londoner Alfred Dunhill (1872-1959) applied for a patent for a handbag with a little light that went on automatically upon opening the bag. The invention must have sparked the imagination, because between the wars and at the beginning of the fifties various imitations followed.

One particular bag with a light is the leather Lite-on made in 1953 by Amsterdam native L.F.W. Straeter. The model is often wrongly ascribed to Elsa Schiaparelli. In addition to lipstick, comb, cigarette and perfume holders, this bag has a little light so that everything can be found instantaneously. The light also shines out through an opening in the bag so that a keyhole can be found with no difficulty.

English

Dans les années trente, la créatrice de mode Elsa Schiaparelli fait sensation avec ses accessoires de mode et sacs surréalistes. Beaucoup de sacs sont alors des modèles qui sortent de l'ordinaire, comme la pochette en forme du luxueux paquebot de croisière français Normandie, offerte à toutes les passagères de première classe à l'occasion de sa première traversée entre la France et les Etats-Unis en 1935.

En réaction à la sobriété des années de guerre, les sacs à main des années cinquante exploitent toutes les matières et formes les plus inédites et originales pour donner des modèles surprenants. Par exemple, des sacs aux décorations insolites ou images peu conventionnelles seront appréciés à certaines périodes. Les créateurs Enid Collins, Judith Leiber et Lulu Guinness inventent alors de drôles de sacs aujourd'hui prisés par les collectionneurs du monde entier.

Le sac avec une petite lumière est un exemple d'objet insolite. L'idée est née en 1922, lorsque le Londonien Alfred Dunhill (1872-1959) dépose un brevet pour un sac à main doté d'une petite lampe qui s'allume automatiquement à l'ouverture. L'invention excite l'imagination et sera suivie de diverses imitations pendant l'entre–deux-guerres et au début des années cinquante.

L'un de ces sacs à lumière est le modèle « Lite-on » en cuir, créé en 1953 par L.F.W. Straeter à Amsterdam mais souvent attribué à tort à Elsa Schiaparelli. Outre ses compartiments pour rouge à lèvres, peigne, cigarettes et parfum, il possède une petite ampoule pour trouver aussitôt l'objet recherché et éclairer à travers un orifice le trou de serrure.

Modeontwerpster Elsa Schiaparelli baarde al in de jaren dertig opzien met haar surrealistische modeaccessoires en tassen. In die jaren werden meer tassen gemaakt met volstrekt afwijkende modellen, zoals de onderarm-tas in de vorm van het luxeuze Franse cruiseschip de Normandie. Tijdens de *maiden trip* van Frankrijk naar de Verenigde Staten in 1935 ontvingen alle eersteklas-passagiers een exemplaar.

Als reactie op de sobere oorlogsjaren werden in de jaren vijftig tassen vervaardigd die opvallend en ver-nieuwend waren door hun materiaalgebruik en vorm. Een ontwikkeling die tot verrassende tasvormen heeft geleid. Daarnaast waren in bepaalde periodes tassen met ongebruikelijke versieringen of met onconventionele afbeeldingen populair. Ontwerpsters Enid Collins, Judith Leiber en Lulu Guinness ontwierpen opvallende tassen die tegenwoordig gewild zijn bij verzamelaars over de hele wereld.

Een voorbeeld van zo'n ongewoon exemplaar is een tas met een lampje. Het eerste idee voor een dergelijke tas stamt uit 1922. De Londenaar Alfred Dunhill (1872-1959) vroeg dat jaar patent aan voor een handtas met een lampje dat bij het openen van de tas automatisch aan-ging. De uitvinding moet tot de verbeelding gesproken hebben, want tijdens het interbellum en begin jaren vijftig volgden diverse imitaties.

Een bijzondere tas met verlichting is de leren Lite-on, gemaakt in 1953 door de Amsterdammer L.F.W. Straeter. Het model wordt ten onrechte vaak toegeschreven aan Elsa Schiaparelli. Naast een lipstick-, kammen-, sigaretten-en parfumhouder heeft deze tas een lampje, zodat in één oogopslag alles te vinden is. Door een opening in de tas schijnt het licht ook naar buiten, zodat ook een sleutelgat zonder moeite gevonden kan worden.

français

nederlands

En la década de 1930, la diseñadora de moda Elsa Schiaparelli causó sensación con sus bolsos y accesorios de moda surrealistas. Era una época en la que muchos bolsos se confeccionaban con patrones completamente fuera de lo ordinario, como es el caso de aquel que reproduce la forma del crucero de lujo francés *Normandie*. En su viaje inaugural de Francia a Estados Unidos de 1935 todos los pasajeros de primera clase fueron obsequiados con un ejemplar.

Como reacción a los sobrios años de guerra, en los años cincuenta los bolsos se diseñaban de modo que tanto los materiales como la forma resultaran sorprendentes y novedosos, una tendencia que produjo modelos que causaban admiración. Y, en algunos momentos, se pusieron de moda los bolsos con motivos decorativos extraños o con imágenes no convencionales. Las diseñadoras Enid Collins, Judith Leiber y Lulu Guinness crearon bolsos chocantes que hoy en día buscan coleccionistas de todo el mundo.

Un ejemplo de estos modelos tan poco comunes es un bolso con una pequeña luz. La idea para realizar dicho bolso se engendró en 1922. Ese año el londinense Alfred Dunhill (1872-1959) solicitó la patente para un bolso con una lucecita que se encendía de forma automática al abrir el bolso. El invento debió disparar la imaginación de los diseñadores posteriores, pues en el período de entreguerras y a principios de los años cincuenta aparecieron diversas imitaciones.

Un bolso especial con luz es el Lite-on, realizado en cuero en 1953 por el diseñador oriundo de Amsterdam L. F. W. Straeter. A menudo esta pieza se atribuye por error a Elsa Schiaparelli. Además de pintalabios, peine, compartimentos para cigarrillos y perfume, este bolso cuenta con una pequeña luz para que la usuaria pueda encontrarlo todo al instante. La luz también sale del bolso a través de una abertura a fin de que pueda encontrarse el ojo de la cerradura sin dificultades.

Negli anni Trenta, la stilista Elsa Schiaparelli destò sensazione con i suoi accessori e le sue borsette in stile surrealista. All'epoca, molte borsette erano ispirate a modelli stravaganti: ne è esempio la pochette la cui forma riproduce la lussuosa nave da crociera francese Normandie. In occasione del viaggio inaugurale di questa nave dalla Francia agli Stati Uniti, nel 1935, tutte le passeggere di prima classe ne ricevettero una in omaggio.

Come reazione all'austerità degli anni della guerra, negli anni Cinquanta si produssero borsette originali e innovative sia nei materiali impiegati, sia nella forma, tanto che vennero create alcune borsette di forma decisamente bizzarra. E in alcuni periodi, divennero popolari borsette con decorazioni inconsuete o anticonvenzionali. Le stiliste Enid Collins, Judith Leiber e Lulu Guinness idearono borse particolarissime che oggi sono molto ricercate da collezionisti di tutto il mondo.

Un esempio di questi oggetti inconsueti è una borsetta provvista di lampadina interna. L'idea originaria di questa borsa risale al 1922, quando il londinese Alfred Dunhill (1872-1959) richiese il brevetto per una borsetta provvista di una lampadina che si accendeva automaticamente quando la borsetta veniva aperta. Questa invenzione deve aver colpito l'immaginazione di molte persone, perché nel periodo compreso tra le due guerre e all'inizio degli anni Cinquanta se ne produssero diverse versioni.

Una particolare borsetta con lampadina è la Lite-on di pelle, un modello che spesso viene attribuito erroneamente a Elsa Schiaparelli, ma che in realtà venne fabbricato nel 1953 dall'olandese di Amsterdam L. F. W. Straeter. Oltre a scomparti per il rossetto, il pettine, le sigarette e il profumo, questa borsetta era munita di una lampadina che permetteva di trovare facilmente ogni cosa. Inoltre, si poteva anche indirizzare il fascio di luce all'esterno attraverso un'apertura della borsa, ad esempio per trovare senza problemi il buco della serratura.

Español

Italiano

In den 30er Jahren sorgte die Modedesignerin Elsa Schiaparelli mit ihren surrealistischen Taschen- und Accessoire-Kreationen für großen Aufruhr. Zu dieser Zeit entstanden die gewagtesten Modelle. So zum Beispiel eine Unterarmtasche in Form des französischen Luxusdampfers Normandie: Auf ihrer Jungfernfahrt von Frankreich nach Amerika im Jahre 1935 erhielten alle Erste-Klasse-Passagiere ein Exemplar.

Als Reaktion auf die ernüchternden Kriegsjahre entstanden in den 50er Jahren Handtaschen, die sowohl was die Materialien als auch die Formen betrifft, ausgesprochen originell waren. Eine Entwicklung, die die seltsamsten Formkreationen mit sich brachte. Taschen mit manchmal völlig ungewöhnlichen Verzierungen oder unkonventionellen Abbildungen waren sehr beliebt. Die Designer Enid Collins, Judith Leiber und Lulu Guinness schufen umwerfende Modelle, die in internationalen Sammlerkreisen mittlerweile heiß begehrt sind.

Ein Beispiel für eines dieser ungewöhnlichen Modelle ist diese Tasche mit einem kleinen Licht. Die erste Idee zu einer derartigen Tasche stammte aus dem Jahr 1922. Der Londoner Alfred Dunhill (1872-1959) meldete ein Patent an für diese Handtasche mit Licht, das automatisch angehen sollte, wenn die Tasche geöffnet wurde. Diese Erfindung schien großen Anklang gefunden zu haben, denn zwischen den Kriegen und in den 50er Jahren folgten zahlreiche Imitationen.

Ein ganz besonderes Beispiel dieser Lichttaschen ist die sogenannte Lite-on, die im Jahre 1953 von dem aus Amsterdam stammenden L.F.W. Straeter entworfen wurde. Fälschlicherweise wird dieses Modell häufig der Designerin Elsa Schiaparelli zugeschrieben. Neben Lippenstiftfach, Kamm, Zigarettenfach und Parfumtäschchen besaß diese Tasche eine Innenbeleuchtung, mit der problemlos in der Nacht alles zu finden war. Im Dunkeln schien das Licht durch eine Öffnung der Tasche nach außen, so dass auch das Schlüsselloch ohne Schwierigkeit gefunden werden konnte.

30 年代にファッションデザイナーのエルザ・スキャパレリがシュールレアリスト調のアクセサリーやバッグで旋風を巻き起こしました。その当時バッグ類は、フランスの豪華客船ノルマンディーを模ったクラッチバッグなど、完全に非日常的なものを元に作られたものが数多くありました。1935 年、ノルマンディーのフランスからアメリカ合衆国までの処女航海で、一等乗船客の全員にこのバッグが贈られました。

地味な戦争時代に対する反動で、50 年代のハンドバッグは印象的で奇抜な素材や形を取り入れ、目を見張るような形のバッグへと発展します。そして、一定期間、風変わりな装飾な型破りな絵柄が好評だった時期がありました。エニッド・コリンズ、ジュディス・レイバー、ルル・ギネスといったデザイナーが風変わりなバッグを作成し、現在では世界中でコレクターたちが探し求めています。

そのような風変わりなバッグを代表するものが、小型ライト付きバッグです。このようなバッグの発想は 1922 年に始まりました。バッグ発明がイマジネーションを刺激したのでしょう。なぜなら戦争の合い間と 50 年代の初めにさまざまな類似品が続出したからです。

特殊なライト付きバッグとして挙げられるのは 1953 年に作られたレザー製ライトオン（Lite-on）です。口紅、コーム、煙草、香水ホルダーに加え、このバッグには小さなライトがついて中のもの全てが瞬時に探せるようになっています。ライトはバッグの開き口から外に向けて照らすことが可能で、ドアの鍵穴も簡単に見つけられる仕組みになっていました。

deutsch

日本語

▲ Leather handbag 'Lite On' with light, Straeter
The Netherlands, 1953.

THE NETHERLANDS

▲Leather handbag with decoration in beads and strass, Berger Bags France, 1950s.

▼ Leather handbag in shape of umbrella with brass frame England, 1930s.

◄ Leather pochette in shape of 'Normandie' France, 1935.

▲ Leather handbag in shape of accordion, Milch U.S.A, 1951.

▼ Tin shoulder-bag in shape of film-box The Netherlands, 1980s.

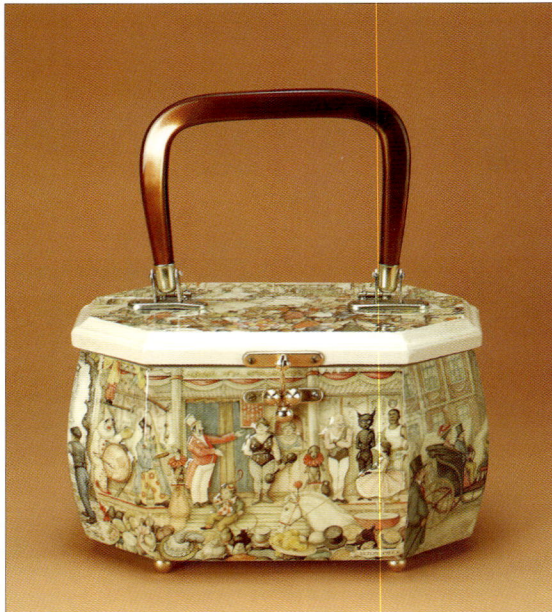

▲ Printed fabric bag with a fabric horse and rider picture and plastic lamination U.S.A., 1950s.
▼ Velvet and brass evening bag with cigarette-box, powder-case in lid France, 1950s.

▲ Wooden and plastic box bag with decoration by Anton Pieck U.S.A., 1970s.
▼ Leather handbag, Anne-Marie of France France, 1940s.

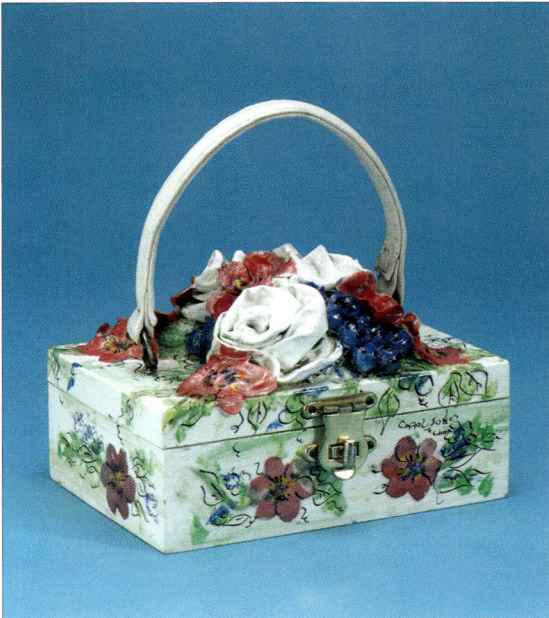

▲ Fabric pochette with matching umbrella England, 1930s.
▼ Painted wooden box bag with brass lock and leather handle,
Carol Jones U.S.A., 1950s.

▲ Satin evening bag embroidered with beads, Isabel Canovas
France, 1992.
▼ Three magazine pochettes Hong Kong, 1960s.

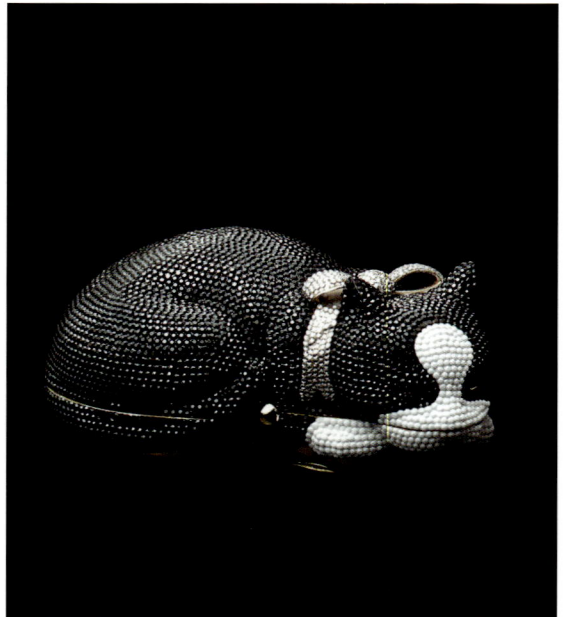

▲ Satin handbag with embroidery and leather roof, Lulu Guinness
England, 2000.
▼ Velvet handbag in shape of Citroen's 2CV, Nathalie Müller
The Netherlands, 1998.

▲ Handbag made of silk ties, Carmen Hempe The Netherlands, 2002.
▼ Evening bag 'Socks', named after the cat of The Clintons, Judith
Leiber U.S.A., 1990s.

▲ Plastic wicker handbag U.S.A., 1950s.

▶ Plastic shoulderbag with clock, Spartus U.S.A., 1980s.
▶▶ Leather handbag with functioning telephone, Dallas Handbags
U.S.A., 1980s.

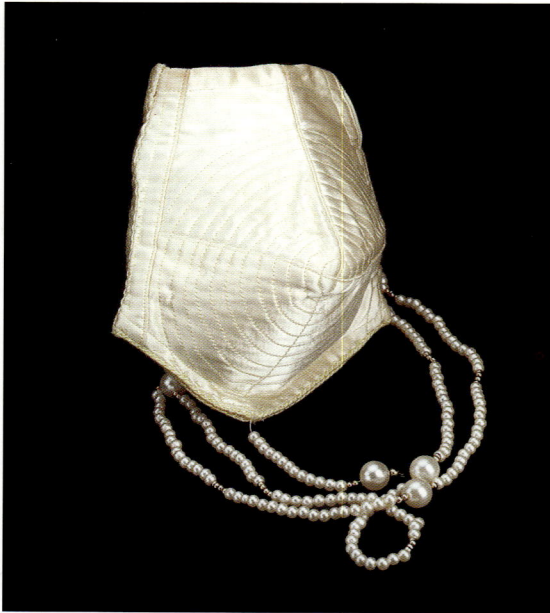

▲ Small silk bag in shape of bra with imitation pearls, Karin Aviaz
Israel, 2002.
▼ Fabric and plastic children's backpack, Oilily The Netherlands, 2003.

▲ Fabric bag decorated with embroidery, lace and print 'Barrel
Organ', Joke Schole The Netherlands, 2003.
▼ Embroidered evening bag, studio Lesage, designed by Gerard
Tremolet France, 1988.

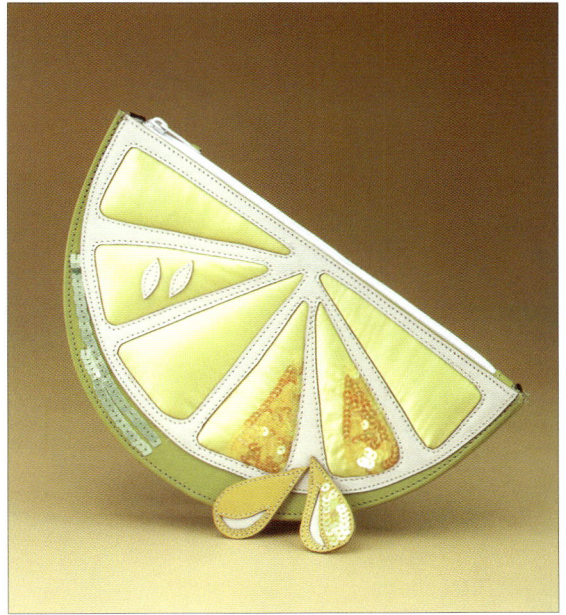

▲ Leather shoulderbag named 'Kosmos', Elly Kersten
The Netherlands, 2000.
▼ Fabric evening bag in shape of evening dress, Lulu Guinness
England, 2004.

▲ Leather and silk handbag in shape of a lemon, Christian Lacroix
France, 2002.
▼ Handmade leather handbag, '3D-Ladybird', Ulrich Czerny
Germany, 2003.

Classic models

Modèles classiques

Klassieke modellen

Modelos clásicos

Modelli classici

Klassische Modelle

古典的なバッグ

In addition to designing clothing, many fashion designers and fashion houses keep busy by designing things like women's handbags. Initially this occurred in order to provide accessories to match the clothes, but later on brands also developed perfumes and other accessories to give their name more recognition. Some logos are widely recognised, such as D&G (Dolce & Gabbana) or the double C (Chanel). In 1896, the Louis Vuitton luggage house introduced its world-famous canvas with the LV monogram.

Well-known leathergoods brands have always come along with new models or put classic models into production again. One such classic model was the pochette or clutch bag, which was carried under the arm or in the hand. Along with the handbag, it was the most popular bag in the twenties and thirties. Around the Second World War, the clutch bag gave way to the shoulder bag. Later on, it became popular again in the refined fashion of the New Look (1947). At the moment, it is often used as an elegant evening bag. There are several classic variations on the shoulder bag or handbag. The best known is perhaps the Chanel bag in quilted leather with a gold-coloured chain. The official name of the bag is 2.55, based on its release in February 1955. Another classic is the Kelly bag from Hermès. It had already existed as a handbag in the thirties, but since 1955 it has owed its name and fame to Grace Kelly, who carried it a lot. A new shoulder bag, already a classic, is the 1998 Baguette from Fendi. This bag with a short shoulder strap is clasped under the arm like a French loaf.

The backpack as a fashion trend is not so longstanding. Prada, in fact, launched the backpack as an accessory with its release of a black nylon model in 1985.

English

Outre les vêtements, beaucoup de créateurs et de maisons de mode gardent la main en créant d'autres objets comme les sacs à main. Il s'agissait au départ de fournir des accessoires assortis aux vêtements ; par la suite cependant, des marques ont commercialisé parfums et autres accessoires pour accroître leur reconnaissance. Certains logos sont aujourd'hui universellement connus, comme D&G (Dolce & Gabbana) ou le double C (Chanel). En 1896, le fabricant de bagages Louis Vuitton lance son célèbre sac en tapisserie orné du monogramme LV.

Les grandes marques de maroquinerie ont toujours à la fois sorti de nouveaux modèles tout en relançant la production de modèles classiques. Tel est le cas de la pochette à porter sous le bras ou dans la main. Avec le sac à main, elle sera le modèle le plus vendu des années vingt et trente puis, au moment de la Deuxième Guerre mondiale, elle cèdera sa place au sac à bandoulière. Elle connaîtra ensuite un regain de popularité au moment de la mode New Look (1947) pour servir souvent de sac du soir élégant. Quant au sac en bandoulière ou sac à main, il en existe plusieurs variantes classiques, dont la plus connue est peut-être le sac Chanel en cuir capitonné à chaîne dorée. Son nom officiel est 2.55 car il a été lancé en février 1955. Autre classique, le sac Kelly d'Hermès existait déjà dans les années trente mais doit son nom et sa notoriété depuis 1955 à Grace Kelly, fidèle utilisatrice. Enfin, un autre sac en bandoulière déjà classique est le Baguette de Fendi, créé en 1998 et qui, avec sa bandoulière courte, se porte serré sous le bras comme une baguette.

La mode du sac à dos ne remonte pas si loin. C'est Prada qui le lance comme accessoire de mode avec la sortie de son modèle en nylon noir en 1985.

Veel modeontwerpers en modehuizen houden zich – uiteaard naast het ontwerpen van kleding – bezig met het ontwerpen van zaken als damestassen. Aanvankelijk gebeurde dit om bij de kleding een passend accessoire te verzorgen, maar later ontwikkelden merken ook parfums en andere nevenartikelen om hun naam meer bekendheid te geven. Sommige logo's zijn overbekend, zoals D&G (Dolce & Gabbana) of de dubbele C (Chanel). In 1896 introduceerde het koffermerk Louis Vuitton zijn wereldberoemde canvas met LV-monogram.

Van oudsher bekende lederwarenmerken kwamen met nieuwe modellen of brachten klassieke modellen opnieuw in productie. Zo'n klassiek model was de pochette of enveloptas, die onder de arm of in de hand werd gedragen. Het was naast de handtas de populairste tas in de jaren twintig en dertig. Rond de Tweede Wereldoorlog maakte de enveloptas plaats voor de schoudertas. Later werd hij opnieuw populair bij de elegante mode van de New Look (1947). Tegenwoordig wordt hij vaak gebruikt als elegante avondtas.

Van de schoudertas en handtas bestaan diverse klassieke varianten. De bekendste is misschien wel de Chanel-tas van doorgestikt leer, met goudkleurige ketting. De officiële naam van de tas is 2.55, naar de presentatie in februari 1955. Een andere klassieker is de Kelly-bag van Hermès. Hij bestond als handtas al in de jaren dertig. Sinds 1955 dankt de tas zijn naam en bekendheid aan de actrice Grace Kelly, die hem veel gedragen heeft. Een nu al klassieke schoudertas is de Baguette van Fendi uit 1998. Deze tas met korte schouderband wordt als een stokbroodje onder de oksel geklemd.

De rugtas is als modeverschijnsel nog niet zo oud. Het was vooral Prada die met de introductie van een zwart nylon model in 1985 de rugtas als assecoire lanceerde.

français   nederlands

Además de diseñar ropa, muchos diseñadores y casas de moda se entretienen en diseñar objetos tales como bolsos femeninos. En un principio con ello se ofrecían accesorios que hicieran juego con las prendas, pero posteriormente las diversas marcas también diseñaron perfumes y otros accesorios en vistas a popularizar su nombre. Algunos nombres eran ampliamente conocidos como D&G (Dolce & Gabbana) o la doble C (Chanel). En 1896, la empresa de maletas Louis Vuitton comenzó a utilizar su mundialmente famosa lona con el monograma LV.

Algunas marcas de marroquinería de renombre siempre presentan nuevos modelos o vuelven a producir modelos clásicos. Uno de ellos fue el *pochette* o *clutch*, que se llevaba bajo el brazo o en la mano. Junto con el bolso de mano fue el bolso más en boga durante las décadas de 1920 y 1930. En torno a la Segunda Guerra Mundial, dio paso al bolso de hombro. Posteriormente, volvió a popularizarse en la refinada moda del New Look (1947). En la actualidad, a menudo se usa como elegante bolso de noche. Existen diversas versiones clásicas del bolso de mano o de hombro. Tal vez el más conocido es el de Chanel, realizado en piel acolchada y con una cadena dorada. El nombre oficial de este bolso es 2.55, pues salió al mercado en febrero de 1955. Otro clásico es el bolso Kelly de Hermès. Ya existía como bolso de mano en la década de 1930, pero desde 1955 debe su nombre y fama a Grace Kelly, que lo lucía a menudo. Otro ejemplo de bolso de hombro que constituye ya un clásico es el bolso Baguette de Fendi, de 1998. Este bolso, con una correa corta, se coloca bajo el brazo como si fuera una barra de pan francés.

La mochila como tendencia de moda no perdura tanto tiempo. De hecho, Prada lanzó la mochila como accesorio cuando presentó un modelo de nailon negro en 1985.

Oltre agli abiti, molti stilisti e grandi case di moda creano anche accessori, come le borsette. All'inizio, si limitavano a disegnare accessori che si abbinassero bene ai loro vestiti, ma in seguito le grandi case di moda cominciarono a sviluppare le proprie linee di profumi e di accessori vari per ampliare ulteriormente la propria fama. Alcuni loghi, come la D&G degli stilisti Dolce & Gabbana o la doppia C di Chanel, si riconoscono ormai a colpo d'occhio. Nel 1896, la pelletteria Louis Vuitton lanciò la sua tela decorata con il monogramma LV, che divenne famosa in tutto il mondo.

Le maggiori case di pelletteria producono modelli sempre nuovi o rilanciano i propri modelli classici. Uno di questi modelli classici è stato la pochette, portata sotto il braccio oppure tenuta in mano. Insieme alla borsa con manici corti, la pochette è stata la borsetta più popolare negli anni Venti e Trenta. Intorno alla seconda guerra mondiale, la pochette cedette il passo alla tracolla, ma in seguito conobbe un revival con l'avvento della moda raffinata del New Look (1947). Attualmente, viene utilizzata spesso come borsetta elegante da sera. La tracolla e la borsa con manici corti presentano diverse varianti classiche: la più conosciuta è forse la borsetta Chanel, in nappa con impuntura a losanghe e tracolla di catenella d'oro. Il nome ufficiale di questa borsetta è 2.55, perché venne lanciata nel febbraio 1955. Un altro classico è la borsa Kelly di Hermès, un modello che esisteva già negli anni Trenta, ma che divenne famoso e prese il suo nome attuale a partire dal 1955, grazie al fatto che l'attrice Grace Kelly la portava spesso. Una borsetta recente ma che è già diventata un classico è la Baguette di Fendi, lanciata nel 1998. Questo modello dalla tracolla molto corta si tiene sotto il braccio, proprio come lo sfilatino di pane francese che le dà il nome.

Lo zainetto utilizzato come borsetta è entrato in voga relativamente di recente. Infatti, il primo zainetto è stato lanciato nel 1985, quando Prada ne propose un modello in nylon nero.

Español

Italiano

Viele Modehäuser und Designer entwerfen neben Kleidung ständig neue Modelle für Damenhandtaschen. Ursprünglich ging es darum, zur Garderobe auch die entsprechenden Accessoires zu gestalten. Später brachten die Modemarken auch eigene Parfüms und andere Artikel mit ihren Markennamen auf den Markt, um das Ansehen ihrer Marken zu erhöhen. Die meisten Logos sind allgemein bekannt, so wie D&G (Dolce & Gabbana) oder das doppelte C von Chanel. Im Jahre 1896 lancierte der Kofferhersteller Louis Vuitton sein weltberühmtes Leinen mit dem LV-Monogramm. Bekannte Lederwarenhersteller bringen immer wieder neue Modelle auf den Markt oder nehmen die Produktion klassischer Modelle wieder auf. Einer dieser Klassiker ist die Unterarmtasche oder Kurvettasche, die unter dem Arm oder in der Hand getragen wurde. Neben der Handtasche war sie die beliebteste Tasche der 20er und 30er Jahre. In der Zeit um den Zweiten Weltkrieg trat die Unterarmtasche in den Hintergrund. Man trug nun immer mehr Umhängetaschen. Später wurde sie jedoch im Zuge des eleganten New Looks im Jahre 1947 wieder aufgenommen. Im Moment wird dieser Taschentyp häufig als elegante Abendtasche getragen. Es existieren zahlreiche klassische Versionen der Umhänge- oder Handtasche. Die bekannteste ist wohl das Chanel-Modell aus gestepptem Leder mit gold-farbener Kette. Ihr offizieller Name ist 2.55 - als Hinweis auf ihre Präsentation im Februar 1955. Ein anderer Klassiker ist die sogenannte Kelly-Tasche von Hermès. Sie existierte als Handtasche bereits in den 30ern. Erst 1955 erhielt sie ihren neuen Namen nach der Schau-spielerin Grace Kelly, die dieses Modell besonders gerne trug. Eine neue Schultertasche aus dem Jahre 1998 ist die Baguette-Tasche von Fendi, bereits heute ein Klassiker. Diese Tasche mit einem nur kurzen Henkel wird unter den Arm geklemmt wie ein französisches Baguette.

Der Rucksack als Modetrend ist noch nicht so alt. Die Firma Prada war es, die den Rucksack, elegant aus schwarzem Nylon, im Jahre 1985 als modisches Accessoire auf den Markt brachte.

洋服のデザインに加え、多くのファッションデザイナーやブランドが婦人用ハンドバッグなどのデザインに精力をつぎ込みました。当初、この動きは洋服にマッチしたアクセサリーを提供するために始まりましたが、後にブランドの知名度を高める目的で香水や他のアクセサリーの開発にも着手するようになりました。ブランドのロゴでD&G（ドルチェ＆ガバナ）や2つのC（シャネル）など広く知れ渡るようになったものもあります。1896年にはルイヴィトン旅行鞄店がかの世界的に有名なキャンバス地にLVのモノグラムをあしらった鞄を売り出します。

有名レザーグッズのブランドは常に、新しいバッグとともに浮上するか古典的なバッグの生産再開とともに芽を出してきました。古典的なバッグのひとつに挙げられるのがポシェットまたはクラッチバッグで、小脇に抱えるか手で持つバッグのことです。ハンドバッグと並んで、この手のバッグは20年代、30年代において最も人気の高いバッグでした。第二次世界大戦頃クラッチバッグはショルダーバッグに人気を奪われてしまいます。その後、洗練されたニュールック（1947年）ファッションの中で再び人気が上昇しました。現時点ではエレガントなイブニングバックとして使用されています。ショルダーバッグやハンドバッグにもいくつか古典的な型の種類が存在します。最もなじみの深いものは、おそらくキルティングを施したレザーのバッグに金色のチェーンを取り付けてあるシャネルのそれでしょう。バッグの正式名称は「2.55」で、1955年の2月に発売が開始されたことかた付けられた名称です。もうひとつの古典的な代表作はエルメスのケリーバッグです。すでにハンドバッグとして30年代に存在していたものですが、1955年以来バッグを愛用していたグレース・ケリーによって名称の面でも知名度の面でも恩恵を受けました。現在ではすでに古典的なものとなりましたが、当時新型のショルダーバッグだったものがフェンディの1998年製バゲットです。この短いショルダーストラップ付きバッグはフランスパンのように小脇に抱えて持ちます。

バックパック（リュックサック）はファッショントレンドとしての歴史はそれほど長くありません。事実、プラダが独自の黒いナイロン製バックパックをアクセサリーとして売り出したのは1985年のことでした。

deutsch

日本語

▲ Beaded handbag, Jeanne Lanvin France, 1910-1930.
▼ Silk envelop bag handpainted with granular paint, Waldybag
England, 1950s.
◄ Brocade bag with brass and turquoise decoration, accordion
closure, Henry a la Pensée France, 1901.

▲ Handbag made of antique fabric, Mayer France, ca. 1930.
▼ Fabric pochette embroidered with silk, matching gloves,
Alexandrine France, 1930s.

▲ Leather and suede clutch bag, Elsa Schiaparelli France, 1930s.
▼ Leather handbag with Galalith handle, Charles Jourdan
France, 1950s.
◄ Suede handbag with mother-of-pearl inlay and brass frame
and handle, Tyrolean U.S.A, 1950s.

▲ Patent leather shoulderbag decorated with metal plates, Pierre
Cardin France, 1960s.
▼ Leather handbag with chrome ring as closure, Zumpolle
The Netherlands, 1950s.

▲ Leather handbag decorated with printed map of London, Golden Age England, 1930s.
▼ Linen and leather 'Cable Car' handbag, Enid Collins of Texas U.S.A., 1964.

▲ Velvet handbag with gold-coloured frame and chain, Emilio Pucci Italy, 1960s.
▼ Linen and leather 'Love Birds' handbag, Enid Collins of Texas U.S.A., 1965.

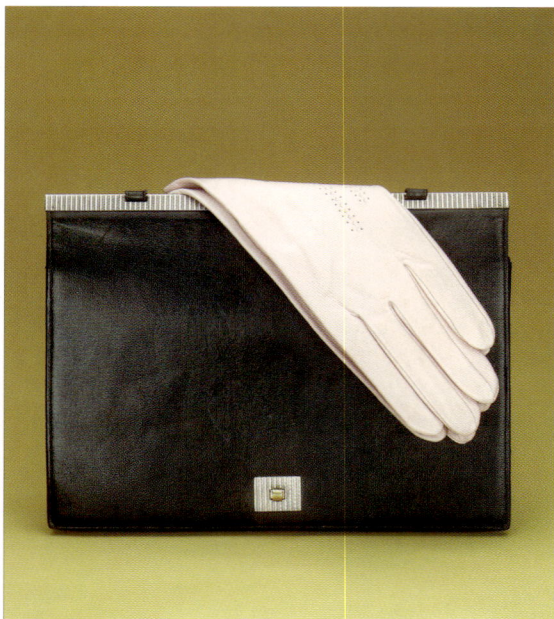

▲ Leather handbag with plastic grip, Lederer France, 1930s.
▼ Leather handbag with silver frame and lock, Dunhill England, 1962.
◀ Silk bag with matching shoes, Saks Fifth Avenue, bag: Coblentz, shoes: Roger Vivier, Paris U.S.A., 1960s.

▲▼ Leather vanity bag with metal frame, Elizabeth Arden U.S.A., ca. 1950.

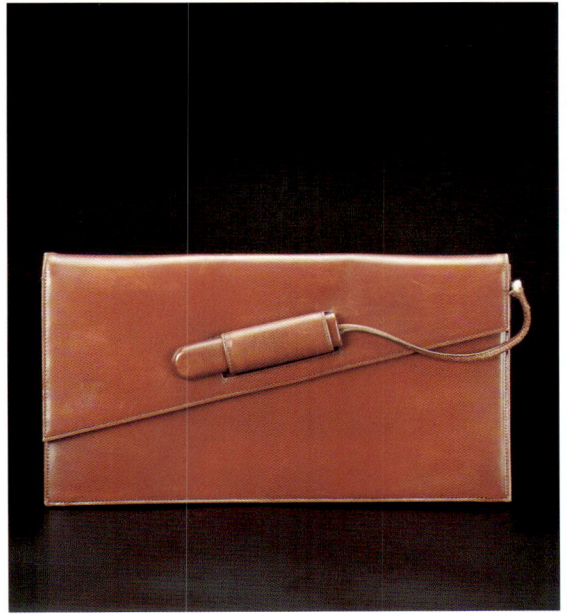

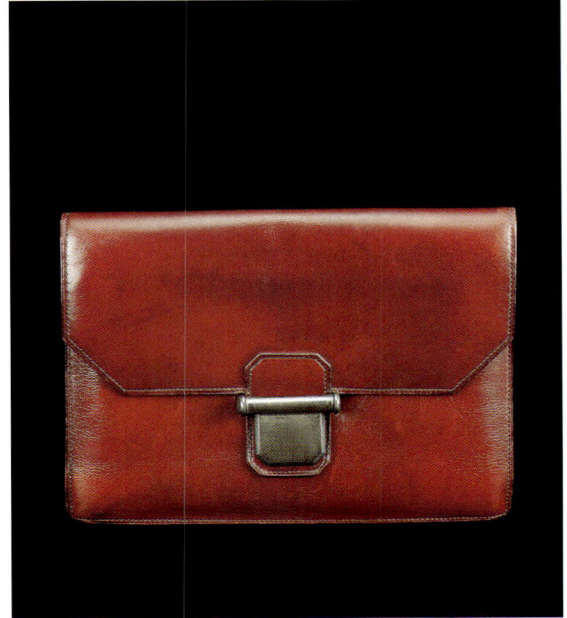

▲ Imitation suede shoulderbag with bijou lock, Mario Valentino and necklace by Pierre Cardin Italy, 1970s.
▼ Leather handbag, Delvaux Belgium, 1970s.

▲ Leather envelop bag, Lederer France, early 1960's.
▼ Leather pochette with metal lock, Hermès France, 1935.

▲ Snakeskin handbag, Blok van Heijst The Netherlands, 1970.

▲ Leather shoulder bag with gold-coloured chain, Chanel (f); printed canvas shoulder bag, Dior (m) and leather handbag with bamboo handle and lock, Gucci (b) France, 1970s; France, 1980; Italy, 1970s.

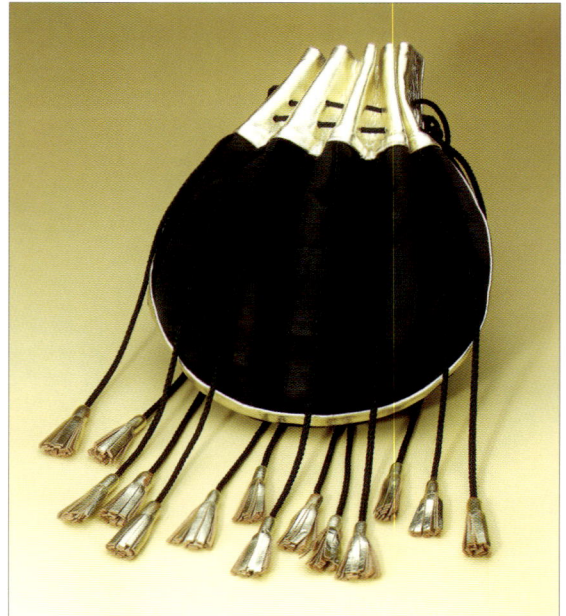

▲ Suede cosmetics bag, Moschino Italy, 1998.
▼ Silk evening bag with gold-coloured chain and decoration with strass, Chanel France, 1980s.

▲ Suede handbag with gold-coloured leather decoration, Cameleon The Netherlands, 1970s.
▼ Fabric and gold-coloured leather handbag, Yves Saint Laurent France, 1970s.
▶ Chain-link shoulderbag, Paco Rabanne France, 1966.

▲ Embossed leather handbag with matching shoes, Stephane Kelian
France, 2001.
▼ Leather handbag with matching shoes, Dolce & Gabbana
Italy, 1999.

▲ Leather handbag with silver-coloured rings, Claudio Ferrici
The Netherlands, 2004.
▼ Satin handbag with suede flap, Christian Lacroix France, ca. 1990.

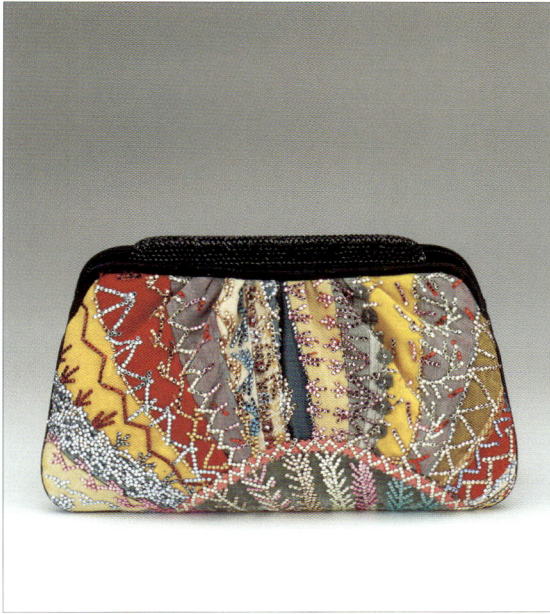

▲ Quilt clutch bag embroidered with beads, Judith Leiber
U.S.A., 1994.

▼ Suede handbag in shape of rose, Yves St Laurent, designed by
Tom Ford France, 2003.

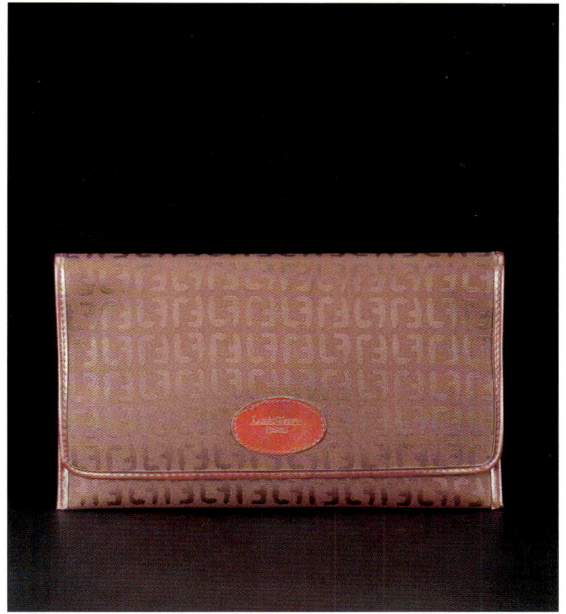

▲ Textile envelop bag with leather border, Louis Ferraud
France, 1980s.

▶ Handbag carried by Madonna at première of the movie Evita,
Gianni Versace Couture Italy, 1997.

▶▶ Leather handbag, Paloma Picasso France, 1998.

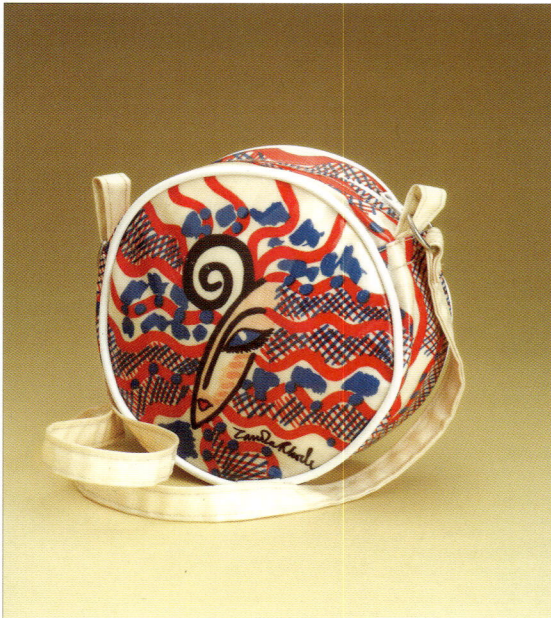

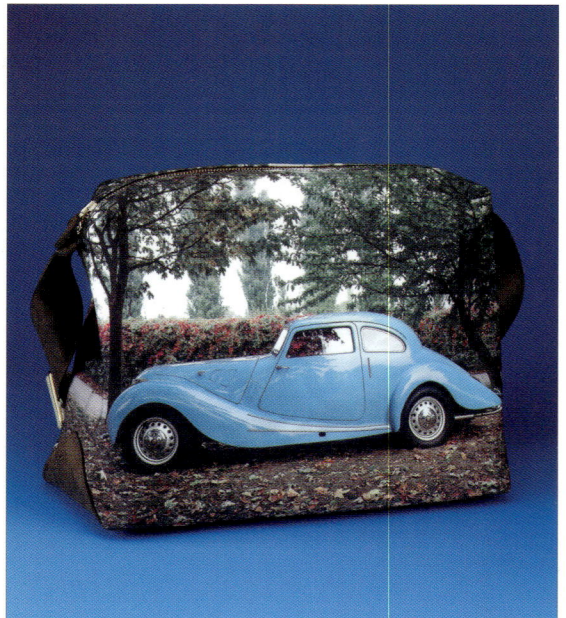

▲ Handbag with print of Marilyn Monroe, Bulaggi
The Netherlands, 2004.
▼ Plastic shoulderbag, Zandra Rhodes England, 1980s.

▲ Fabric handbag decorated with feathers and plastic beads,
Alexander McQueen England, 2003.
▼ Printed fabric shoulderbag, Paul Smith England, 2003.

▲ 'Baguette' shoulderbag embroidered with beads, Fendi Italy, 2001.   ▶ Fabric and leather shoulderbag with matching shoes, Coccinelle Italy, 2003.
▶▶ Cotton and leather handbag, Dolce & Gabbana Italy, 2001.

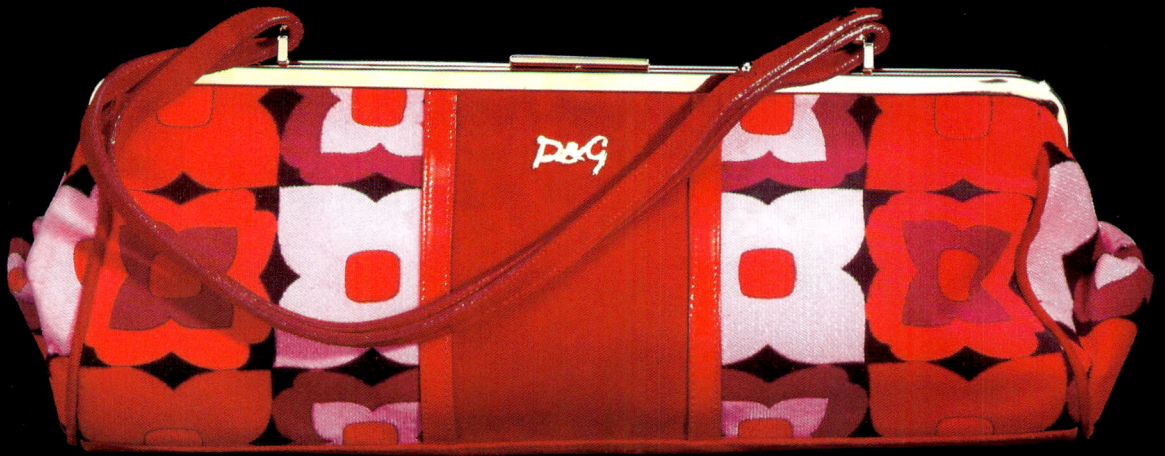

Present day designs

Créations contemporaines

Hedendaagse ontwerpen

Diseños actuales

Modelli attuali

Zeitgenössisches Design

今日のデザイン

The development of handbag design is strongly influenced by the fashion scene. The handbag is still used to accessorise clothes, and it continues to adapt to changing trends.

Designers have various starting points: functionality, form, material, fashion and emotion. There are designers influenced by architecture who make bags with geometrical shapes in combination with daring colour combinations. For other designers, the handbag is an implement which must be durable. They especially look at the practical demands the bag must fulfil and make use of strong materials and handy compartments for the telephone and keys. Emotion plays a role for some designers. Portraits, Madonnas and angels turn bags into personal statements. And the 'memory bag' is a collection of souvenirs from the designer.

English

L'évolution des tendances dans le sac à main est très fortement influencée par la mode. Il continue en effet d'être choisi pour accessoiriser les vêtements et ne cesse d'évoluer.

Les créateurs prennent divers points de départ : fonctionnalité, forme, matière, mode et coup de cœur. Certains s'inspirent de l'architecture et créent des sacs aux formes géométriques et aux combinaisons de couleurs hardies. Pour d'autres, le sac à main est un accessoire fait pour durer et ils observent de près les exigences pratiques en choisissant des matières résistantes et des compartiments utiles pour le téléphone ou les clés. Enfin, pour d'autres encore, les sentiments l'emportent et des portraits, madones ou anges font du sac une déclaration de personnalité. Quant au « memory bag », il regroupe un ensemble de souvenirs du créateur.

De ontwikkeling van het tasontwerp wordt sterk beïnvloed door het modebeeld. De tas is nog steeds het attribuut dat de kleding completeert, en het blijft zich aanpassen aan veranderende gewoontes.

De ontwerpers hebben verschillende uitgangspunten: functionaliteit, vorm, materiaal, mode en emotie. Er zijn ontwerpers die beïnvloed worden door architectuur. Zij maken tassen met geometrische vormen, in combinatie met gewaagde kleurcombinaties. Voor andere ontwerpers is de tas een gebruiksvoorwerp waarmee je intensief moet kunnen leven. Zij kijken vooral naar de praktische eisen waaraan de tas moet voldoen, zoals sterk materiaal en handige vakjes voor de telefoon en sleutels. Bij sommige ontwerpen speelt emotie een rol. Tassen met portretten, madonna's en engelen maken de tas dan tot een persoonlijk document. Zo is de 'memory bag' een verzameling van souvenirs van de ontwerper.

El desarrollo del diseño de bolsos de mano se ve fuertemente determinado por el mundo de la moda. El bolso sigue utilizándose para complementar prendas de ropa y no deja nunca de adaptarse a las tendencias que se van sucediendo.

Los diseñadores parten de varios puntos: la funcionalidad, la forma, el material, la moda y la emoción. Hay diseñadores que se dejan influir por la arquitectura y que crean bolsos de formas geométricas combinados con osadas combinaciones de colores. Para otros diseñadores, el bolso es un complemento que debe durar. Ponen especial atención a las demandas prácticas que debe satisfacer y por ello se sirven de materiales fuertes y los dotan de cómodos compartimentos para el teléfono y las llaves. También las emociones desempeñan un papel importante para algunos diseñadores: los retratos, las madonas y los ángeles convierten los bolsos en afirmaciones personales. Finalmente, el "bolso de recuerdos" es una evocación de los recuerdos del diseñador.

Lo sviluppo dei modelli di borse è fortemente influenzato dal mondo della moda. La borsetta, infatti, è ancora utilizzata come accessorio per gli abiti, e continua ad adattarsi ai mutamenti di tendenza nell'abbigliamento. Nel creare i loro modelli, gli stilisti possono muovere da diversi punti di partenza: funzionalità, forma, materiale, moda ed emozione. Ci sono stilisti influenzati dall'architettura che disegnano borsette di forma geometrica e con ardite combinazioni di colori. Per altri stilisti, la borsetta deve essere soprattutto funzionale: prestano particolare attenzione alle funzioni pratiche che la borsa deve svolgere e utilizzano materiali robusti e comodi scomparti per oggetti come il cellulare e le chiavi. Per altri stilisti ancora, l'emozione ha un ruolo fondamentale: ritratti, madonne e angeli trasformano queste borsette in vere dichiarazioni di principio. Inoltre si è affermata anche la "*memory bag*", una raccolta di ricordi dello stilista.

Español

Italiano

Die Entwicklung im Taschendesign steht unter dem starken Einfluss der Modewelt. Die Handtasche ist immer noch *das* modische Accessoire und passt sich den ständig wechselnden Trends der Kleidermode an. Designer berücksichtigen verschiedene Kriterien: Wichtig sind Funktionalität, Form, Material, Mode und Emotion. Manche inspirieren sich an der Architektur und kreieren Taschen in geometrischen Formen, in Kombination mit gewagten Farbkombinationen. Für andere Designer wiederum ist die Tasche ein täglich verwendeter Gebrauchsgegenstand, der praktisch und robust sein sollte. Sie legen Wert auf den speziellen Verwendungszweck des Gegenstand. Daher verwenden sie strapazierfähige Materialien und denken an praktische Seiten- oder Innentaschen für Schlüssel und Handy. Emotionen spielen zuweilen ebenso eine wichtige Rolle. Taschen mit einem Portrait berühmter Personen, Madonnen oder Engelchen stellen eine persönliche Verbindung zum Träger her. Die „Memory Bag" ist eine Souvenirsammlung des Designers.

ハンドバッグのデザイン開発はファッションシーンの影響を多大に受けています。ハンドバッグは今でも洋服を引き立てる小物として使用され、これからもトレンドの変化に対応し続けます。
デザイナーはいくつかの始発点を持っています。機能性、形、素材、流行、感情などがそれに当たります。中には建築物からひらめきを得て、幾何学的な形を大胆な色彩と組み合わせたバッグなどを作成しているデザイナーがいます。また、ハンドバッグは用具であり、したがって丈夫でなければならないと考えるデザイナーもいます。後者はバッグが満たすべき実用的な要求面にとりわけ着目し、丈夫な素材や形帯電話や鍵を収納できる便利性の高い仕切りなどを取り入れます。感情がバッグのデザインに役立てるデザイナーも中にはいます。肖像画、聖母、天使などによって普通のバッグが個人的な思いのこもったバッグに一変します。この「思い出のバッグ」はそのデザイナーが生み出した記念品的バッグのコレクションです。

deutsch

日本語

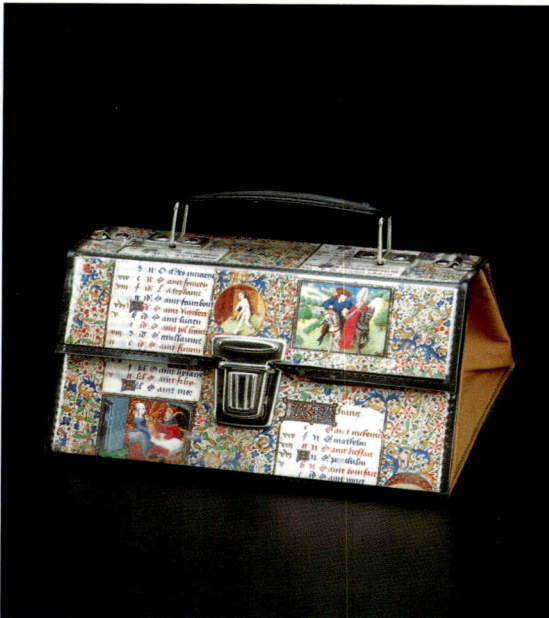

▲ Painted fabric handbag decorated with coin purses, Petra Hartman The Netherlands, 2002.

▼ Handbag decorated with laminated prints, Hil de Jong The Netherlands, 1998.

▲ Fabric shoulderbag with 'Madonna' print, Carmen Hempe The Netherlands, 2002.

▼ Fabric handbag decorated with embroidery, lace and imitation nails, Hester Slaman The Netherlands, 2003.

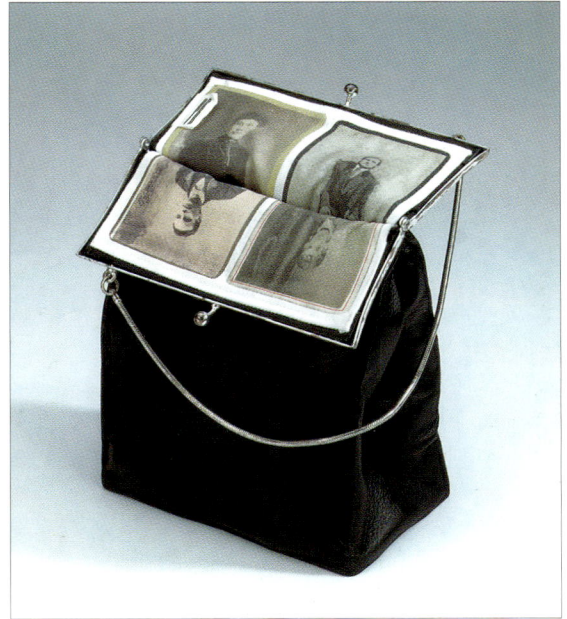

▲ 'Hyères' handbag made of antique postcards, Georgette Koning
The Netherlands, 1990.
▼ Velvet handbag decorated with glass stones, Helmie van de Riet
The Netherlands, 2002.

▲ Velvet rucksack with artificial fur named 'Bull', Margriet Stegmeijer
The Netherlands, 1996.
▼ Leather handbag with printed 19th century photographs, Petra
Reuvers The Netherlands, 2001.

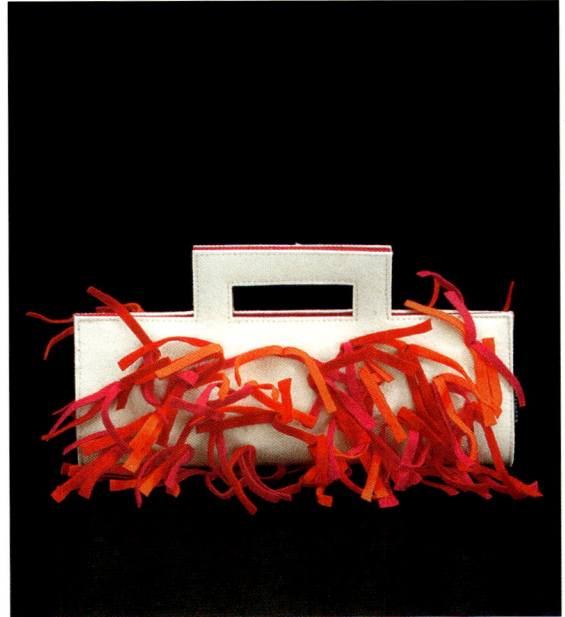

▲ Felt handbag embroidered with lace, Bouwjaar '63
The Netherlands, 2003.
▼ Leather handbag decorated with many different 'Memories',
Frida Badoux   The Netherlands, 2003.

▲ Plastic 'Digital Desire' shoulderbag, Paula Pontes
The Netherlands, 2003.
▼ Felt handbag, Bouwjaar '63   The Netherlands, 2004.

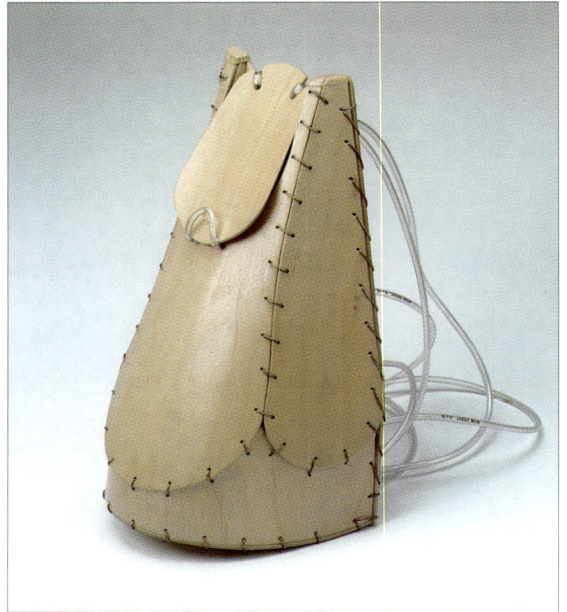

▲ Small wooden shoulderbag with leather strap, Peter van der Waal
The Netherlands, 1996.
▼ Leather chatelaine-style handbag; Designer: Sandra van Vliet
The Netherlands, 1994.

▲ Wooden rucksack, Ferdi Wouters The Netherlands, 2003.
▶ Suede handbag decorated with stones from a French beach,
Julia Russia, 1998.

◀ Handbag made of small nylon discs, Dana van der Bijl
The Netherlands, 2002.

▲ Two synthetic fabric shoulderbags 'Mailbox' (b) and 'Bow' (f), Door
Thomassen The Netherlands, 2002.

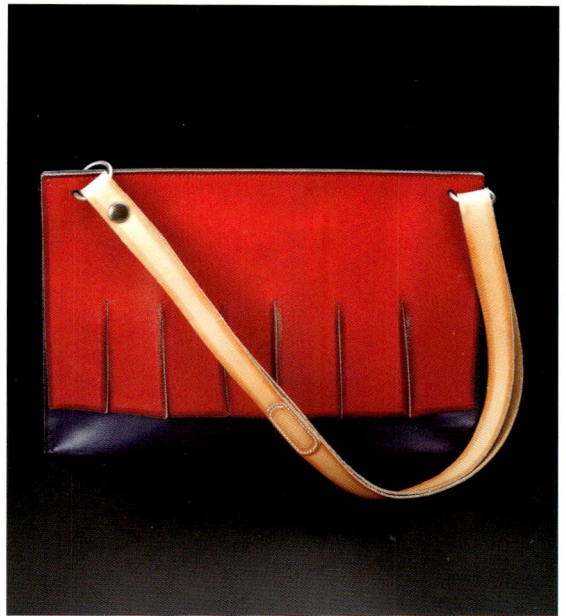

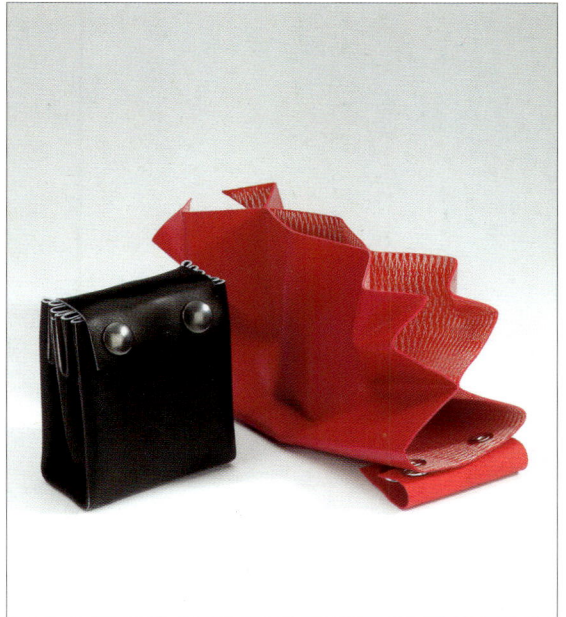

▲ Fabric shoulderbag with zippers and lined with spinnaker-cloth, Sandra van Zanten The Netherlands, 1997.
▼ Handmade leather handbag, Kathrin Hempel Germany, 2003.

▲ Leather shoulder bag, Uwe Seyferth The Netherlands, 2004.
▼ Two folding leather coin purses, Ferry Meewisse
The Netherlands, 2002.

▲ Suede pochette with magnetic closure, ZetBe Germany, 1990s.

▲ Leather 'Saffiano' shoulderbag, MK Accessoires
The Netherlands, 2003.

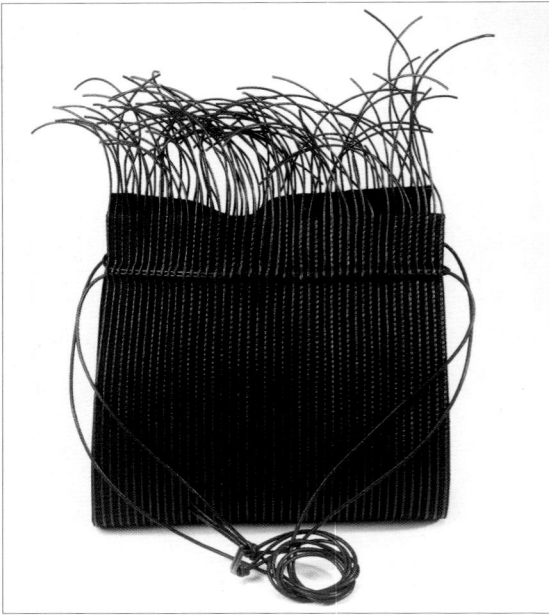

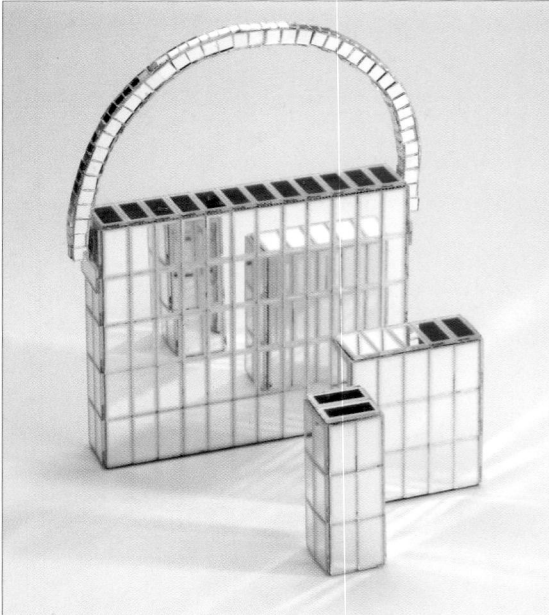

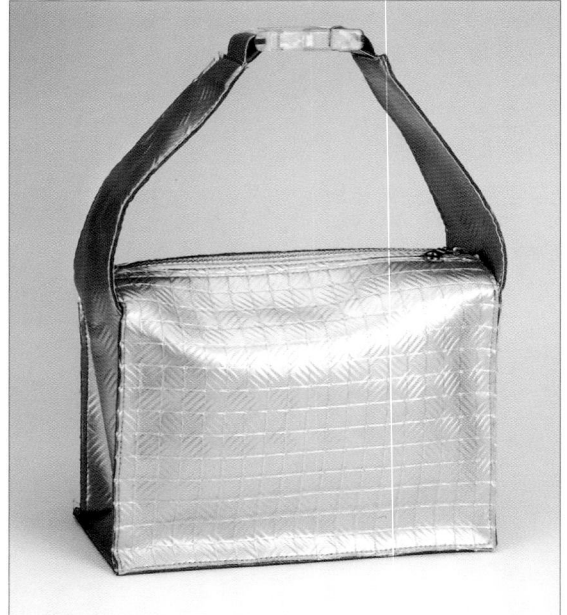

▲ Woven leather shoulderbag, Claudia Eckert & Coco Syring
Germany, 2003.
▼ Vanity bag made of small mirrors 'Mirror in the Hand', Georgette
Koning The Netherlands, 2001.

▲ Coated leather 'Square' shoulderbag, Mariëlle Willems
The Netherlands, 2000.
▼ Handbag made of plastic, Lenny Moeskops The Netherlands, 2000.

▲ Suitcase made of leather and wire, Maria Hees
The Netherlands, 1979.

▲▶ Folding leather handbag, Ferry Meewisse The Netherlands, 2002.

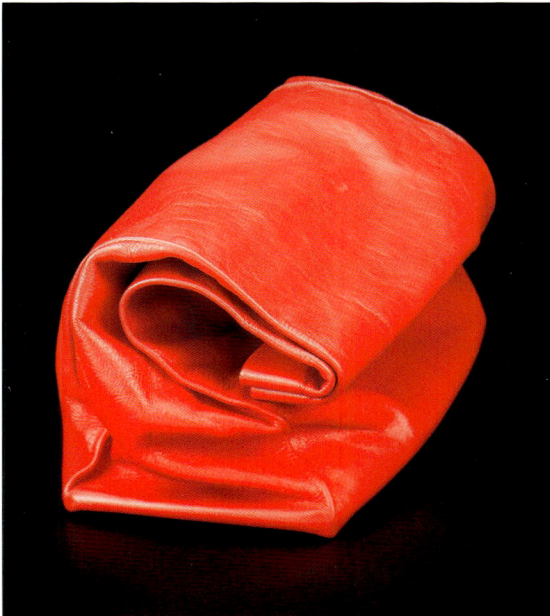

▲ Leather handbag named 'Twister', Hester van Eeghen
The Netherlands, 1998.
▼ Leather bag in shape of paperbag, Gilberthe Akkermans
The Netherlands, 1990s.

▲ Leather wallet with 'Serpentine' shoulder-strap, Hester van Eeghen
The Netherlands, 1990s.

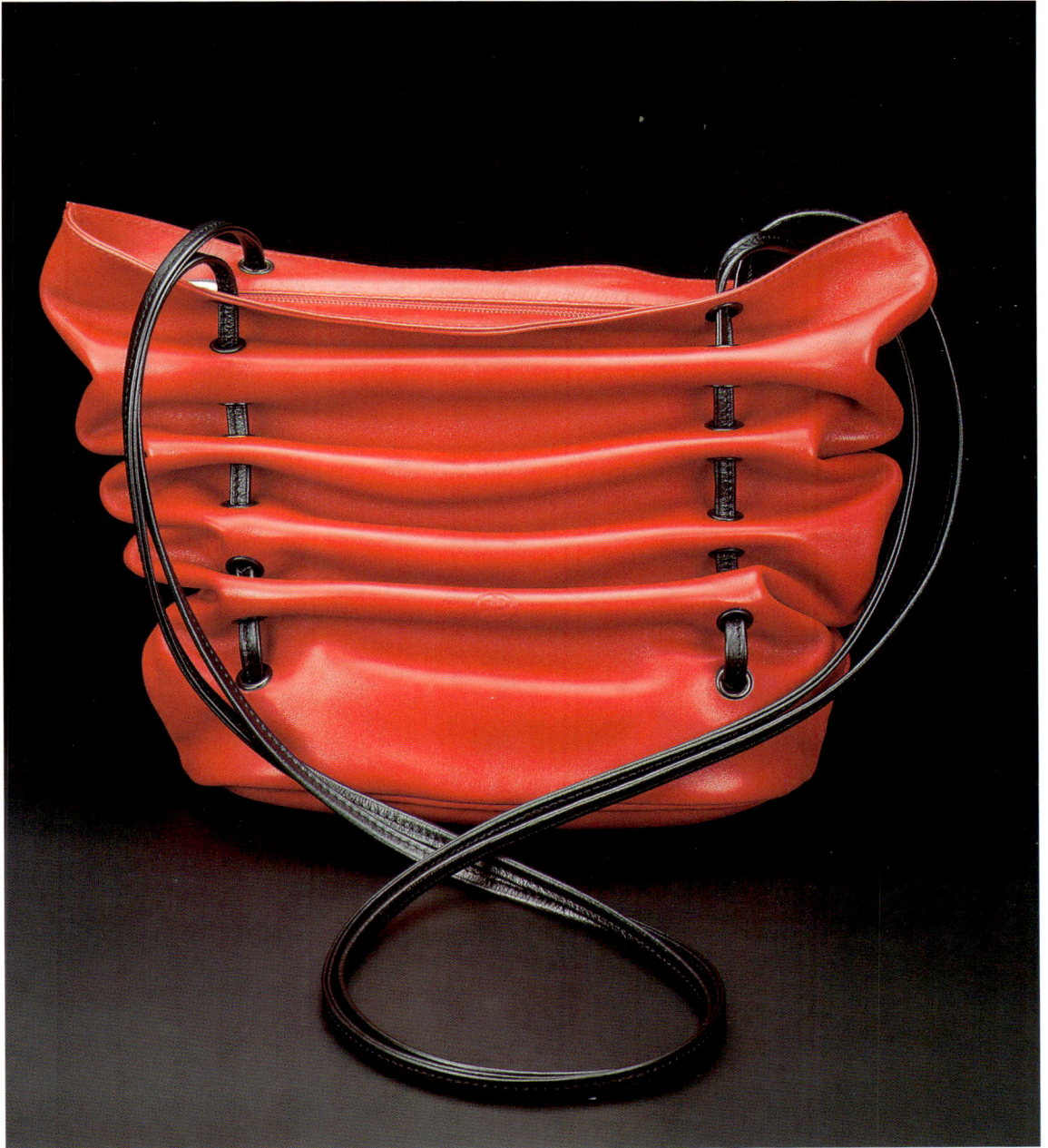

◄ Leather 'Drop' shoulderbag, Hester van Eeghen
The Netherlands, 1990s.

▲ Leather 'Accordion' shoulderbag, Hincke Elgersma
The Netherlands, 2000.

.., Sylvie, *Classic Plastics, from Bakelite to High-Tech*, London 1988 (1984).

Kurz, Sabine and Mary Sue Packer, *Strass, Internationaler Modeschmuck von den Anfängen bis Heute*, München 1997.

Mihm, Andrea, *Packend....Eine Kulturgeschichte des Reisekoffers*, Marburg (Ger.) 2001.

Pina, Leslie and Donald-Brian Johnson, *Whiting & Davis Purses, The perfect mesh*, Atglen, PA (USA) 2002.

Salmon, Larry, "Ballooning: accessories after the fact", *Dress*, (1976) 2., p. 1-9.

Scheuer, N. and E. Maeder, *Art of Embroiderer by Charles Germain de Saint-Aubin, Designer to the King 1770*, Los Angeles (Los Angeles County Museum of Art) 1983.

Schmuttermeier, Elisabeth, a. o., *Cast Iron from Central Europe, 1800-1850*, catalogue of exhibition. Vienna/New York (Austrian Museum of Applied Arts) 1994.

Schürenberg, Sabina, *Glasperlarbeiten Taschen und Beutel, von der Vorlage zum Produkt*, München 1998.

Serena, Raffaella, *Embroideries and patterns from 19th century Vienna*, Milan/Woodbridge 1998.

Raulet, Sylvie, *Van Cleef & Arpel*, Paris 1986.

Wiener Werkstätte, Lederobjekte, Cat.Wien (Österreichischen Museums für angewandte Kunst), Wien 1992.

Ulmer, R. en J. Srasser, *Plastics Design +*, catalogue of exhibition. München (Die Neue Sammlung, Staatliches Museum für Angewandte Kunst), München 1997.

Ulzen, Evelyn, *Glasperlen, Herstellung und textiler Verbund*, Berlin 1993.

Warren, E., *Treasures in needlework, comprising instructions in knitting, ...*, London 1855.

Wilcox, Claire, *A century of bags, icons of style in the 20th century*, Londen 1997.

Wilcox, Claire, *Bags*, Cat. London (Victoria and Albert Museum) 1999.

Magazines and trade catalogues

Au Bon Marché, *Nouveautés d'Hiver*, Paris 1927-1928.

De Bazar, 1865-1886.

Elegance, Amsterdam 1947-1956.

Femina (UK ed.) 1920-1921.

Femina, Paris 1901-1948 (incomplete).

La Femme Chic, Paris 1913 -1961 (incomplete).

Harrods News, London 1902, 1904, 1906-1914, 1916, 1919-1984.

Harpers' Bazaar, New York 1950-1955.

Journal des Dames et des Modes (new ed.) 1913, 1916.

Lederwaren, Doetinchem 1938-1968.

Liberty Gifts, London 1926, 1931-1933 (incomplete).

Liberty Christmas gifts, London 1930-1931, 1933-1934.

Liberty Yule-tide gifts, London 1908-1920, 1923-1932 (incomplete).

La Mode illustrée, Paris 1875-1919 (incomplete).

Les Modes, Paris 1901-1921 (incomplete).

Penelopé, Amsterdam 1821-1835.

Vogue (UK ed.) 1924-1926, 1930-1940 and 1951.

Vogue (French ed.) 1925-1937 and 1953.

Vogue (USA) 1932, 1950-1955.

Archives

Dunhill archives (archives from Alfred Dunhill Limited, London).

Wiener Werkstätte archives in the Austrian Museum of Applied Arts.